Living with Racism

D0067811

LIVING WITH RACISM

THE BLACK MIDDLE-CLASS EXPERIENCE

JOE R. FEAGIN
MELVIN P. SIKES

Beacon Press
Boston

Beacon Press
25 Beacon Street
Boston, Massachusetts 02108-2892

Beacon Press books
are published under the auspices of
the Unitarian Universalist Association of Congregations

© 1994 by Joe R. Feagin and Melvin P. Sikes
All rights reserved
Printed in the United States of America

99 98 97 96 95   8 7 6 5 4 3 2

Text design by Lisa Diercks

Library of Congress Cataloging-in-Publication Data

Feagin, Joe R.
    Living with racism: the black middle-class experience /
Feagin and Melvin P. Sikes.
        p.   cm.
    Includes bibliographical references and index.
    ISBN 0-8070-0924-5 (cloth)
    ISBN 0-8070-0925-3 (paper)
    1. Afro-Americans—Social conditions—1975– 2. Racism—United
States. 3. Middle class—United States. 4. United States—Race
relations. I. Sikes, Melvin P. II. Title.
    E185.86.F43   1994
305.96'073—dc20   93-37530

Contents

Preface

"WHAT is it like to be a black person in white America today? One step from suicide! What I'm saying is—the psychological warfare games that we have to play everyday just to survive. We have to be one way in our communities and one way in the workplace or in the business sector. We can never be ourselves all around. I think that may be a given for all people, but us particularly; it's really a mental health problem. It's a wonder we haven't all gone out and killed somebody or killed ourselves."

Our interviews began with this statement from a successful black entrepreneur, the first respondent of 209 African Americans we interviewed in a number of cities across the United States. She challenges us to see the personal and family losses that have resulted from decades of dealing with prejudiced whites. She summons us to understand the great tension between conforming to white standards and trying to maintain personal integrity and black identity. She dares us to look beyond the statistics of inequality conventionally provided by scholars and journalists to experience the reality and pain of recurring racial discrimination, raising the questions: How are the unique vicissitudes of my life defined? How have I survived? And at what price?

A common white credo about racial relations today holds that discrimination is no longer a serious and widespread problem and that whatever blatant antiblack hostility remains is mostly that of isolated white bigots and Klan-type groups. In particular, middle-class African Americans are not viewed as victims of discrimination, but are seen as prosperous examples of the success of equal opportunity and affirmative action programs. Indeed, middle-class black Americans are thought by many whites to be the beneficiaries of racial quotas that have gone too far, to the point of "reverse discrimination."

Middle-class black Americans appear to most whites to have secured the promises of the American dream. They and their families have sacrificed to get a good education; they have worked very hard; and they have done everything said to be required to achieve the American dream. All have achieved or will soon achieve some signs of material success—the good income, the credit cards, the nice car. They appear to be well integrated into middle-class America, and from a white perspective they have no real reason to link problems in their lives to skin color.

Yet when one engages in extended conversations with middle-class African Americans about their efforts, achievements, and obstacles, their often vivid accounts of the white hostility and discrimination they have experienced tell a different story. In this book we hope to show the image of untrammeled black middle-class prosperity and integration to be a white illusion, quite out of touch with the daily reality.

Our in-depth interviews provide windows into the black middle-class world, one not only of determination and hard work but also of frustration and rage over persisting discrimination. These African Americans show in their personal accounts that they have not been accepted as equals by many of the working-class and middle-class whites they encounter in their daily lives. In our analysis we address the character of the hostility and discrimination these middle-class respondents have experienced in public places and in traditionally white workplaces, business arenas, residential complexes and neighborhoods, and schools and colleges. They present a tragic and terrible portrait of recent and continuing experiences with white racism.

But there is more to our argument than the contention that middle-class African Americans face serious discrimination. Our data say something even more profound about the state of this nation. Clearly, no amount of hard work and achievement, no amount of money, resources, and success, can protect black people from the persisting ravages of white racism in their everyday lives. Our respondents are alternately baffled, frustrated, shocked, and outraged that the strong evidence of their hard work and personal achievements does not protect them from white discrimination. Moreover, while they may have greater resources with which to respond to discrimination than less affluent black Americans, the presence and use of these resources appear to have had little lasting effect on the magnitude of white racism in the United States today. Racial stereotyping, prejudice, and hostility still operate indiscriminately, despite the actual identities and achievements of the black individuals discriminated against. In the everyday experience of our black middle-class respondents the full attainment of the American dream is "for whites only." The implications of this continuing racism for the fundamental democratic values of this society are far-reaching. The classic American creed promises the inalienable rights of "life, liberty, and the pursuit of happiness" today for all citizens of this democratic nation. Yet after several centuries of struggle these rights are not even close to being secured for black Americans, including middle-class black

Americans. Perhaps the greatest tragedy in our findings of widespread racism is that they reveal the much-celebrated American creed to be little more than hollow words.

Over the past decade or two, mainstream white media commentators, intellectuals, and government policymakers have rarely accorded value to critical black middle-class voices. This book evolved from our own conversations as professional colleagues, one white (Feagin) and one black (Sikes). As Sikes recounted his many and dramatic experiences of racial discrimination, Feagin was moved and angered. We both found our exchanges eye-opening, and Feagin pressed Sikes to write of these experiences in an autobiography. Yet Sikes felt unable to do so, because the task would be too painful and probably fruitless, particularly after more than four decades of experience with white editors and publishers uninterested in publishing strong black accounts of everyday racism. Eventually, then, our discussions led to the decision to collect and compile accounts of the everyday experiences of a large group of middle-class African Americans.

This book has grown beyond the initial attempt to record black middle-class experience to a deep analysis of the character and impact of white racism in this society. A primary goal is to help voice rarely expressed middle-class realities, using a richness of material unavailable in surface-level analyses based on surveys and opinion polls. We hope this book is as true as it can be to the life experiences of middle-class African Americans; to the racial barriers they face; to the pain and rage they feel; and to how they react, fight, and survive.

As a current expression among African Americans puts it, "Racism in America is alive and well!" Grounded in black experience, this book is a plea for better-enforced civil rights laws and for new social policies in the public and private sectors designed to confront and extirpate persisting white racism in its many modern faces and disguises.

Acknowledgments. In conducting this research study and preparing this manuscript we incurred more intellectual debts than we can ever repay. We are especially grateful to the many African Americans who gave of their time and energy to provide us with the extensive interview materials on which this book is based. We have not been able to quote all of them in the text, but all the interviews have informed our analysis whether quoted or not. We are indebted to many other people as well. We are indebted to the many black journalists (especially Isabel Wilkerson) and other black professionals around the country who took time out to talk with us about our research materials and their own life experiences. We would like to thank Hernan Vera, Nijole Benokraitis, John Goering, Christine Williams, Raphael Allen, Charles Tilly, John S. Butler, Tony Orum, Nestor Rodriguez, Sharon Collins, Janice Allen, Nikitah Imani, Michael Hodge, and Suzanne Harper for their insightful comments on earlier drafts of this manuscript, and Nijole Benokraitis, Beth Anne Shelton, Bob Parker, Diane Smith, Robert Adams, Yanick St. Jean, Leslie Inniss, Debi Van Ausdale, Cedric Herring, Marsha Herring, Lory Jennell Dance, Barbara McDade, Bob Bullard, L. M. Bullard, Yoku Shaw-Taylor, Charles Shepherd, Brenda Shepherd, Wilmer Roberts, Megan Pulliam, Annette Adams, Kellie Barr, Joseph Delphonse, Nishon M. Holmes, Robert L. Mayers, Pansy Mcdowell, Richard Newton, Mattie Lucas, Tammy Edwards, and Virginia Reid for interviewing and research assistance. We are indebted to Clairece Feagin and Zeta Sikes for their assistance and personal support.

We would like to thank the Hogg Foundation for Mental Health and the University of Florida Division of Sponsored Research and College of Liberal Arts and Sciences for financial support for certain portions of our research. We also would like to thank the University of Oklahoma Center for Research on Minority Education for support of a working paper that developed into part of chapter 3 and the United Church of Christ's

Commission on Racial Justice for allowing us to develop an initial version of some material found in chapter 6 at their December 1991 National Symposium on Race and Housing. We would like to thank two journals for permission to use portions of two articles. An early form of portions of chapter 2 appeared as Joe R. Feagin, "The Continuing Significance of Race: Antiblack Discrimination in Public Places," *American Sociological Review* 56 (February 1991), pp. 101–116; and an early rendering of parts of chapter 3 appeared in Joe R. Feagin, "The Continuing Significance of Racism," *Journal of Black Studies* 22 (June 1992), pp. 546–578.

Chapter One

The Continuing Significance of Racism

Everything, everywhere I look, everywhere I turn, right, left, is white. It's lily white, it's painted with white. And it's funny, because I was reading this article about how America is synonymous with white people. I mean, I'm sure when Europeans, or Asians or Africans for that matter, think of America, they think of white people, because white people are mainstream, white people are general. "White is right," as my daddy tells me. White is right, at least they think it is. So, if you're a black person trying to assert yourself, and express your culture, there's something wrong with you, because to do that is to be diametrically opposed to everything this country stands for. And everything this country stands for is what is white.

—Student at a historically white university

THE United States and its founding documents stand for democracy, liberty, and justice around the world. Yet the founding documents, especially the U.S. Constitution, buttressed the long-term enslavement of African Americans. Centuries of slavery and decades of legal segregation finally came to an end with the civil rights revolution of the 1950s and 1960s. During the period of legal segregation white prejudice was overt and frequently crude, and the material, physical, and psychological impact of blatant discrimination on African Americans was severe. Without societal backing in the form of civil rights laws, few blacks had the resources and power to fight discrimination successfully.

Widespread societal changes came in the 1960s as African Americans moved into areas of society formerly off limits to them. Federal and state governments began the task of dismantling the legal foundations of a segregated society and granted black Americans formal equality. Some government and private employers implemented modest affirmative action programs to overcome the consequences of past discrimination. In the years of the civil rights revolution, legal segregation was gradually destroyed, and for a time the old racial order seemed to be targeted for thoroughgoing destruction. Between the mid-1970s, and the early 1990s, however, many white decisionmakers in the private and public sectors abandoned aggressive programs to redress racial discrimination and retreated to a rhetoric of formal equality. As a result, in the 1990s racial discrimination remains at the heart of U.S. society.

Yet today most white Americans do not see racial discrimination as a widespread or deeply entrenched problem in traditionally white workplaces, law courts, schools, and other institutions. White and black Americans had quite different views about the role of racism in causing the 1992 Los Angeles riot. Local and national polls after the riot found that a large majority of black Americans did not feel that they received fair treatment in the U.S. courts. In the same surveys most whites felt the courts were fair.[1] Numerous other opinion polls over the past decade have shown that the majority of white Americans do not

2

view racial injustice in employment and other areas as a major American dilemma in need of aggressive government action. The majority of whites appear to view "racism" as certain extreme views about white superiority, as "racism in the head," to use Judith Lichtenberg's apt term.[2] Apparently, when they think about it, the majority of whites tend to look at serious racism as the prejudices and actions of extreme bigots not considered to be representative of the white majority. Even the growing number of "hate crimes" targeting black Americans tend to be blamed on a few white "extremists."[3] Whites have the luxury of looking at matters of racial discrimination with detachment. This viewpoint makes it easier for whites to deny the reality of much of the racism reported by blacks. In contrast, black Americans view racism not with detachment but in terms of their own and their relatives' *experiences* in past and present encounters with white people. Marian Wright Edelman, an African American lawyer and the founder of the Children's Defense Fund, captured this eloquently in her recent book, *The Measure of Our Success: A Letter to My Children and Yours*: "It is utterly exhausting being Black in America—physically, mentally, and emotionally. . . . There is no respite or escape from your badge of color."[4]

In this book we generally use the term *racism* in a broad sense to refer not only to the prejudices and discriminatory actions of particular white bigots but also to institutionalized discrimination and to the recurring ways in which white people dominate black people in almost every major area of this society. A National Council of Churches work group has provided a summary of this institutionalized racism: "Both consciously and unconsciously, racism is enforced and maintained by the legal, cultural, religious, educational, economic, political, environmental and military institutions of societies. Racism is more than just a personal attitude; it is the institutionalized form of that attitude."[5]

3

Racism is racial prejudice backed by power and resources. White domination is often rationalized by the belief that the inferiority or superiority of a group's abilities, values, and culture are linked to physical characteristics such as skin color. In the chapters that follow we provide strong evidence of the blatant, subtle, and covert discrimination that cumulates to the intricate structures and processes of institutionalized racism. Contrary to a common white view, modern racism does not consist mainly of the isolated acts of scattered white bigots, but rather has been inescapable in the everyday worlds of African Americans. Almost any encounter with whites, in workplaces, schools, neighborhoods, and public places, can mean a confrontation with racism.

The Denial of White Racism

For a short period during the late 1960s and early 1970s a new intellectual discourse characterized much scholarly and media commentary on racial relations in the United States. The earlier "culture of poverty" language was abandoned for terms such as *white racism*, *racial discrimination*, and *institutional racism*. To cite perhaps the most important example, the 1968 National Advisory Commission on Civil Disorders, a mostly white group of prominent Americans appointed by President Lyndon B. Johnson to investigate the ghetto riots of the 1960s, concluded: "Our Nation is moving toward two societies, one black, one white—separate and unequal."[6] The first pages of the commission's final report minced no words about whites' responsibility for the condition of black Americans: "Discrimination and segregation have long permeated much of American life. . . . White society is deeply implicated in the ghetto. White institutions created it, white institutions maintain it, and white society condones it. . . . White racism is essentially responsible for the explosive mixture which has been accumulating in our cities since the end of World War II."[7] For a time many white analysts in academia, government, and the mass media interpreted the oppressive conditions of black Americans in the same terms.

The perspective criticizing and blaming whites and white institutions did not last. By the mid- to late-1970s there was much discontent and resentment among whites, including many in positions of power, over race-conscious remedies and the growing power of black Americans in the economy, universities, and politics. Since that time there has been a significant shift in how many prominent white scholars, journalists, politicians, and jurists have analyzed racial issues and problems. Terms like "institutional racism" and "white racism" have become rare, apparently because they have been seen by mainstream white analysts and some black neoconservative analysts as too harsh or radical. Instead, numerous articles have been written on the theme of the declining significance of race in U.S. society. Racial discrimination has often been downplayed as a major national problem. On March 7, 1988, the authors of a *Newsweek* article argued, without conducting research on racial discrimination, that "mercifully, America today is not the bitterly sundered dual society the riot commission grimly foresaw."[8] In the Winter 1988 issue of *Policy Review*, journalist Thomas Bray argued that racism was not a central motivating factor behind the 1960s riots, that the 1968 National Advisory Commission's analysis was "deeply flawed" and its central concept of institutional racism useless for analyzing U.S. racial relations then or now.[9]

With the demise of a highly visible black civil rights movement in the 1970s and 1980s, a new language was developed by many white intellectuals, media commentators, and politicians to analyze U.S. racial relations. Terms such as *the black underclass*, *reverse discrimination*, and *the privileged black middle class* have been used by commentators as influential and diverse as Nathan Glazer, Ben Wattenberg, Thomas and Mary Edsall, Nicholas Lemann, Ken Auletta, Daniel Patrick Moynihan, Thomas Sowell, Bayard Rustin, William J. Wilson, Stephen Carter, Shelby Steele, and Jim Sleeper. These writers often stress the existence of a pathological black underclass and of a pampered and prosperous black middle class, at the same time playing down the reality of persistent discrimination against all African Americans.

Nathan Glazer, in his influential book *Affirmative Discrimination* (1975), was one of the first to articulate these themes. There he argued that the United States was winning the battle against racism, that "no one is now excluded from the broadest access" to what the U.S. economy and society make possible. Glazer celebrated the new black prosperity and attributed continuing black problems not to discrimination but mostly to a tangle of ghetto pathologies. In addition, he argued that affirmative action was wrongheaded and would not benefit impoverished blacks.[10] Writing in 1973, demographic analysts Ben Wattenberg and Richard Scammon likewise exaggerated black progress, arguing from statistical data that the number of middle-class blacks "can reasonably be said to add up to a majority of black Americans."[11] For these prominent white scholars the expansion of the black middle class seemed to signal an end to the old racist order in the United States.

Since the mid-1970s scholars in a variety of fields have developed and embellished these and related arguments. In a 1981 book *Wealth and Poverty*, once called the "Bible of the Reagan-Bush administrations," economist George Gilder declared there was no need for government action to assist black Americans because it was virtually impossible to find a serious racist in a position of power and because major discrimination had been effectively abolished in the United States.[12] Reviewing much research done on higher education in the 1980s, education professor George Keller has attributed the lack of recent black advancement in higher education to causes mostly within the black community. He downplayed racism as a major factor in blacks' problems at white colleges and universities and emphasized instead individual and family factors, including an alleged lack of black middle-class leadership.[13]

Not only white scholars but also a few black scholars discussed the decline in racial discrimination and contrasted an underprivileged underclass with a very privileged middle class. In a much cited 1978 book that triggered national discussion about race and class, *The Declining Significance of Race*, University of Chicago sociologist William J. Wilson argued that the growth of the black middle class resulted from declining racial discrimination, government remedial programs, and improving economic conditions in the 1960s and 1970s. In his view, "talented and educated blacks are experiencing unprecedented job opportunities in the growing government and corporate sectors, opportunities that are *at least* comparable to those of whites with equivalent qualifications."[14] In a later book, *The Truly Disadvantaged*, Wilson reiterated these arguments in a critique of conservative underclass theories. There he suggested that the major problem of the 1964 Civil Rights Act was its failure to improve the economic situation of the underclass, not its failure to abolish discrimination for all black Americans. Moreover, in an *Atlantic* book review, former civil rights activist Bayard Rustin went so far as to say that arguments focusing on racial discrimination and the lack of black progress only served "to alienate whites." He argued that continuing obstacles to economic and social integration for black Americans were "not primarily a result of racism" but rather had to do with family breakups and economic recessions. Since the 1970s even some black analysts like Wilson and Rustin have focused on economic and family conditions, not on antiblack discrimination, in evaluating U.S. racial relations.[15]

In *The Content of Our Character*, Shelby Steele, an English professor and a black neo-conservative analyst, deemphasized the significance of discrimination as a factor in black problems and argued that "our oppression has left us with a dangerously powerful memory of itself that pulls us into warlike defensiveness." Steele argued that this memory of past oppression is a major reason blacks do not take advantage of current opportunities. Steele further argued that a black American is "basically as free as he or she wants to be. For every white I have met who is a racist, I have met twenty more who have seen me as an equal."[16] Similarly, Yale law professor Stephen Carter has maintained that racism is "no longer the all-encompassing force it once was, and it no longer holds the entire black race in desperate thrall." The significance of racism for middle-class blacks "really *is* receding." Drawing on earlier analyses, Carter also suggested that discrimination has largely been replaced by problems of the underclass.[17]

One feature of discussions of middle-class blacks in the scholarly literature and media is a focus on the positive side of their experience, especially upward economic mobility. This approach can be found in official reports from national organizations and governmental agencies. The National Research Council (NRC) report on black Americans in the late 1980s, *A Common Destiny*, offers lengthy discussions of the problems of less well-off blacks but only a brief and generally positive assessment of the situation of the middle class.[18] Other major research reports, including *Closing the Gap*, a report from the Rand Corporation, and the *Economic Progress of Black Men in America*, a report of the U.S. Commission on Civil Rights, have emphasized the economic success of black Americans, including the middle class.[19]

Government officials joined the chorus, sometimes citing the aforementioned scholarly reports as support for government's retreat from aggressive economic opportunity and civil rights programs. In a January 1989 television interview, outgoing

President Ronald Reagan argued that civil rights leaders such as Jesse Jackson and Coretta Scott King were intentionally overstating the extent of racial discrimination and were "doing very well leading organizations based on keeping alive the feeling that they're victims of prejudice."[20] In recent years Supreme Court decisions have communicated the same official government attitude. Dissenting from a conservative decision on employment rights in 1989, liberal Justice Harry Blackmun described the attitude of the (white) majority on the nation's highest court: "One wonders whether the majority still believes that race discrimination—or, more accurately, race discrimination against nonwhites—is a problem in our society, or even remembers that it ever was."[21]

Commentators in the mass media have likewise concentrated on the prosperity and privileges of the middle class and the dilemmas of the underclass. Those in the black middle class, especially the well-educated professionals and managers, have been viewed as having achieved the American dream like the middle classes of white ethnic groups before them. The major difference between the 1960s and 1980s, suggested a *Newsweek* article celebrating black middle-class affluence, is the "emergence of an authentic black middle class, better educated, better paid, better housed than any group of blacks that has gone before it."[22] Writing in 1991 in the *Atlantic* about black middle-class prosperity and the "extraordinary integration of the races," Thomas and Mary Edsall blamed the political misfortunes of the Democratic Party in the 1970s and 1980s on white hostility toward a dangerous black underclass that whites viewed as coddled by liberal elites and government programs. In a best-selling book, *Chain Reaction*, the Edsalls, like many white media analysts, have argued that among whites there has been a "public repudiation of racism" and a "stigmatization of overly racist expression" since the 1960s.[23]

According to a 1989 article by the literary editor of *The New*

Republic, Leon Wieseltier, black leaders have exaggerated white racism as a root cause of inner city drug problems.[24] He argued that this perspective accenting racism is "madness," that "in the memory of [racial] oppression, oppression outlives itself. The scar does the work of the wound. That is the real tragedy: that injustice retains the power to distort long after it has ceased to be real." Wieseltier suggested that the scars and memories of past racial discrimination are far more serious than present racial discrimination. Moreover, in a 1991 book on New York's racial politics, journalist Jim Sleeper poked fun at black arguments about persisting institutional racism and suggested that advantaged middle-class blacks have stopped "burning the midnight oil."[25]

The argument that white racism is no longer a serious and entrenched national problem and that blacks must take individual responsibility for their problems took on juggernaut proportions in the mass media by the late 1980s and early 1990s, as books like those of Steele, Sleeper, and the Edsalls were widely celebrated. The social issues editor of *Business Week*, Elizabeth Ehrlich, praised their arguments profusely and argued that blacks' emphasis on racial victimization and redress for discrimination was both unconstructive and wrongheaded.[26] Moreover, a study of hundreds of thousands of articles and stories in several hundred mainstream magazines and newspapers published between 1978 and 1992 found only nine articles that headlined "white racism." With only two exceptions, they concerned black analysts commenting on white racism. In this fourteen-year period virtually no white journalists or editors took the central part that whites play in modern racism seriously enough to do a major article on the subject. Very few saw *white* racism as a major persisting problem for the country as a whole.[27] Even British journalists writing about the American scene have joined the white chorus, as in this 1993 comment on an African American novelist in the *Financial Times*: "[Her] subject is the central issue facing black Americans in the post civil rights era, which is no longer white racism but rather the question of identity."[28]

Influential whites are not alone in their denial of widespread white racism. A majority of the white population seems to share the view that, while discrimination still exists, it is no longer of great significance. In interviews with whites in the 1970s and early 1980s, Bob Blauner found that virtually all viewed recent decades as an era of great racial progress for U.S. racial relations.[29] In the NRC report *A Common Destiny*, editors Jaynes and Williams noted that by the late 1970s many white Americans believed that the Civil Rights Act of 1964 "had led to broad-scale elimination of discrimination against blacks in public accommodations."[30] By 1976, according to a national survey analyzed by Kluegel and Smith, 71 percent of whites agreed with the statement that "blacks and other minorities no longer face unfair employment conditions; in fact they are favored in many training and job programs." Just 12 percent agreed that "discrimination affects all black people; the only way to handle it is for blacks to organize together and demand rights for all."[31] A 1980 Gallup poll found 68 percent of whites saying that blacks now had equal standing with whites in the society.[32] And a late 1980s Louis Harris survey found that, in the case of executive-level jobs, 70 percent of the white respondents believed that blacks got fair treatment.[33] In the case of white-collar jobs in general, 69 percent of the whites did not think blacks were discriminated against. Similarly, in 1991 a National Opinion Research Center survey asked the respondents why blacks have worse jobs, lower incomes, and less desirable housing than whites. Choosing among alternative explanations, 56 percent of whites said that this was not "mainly due to discrimination."[34] From the perspective of leading white scholars, media commentators, editors, and politicians, as well as the majority of the white public, the problems of racial discrimination

11

and injustice are not systemic or pervasive enough to require aggressive new government action.

The Continuing Significance of Racial Discrimination

In contrast to the common white view, few middle-class African Americans interviewed for this book see the significance of racism in their lives declining. Indeed, in the late 1980s and early 1990s many African Americans perceive an increase in the significance of race. We can anticipate the discussions in later chapters with this brief comment from a black professor at a northern university:

> It's just really scary, you know, to see the skinheads and the Ku Klux Klan and the white power and people like Duke, who was elected in Louisiana, with his views, being able to speak in public and get rewarded for it. . . . Right after the Sixties, there was some shame about rewarding people like that. There was a public set of rules that you just don't do that, and I think that Reagan sort of dispelled all of that. So it's open season again, so that it's okay to be a bigot, it's okay to be a racist, and "we certainly don't need all these *special* affirmative action programs and all these other things." So that sets the national tone, and I think our leadership makes a real difference.

Is this so? What do we know about the realities of racial discrimination today? In recent years a few, mostly minority, scholars have kept alive a critical perspective on the enduring white-racist social order. For example, in September 1978 the Association of Black Sociologists protested the awards given to William J. Wilson's *The Declining Significance of Race* on the grounds that he neglected "the continuing discrimination against blacks at all class levels." Since the early 1970s black scholars such as Manning Marable, Patricia Williams, Bell

12

Hooks, Kesho Yvonne Scott, Lois Benjamin, and Philomena Essed; Latino researchers such as John Fernandez and Rodolfo Alvarez; and white researchers such as Sidney Willhelm, Bob Blauner, and Andrew Hacker have provided important analyses of racial discrimination and inequality, drawn from demographic data, in-depth interviews, and personal experience. With one exception, Andrew Hacker's *Two Nations* (a 1992 book on racism by a white social scientist), these probing analyses have not been published by major New York trade book publishers.

During the 1960s three major surveys of African Americans were conducted by Louis Harris and Gallup and published as cover stories in *Newsweek*; three significant books were published on those surveys by Simon and Schuster. The first national survey of African Americans, conducted by Louis Harris, became a cover story for *Newsweek* in July 1963 and was soon followed by a provocative book, *The Negro Revolution in America*, which analyzed the opinion poll data in more detail in such chapters as "What It's Like to Be a Negro" and "Weapons of the Revolution." Black respondents were frequently quoted, and personal experiences with discrimination and protest were examined. Followup surveys were done in 1966 and 1969, with similar cover stories and summary books entitled *Black and White* and *Report from Black America*, respectively. All three books made use of both quantitative and qualitative data on the lives of black Americans. They, and the related *Newsweek* articles, played an important role in documenting for the white public and white policymakers the dimensions of antiblack discrimination in the 1960s.[35]

Since then no similarly systematic research on the character and breadth of the discrimination faced by black Americans in daily life has been published. A few surveys of black Americans have been conducted, but they have not dealt as much with personal encounters with discrimination as the 1960s surveys, and the data have not been so widley disseminated.[36] A 1991 review of black opinion surveys by Sigelman and Welch and the review of black surveys in *A Common Destiny* have shown that in recent years few researchers have asked black Americans specific questions about the racial discrimination they encounter in their everyday lives. When questions about discrimination have been asked, they have usually been brief and not personal, inquiring, for example, if blacks generally face discrimination in white-collar jobs, as in the 1988 Harris survey. In such surveys substantial proportions of the blacks interviewed in all regions have responded that there is significant discrimination in jobs, income, and housing.

Where a few personal questions have been asked, the answers also suggest significant and widespread discrimination. A 1978 Louis Harris survey asked: "Have you or anyone in your family been discriminated against in trying to get ahead on the job or in trying to get a job?" Thirty-nine percent reported personal or family discrimination, and another 11 percent were uncertain. Two hypothetical questions were also asked. On a job pay question just under half of the black respondents said they would probably get less pay than a white person for the same work. On a hypothetical housing question 45 percent said that if they were to get a house or an apartment "the same as a white person" they would pay more than the white person.[37] Moreover, in a 1986 ABC News/*Washington Post* poll the proportions of blacks answering "yes" to four questions about personal experience with discrimination were as follows: in getting a quality education, one quarter; in getting decent housing, one quarter; in getting a job, 39 percent; and in getting equal wages for a job, 41 percent.[38] These survey questions on black encounters with discrimination are, as Sigelman and Welch point out, "fairly crude" and ignore much racial discrimination "in the daily routines of life." They add that the extent of discrimination might be found to be even "more widespread if our measures of discrimination were more refined."[39] Opinion surveys have been brief and superficial in dealing with antiblack discrimination. They have not asked black Americans about discrimination in such important areas of everyday life as public accommodations, the street, and white-collar workplaces. The major purpose of the chapters that follow is to go beyond the bare-bones survey data to examine the character, range, and depth of the discrimination black Americans encounter, its impact, and the ways in which they cope and respond.

Racism as Everyday Experience

Much of the analysis in this book is shaped by several theoretical propositions derived substantially from close readings of our interviews with middle-class African Americans. We have found existing theories useful for interpretive purposes, but we have relied heavily on the many theoretical insights provided by our respondents. As a group, they are deeply reflective about their lives as African Americans and have constructed their own insightful theoretical frames.[40]

The first of these general propositions is that modern racism must be understood as *lived experience*. The recurring experiences of middle-class and other black Americans with whites who discriminate are the heart of the racial problem in this nation. When our respondents talk about being black in a country dominated by whites, they do not speak in abstract concepts of discrimination or racism learned only from books, but tell of mistreatment encountered as they traverse traditionally white places. Most reflect on their trials, and their interpretations of the black middle-class experience are theories grounded in their everyday lives.

Our analyses of the interviews are based on several close readings of typewritten transcripts. Rather than a collection of unrelated reflections and narratives, the interview accounts we present link together substantively at a number of different levels.

A second proposition gleaned from the interviews is that experiences with serious discrimination not only are very painful and stressful in the immediate situation and aftermath but also have a *cumulative* impact on particular individuals, their families, and their communities. A black person's life is regularly disrupted by the mistreatment suffered personally or by family members. The presence of the pronoun "we" in many black accounts of encounters with whites often suggests the collective character of the African American experience. Recurring encounters with white racism can be viewed as a series of "life crises," often similar to other serious life crises, such as the death of a loved one, that disturb an individual's life trajectory.[41] Sympathetic whites may have an intellectual understanding of the consequences of racial discrimination. Profound understanding or empathy, however, involves feeling the pain and comprehending that discrimination is a series of unforgettable life crises.

The cumulative impact on an individual of repeated personal encounters with racial hostility is greater than the sum of these encounters might appear to be to a casual observer. In addition, discrimination is seldom just a personal matter. A black victim frequently shares the account with family and friends, often to lighten the burden, and this sharing creates a domino effect of anguish and anger rippling across an extended group. An individual's discrimination becomes a family matter. Another aspect of the cumulative effect of discrimination is, of course, historical, for discriminatory incidents are freighted with centuries of racial oppression of which the black victims are consciously or unconsciously aware. Memory is a key factor. Experiences with serious discrimination are stored not only in individual memories but also in family stories and group recollections. As a result, in discussing their negative encounters with whites many respondents move easily from the "I" of their own experiences to the "we" that indicates both a broad racial consciousness and a sense of group solidarity.

The third generalization we suggest is that the repeated experience of racism significantly affects a black person's behavior and understanding of life. It shapes both one's way of living—as family members, as church members, as employees, and as citizens—and one's life perspective. By life perspective we mean one's model, one's paradigmatic assumptions about and understandings of life and of the social world. A black American's life perspective comes to embed a repertoire of responses to hostile and racist acts by whites. Like other black Americans, those we interviewed have learned to cope and contend with racial mistreatment in a variety of creative ways and somehow to maintain their equilibrium.

A fourth proposition we offer is that the daily experiences of racial hostility and discrimination encountered by middle-class and other African Americans are the constituent elements of the interlocking societal structures and processes called "institutionalized racism." Our interviews reveal much about how this discrimination works. Particular encounters with whites often hint at or reveal the influence of the larger context of institutionalized racism, for racial hostility is not inborn but learned. The reflections on black experiences and the incidents recounted in the interviews add together to show the web of intentional and unconscious discrimination across traditionally white spaces. Individual black Americans soon come to see that no amount of hard work or achieved status can protect them from racial oppression across numerous institutional arenas of this society. White discriminators typically see only the color of their skins and not their great efforts, sacrifices, and personal achievements. Moreover, through institutionalized discrimination whites not only restrict individual mobility but also social, economic, and political mobility for black Americans as a group. Indeed, to limit group mobility, to protect white privilege and power, seems to be the underlying reason for institutionalized racism.

In times of group protest by African Americans, such as the urban uprisings in cities from Los Angeles to Miami since the early 1980s, white awareness of U.S. racial problems usually increases significantly; for the most part this is temporary, however, and the majority of whites dodge the real meaning of these events. For a time whites, including scholars and media analysts, may discuss the "race relations problem" as the fault of black Americans or as an abstract problem "out there," not a problem rooted in individual whites themselves or their immediate families, social groups, and workplaces. *Time*'s front cover story soon after the 1992 Los Angeles riot was titled, "Why Race Still Divides America and Its People."[42] In reviewing mainstream media stories after the 1992 urban uprisings in Los Angeles we did not find any sustained media analysis that underscored the point our interviews dramatized: that the discriminatory *actions* of many white Americans in many institutions— and not some vague agent called "racial divisions"—are the major reason for continuing black-white problems and persisting black protest.

The Dimensions of Racial Discrimination

In the relevant social science literature racial discrimination is seldom clearly defined. In the 1944 classic, *An American Dilemma*, Gunnar Myrdal regularly used the concept but never clearly defined it.[43] Other major analysts of black-white relations from the 1940s to the 1980s, such as Blalock and Katz and Taylor, likewise give no explicit definition.[44] Among scholars who have developed definitions since the 1950s, we observe a trend toward emphasizing the macro-social level of group power and

18

institutionalized discrimination over the micro-level of individual interaction. In *The Nature of Prejudice* (1958) Gordon Allport stressed the actions of individuals and small groups and viewed discrimination as denying "individuals or groups of people equality of treatment which they may wish."[45] By the late 1960s and early 1970s many racial relations scholars were emphasizing large groups and institutions. In a pathbreaking 1967 book, *Black Power*, Stokely Carmichael and Charles Hamilton sharply contrasted the new view of institutional racism with the older approach focusing on individual racism.[46] Similarly, Thomas Pettigrew focused on the institutional dimension: "racial discrimination is basically an institutional process of exclusion against an outgroup on largely ascribed and particularistic grounds of group membership rather than on achieved and universalistic grounds of merit."[47] While whites have the power to discriminate as individuals, much of their power to harm comes from membership in white-dominated organizations and social networks, what Randall Collins calls "enforcement coalitions."[48]

Since the 1960s we have witnessed the demise of legal segregation and the emergence of many types of informal discrimination. Blatant discrimination has been joined by much subtle and covert discrimination. Moreover, writing about present-day discrimination in Great Britain, Brittan and Maynard have noted the importance of negotiated interaction: "the terms of oppression are not only dictated by history, culture, and the sexual and social division of labor. They are also profoundly shaped at the site of the oppression, and by the way in which oppressors and oppressed continuously have to renegotiate, reconstruct, and re-establish their relative positions in respect to benefits and power."[49] What begins as one-way action by a white discriminator can become interaction, often to the surprise of the white initiator. One dramatic change in racial interaction in the last two decades is the sizeable increase in the number of middle-class black Americans with the resources to contest discrimination tacitly or explicitly.[50]

We suggest that antiblack discrimination at the interpersonal micro level can be defined as the blatant, subtle, and covert actions taken by white people, willfully or half-consciously, to exclude, restrict, or otherwise harm black people. A particular discriminatory act can become the first stage in a racial negotiation process. In addition, discriminatory actions vary on a number of important dimensions, including these often suggested in our interviews: (1) the site of the action; (2) the range of discriminatory action; (3) the impact on the victim; and (4) the character of the response. A central purpose of this book is to deepen the contemporary analysis of racial discrimination by delineating and documenting these dimensions as they recur in the accounts of our respondents.

The experience of racial hostility can vary with the character of the site where it takes place. In our interviews a black professor contrasted the protection her status gives her in certain settings with the lack of protection in other, more public, surroundings:

> If I'm in those areas that are fairly protected, within gatherings of my own group, other African Americans, or if I'm in the university where my status as a professor mediates against the way I might be perceived, mediates against the hostile perception, then it's fairly comfortable. . . . When I divide my life into encounters with the outside world, and of course that's 90 percent of my life, it's fairly consistently unpleasant at those sites where there's nothing that mediates between my race and what I have to do. For example, if I'm in a grocery store, if I'm in my car, which is a 1970 Chevrolet, a real old ugly car, all those things—being in a grocery store in casual clothes, or being in the car—sort of

advertises something that doesn't have anything to do with my status as far as people I run into are concerned. Because I'm a large black woman, and I don't wear whatever class status I have, or whatever professional status [I have] in my appearance when I'm in the grocery store, I'm part of the mass of large black women shopping. For most whites, and even for some blacks, that translates into negative status. That means that they are free to treat me the way they treat most poor black people, because they can't tell by looking at me that I differ from that.

Protection against overt discrimination is likely to decrease as a black person moves from work settings, such as a department within a white university, into such public places as hotels, restaurants, and stores. Moreover, as black citizens move into public places such as city streets they have the most public exposure and the least protection. We will also see that in many places whites question the presence or actions of blacks. We believe that a significant dimension of modern racism is the racially motivated "blocking of space." A black person venturing into historically white spaces may learn from the attitudes, stares, or actions of whites that such sites are still "for whites only" or, at best, that it is for whites to determine who can reasonably be present.

A second important aspect of racial discrimination is its great range in character and subtlety. Allport once noted that prejudices are expressed in hostile actions ranging from antilocution to avoidance, exclusion, attack, and even genocide.[51] Today antiblack discrimination still ranges across this continuum: (1) avoidance, such as a white clerk avoiding the hand of a black customer; (2) exclusion and rejection, such as blocking a job promotion; (3) verbal attacks, such as yelling "nigger"; and (4) physical attacks, such as beatings by the police and physical assaults on college campuses. These examples are clearly overt.

21

More subtle forms include insults and insensitivities, which are common in everyday racism; our respondents sketch out a number of forms, including insensitivity to subcultural preferences (e.g., in music) in the workplace.

The motivations, stereotypes, and prejudices lying behind the white discrimination we examine in this book are often not clear. Still, some accounts provide some insight into white attitudes. White opinion surveys reviewed in two major books, *Racial Attitudes in America* and *A Common Destiny*, have shown that in certain subject areas white attitudes toward blacks have improved in recent decades.[52] Nonetheless, recent opinion surveys also indicate that large proportions of whites candidly express racial prejudices and stereotypes. Judging from the overtly antiblack responses to questions in 1990s opinion surveys, somewhere between 20 and 35 percent of whites are very negative and exclusionary in their attitudes toward black Americans, in regard to such matters as supporting anti-intermarriage laws and keeping blacks out of white neighborhoods.[53] These percentages are very significant, especially if they do not include, as seems likely, the large proportion of whites who more or less share the same views but are unwilling to say so to a pollster. Yet if only a third or so of whites hold the most hostile antiblack views, then perhaps fifty million whites over eighteen years of age today fall into this category. This number is far greater than the total of all black men, women, and children in the United States. In addition to those whites with very hostile views, the majority of whites interviewed in recent NORC surveys have shown that they accept some racial stereotypes, such as that blacks are less hardworking and more violent than whites.[54]

In fact, in recent years social scientists have conducted few systematic, in-depth research studies of white racial attitudes or of white discriminatory actions in particular settings. Brief responses to short poll questions do not necessarily signal the true feelings of many whites. Most whites share a common historical and cultural heritage of racism centered on African Americans. While much antiblack thinking is conscious, some is so deeply embedded in white assumptions and perspectives as to be half-conscious or even unconscious. It appears that a majority of whites think in racial terms when they make important choices —choosing neighborhoods, employees, business partners, places to go in the city, and mates for themselves and their children. Indeed, the negative reactions that at least two thirds of whites in recent surveys have shown toward interracial marriages are evidence of the depths of this racial heritage.[55] Without having to think much about it, the majority of whites seem to have a racial consciousness that is more than a few prejudices, but rather a broader framework of racialized thought, a way of organizing information about black and white Americans.[56]

Another aspect of discrimination is its lasting impact. In the immediate situation or over the long haul, discrimination can generate determination, embarrassment, frustration, bitterness, anger, rage, and any combination of these feelings. Discrimination is an energy-consuming, life-consuming experience. The enduring, cumulative impact of white racism has rarely been understood by white Americans. We can illustrate it with a brief quote from a black professor who has worked in several regions of the country:

I don't think white people, generally, understand the full meaning of racist discriminatory behaviors directed toward Americans of African descent. They seem to see each act of discrimination or any act of violence as an "isolated" event. As a result, most white Americans cannot understand the strong reaction manifested by blacks when such events occur. They feel that blacks tend to "overreact." They forget that in most cases, we live lives of quiet desperation generated by a litany of *daily* large and small events that, whether

23

or not by design, remind us of our "place" in American society.

Even to empathetic whites discrimination appears as discrete and isolated events. For blacks, the thick skin necessary for survival may make a given individual unaware at the conscious level, or only barely conscious, of the damage some of these instances inflict. As we noted earlier, an individual's own negative experiences are frequently shared with family and friends, relieving the victim's pain but also spreading the psychological costs. And there is the historical context to individual experience, an aspect the professor went on to explain:

> [Whites] ignore the personal context of the stimulus. That is, they deny the historical impact that a negative act may have on an individual. "Nigger" to a white may simply be an epithet that should be ignored. To most blacks, the term brings into sharp and current focus all kinds of acts of racism—murder, rape, torture, denial of constitutional rights, insults, limited opportunity structure, economic problems, unequal justice under the law and a myriad of . . . other racist and discriminatory acts that occur daily in the lives of most Americans of African descent— including professional blacks.

Surprisingly few recent analyses pay much attention to another important dimension of racial discrimination, the responses and strategies for coping of African Americans. Before desegregation in the 1960s, "old-fashioned racism," especially in the South, routinely took the form of an asymmetrical encounter in which blacks were expected to treat whites with deference. Examples included the obsequious words and gestures, the etiquette of race relations, that many black people used to survive segregation and informal mistreatment. Racially deferential behavior can still be found on the part of African

Americans, especially when there is the threat of force (for example, during police harassment) or in work situations not far removed from the old segregation. For example, Rollins found in a northeastern study that black domestic workers were commonly very deferential to white female employers.[57] Today, however, most discriminatory interactions no longer seem to involve an open show of old-fashioned deference by the black victims. Even when whites still expect it, black Americans usually do not oblige.

While many whites assert that blacks jump much too quickly to a cry of "racism," in reality the opposite reaction is more likely the case. Our interviews suggest that black middle-class people frequently respond to possible discrimination by taking a "long look," by evaluating a situation carefully before judging it discriminatory and taking action. One respondent, a clerical employee, described the "second eye" she uses: "I think that it causes you to have to look at things from two different perspectives. You have to decide whether things that are done or slights that are made are made because you are black or they are made because the person is just rude, or unconcerned and uncaring. So it's kind of a situation where you're always kind of looking to see with a second eye or a second antenna just what's going on." The term "second eye" suggests that she and others like her look carefully at white-black interaction through a distinctive lens colored by accumulating personal and group experience. We have noted in our interviews the willingness of many black respondents, using this "second eye," to give whites the benefit of the doubt in many interracial encounters.

Once a black person has spent mental energy in evaluating the situation, the active response to it may vary greatly. One strategy is to leave rather than engage in explicit conflict. Another is to ignore the discrimination and continue with the interaction, a strategy similar to the one Carol Brooks Gardner has reported in her research on women who deal with harassing

25

remarks from men on the street.[58] In some situations resigned acceptance may be the only realistic response. More confrontational responses to hostile white actions include verbal reprimands and sarcasm, physical counterattacks, and lawsuits.

Most people want to be legitimate in the eyes of others, and this includes many white discriminators. This concern for legitimacy can give black victims some leverage in certain discriminatory situations. In subsequent chapters numerous respondents articulate an ideal of "liberty and justice for all." What is especially significant is that the equal rights ideology of these middle-class black Americans is based on this American creed, the basic American principles accepted in the abstract, if not in practice, by most whites. The American creed and the legal system are often silent partners in black battles with an often hostile white world.

What Is the Black Middle Class?

Middle class African Americans are the group within black America that, generally speaking, has had the most recent experience with whites across the broadest array of social situations. They are often the ones who are desegregating historically white arenas and institutions, including upscale restaurants and department stores, business enterprises, corporate and government workplaces, white colleges, and white neighborhoods.

Since the nineteenth century the black middle class has been held up as a model for or sign of black advancement. For many decades the importance of the middle class has been emphasized by black leaders, as in William E. B. Du Bois' advocacy of an educated black elite working for social change.[59] Since the publication of E. Franklin Frazier's *Black Bourgeoisie* in the mid-1950s, a "new black middle class" composed increasingly of white-collar workers has been the subject of some scholarly and general discussion. In this controversial book Frazier criticized the black middle class as a whole for its conspicuous consumption, its obsession with status, and its uselessness within the larger society.[60] Most subsequent assessments of middle-class black Americans have been more balanced and have recognized the important achievements and general significance of this segment of black America.

In the social science literature there is no consensus definition of this black middle class, but several social scientists have used a broad demarcation including white-collar workers, sometimes with the addition of the most skilled blue-collar workers.[61] Historically, this class has grown significantly. In 1910 about 6 percent of blacks and a quarter of whites were in what the Census Bureau defined as trade, government service, professional, and clerical occupations, categories roughly covering that demarcation.[62] A few decades later, in 1940, only 9 percent of employed blacks were in white-collar or skilled blue-collar jobs, compared with just under half of whites. Significant gains came in the next few decades, and by 1970 the proportions had risen to 32 percent of blacks and 62 percent of whites.[63]

Legal equality for blacks under the 1960s civil rights laws generated a significant expansion of a formerly small middle class. In a pathbreaking analysis Bart Landry speaks of the 1960s as creating a "new middle class" whose "emergence marked a major turning point in the life of black people in the United States."[64] Landry and William J. Wilson, among others, have demonstrated the role of Vietnam-war-related economic growth and government antidiscrimination action in opening up job opportunities and spurring the development of the black middle class since the 1960s.

The broad occupational categories used by the Census Bureau were changed in 1980, so that recent data are not strictly comparable to earlier data. However, a 1988 Bureau of Labor Statistics survey found that about half of employed blacks held white-collar or skilled blue-collar jobs, compared with seventy percent of whites.[65] Yet these data probably exaggerate black progress, for those black employees in the Census Bureau's white-collar categories are often disproportionately concentrated in lower-status jobs.

Some researchers have suggested that educational attainment and income position should be considered in estimating accurately the security and size of the black middle class.[66] In many discussions middle-class status for black Americans is associated with higher levels of education, certainly a high school education and usually some college work. In 1989 about two thirds of black Americans over the age of twenty-four had completed high school. About 28 percent had completed at least a year of college, and just 12 percent had secured a college degree.[67] Increasingly, some college work, if not a college degree, seems essential to secure placement in the middle class, and this may especially be true for black Americans. Moreover, in the existing literature there seems to be no consistent standard for what is a middle-class income for black Americans, but one might speculate that an annual income near or above the white median for individuals or families might be a very rough standard for black individuals or families, at least for those with established households. A federal report found that in 1947 only 17 percent of black families had incomes above the white median income. By 1974 the proportion of black families above the white median had grown to nearly one quarter. Since the 1970s blacks have apparently made only small gains relative to whites. From 1988 data one can estimate that a little more than a quarter of black families had incomes above the white median income for that year.[68] Since the 1970s blacks have made only small gains relative to whites. Using these educational and income data, one might estimate that from one quarter to one third of the black population is more or less securely middle class.[69] While there is as yet no consensus on which measures to

use, it is clear that occupational, educational, and income criteria have been used, separately or together, by many analysts to
come up with rough evaluations of the character or size of the
black middle class.

African American Witnesses: Our Middle-Class Respondents

Analyses of the economic and social status of African Americans that rely on Census Bureau data and public opinion surveys are useful, but they lack experiential depth. Examination of
the texture, range, and meaning of black experiences requires
something more than quick responses to survey questions. Sociologist Herbert Blumer once noted that the only way to "get
assurance is to go directly to the empirical world—to see
through meticulous examination of it whether one's premises or
root images of it, one's questions and problems for it, the data
one chooses out of it, the concepts through which one sees and
analyzes it, and the interpretations one applies to it are actually
borne out."[70]
Listening at some length to black witnesses talking about
everyday experiences is particularly important for white analysts who wish to understand the contemporary situations and
experiences of black Americans. It would appear that few white
Americans even begin to understand the character, pain, and
meaning of the contemporary black experience with racial hostility and discrimination. In an article in the *Washington Post*
written a few months before her suicide in 1984, Leanita Mc-
Clain, a prize-winning black journalist, wrote how her feelings
toward the whites she worked with changed as she heard them
viciously attack Harold Washington, the first black mayor of
Chicago: "I had put so much effort into belonging, and the
whites had put so much effort into making me feel as if I be-

longed, that we all deceived ourselves. . . . But none of us had ever dealt with the deeper inhibitions, myths and misperceptions that this society has force-fed us."[71]

Grass-roots theorists, what Antonio Gramsci once called the "organic intellectuals,"[72] frequently develop theory out of the daily experiences of difficulties and oppression. In our research we listened, usually at some length, to the accounts of many middle-class African Americans about their experiences with racial hostility and discrimination in contemporary America. We have received valuable insights from black correspondents and informants in powerful positions in traditionally white institutions across the nation, from middle-class blacks in the audiences where we have presented lectures, and from our own black students. While we make good use of these discussions in the chapters that follow, we draw most heavily on in-depth interviews with a sample of 209 middle-class African Americans, a group that represents a range of middle-class experience. Like other qualitative studies of the contemporary American experience[73] we do not have a systematic random sample, but we have made a strong attempt to talk with a broad and diverse group of middle-class African Americans. Those interviewed were selected, in a snowball design with dozens of different starting points, from the ranks of those reputed to be middle class. All but one were interviewed by black interviewers. The sample is about half male and half female. Just over half are between thirty-six and fifty years old; another third are eighteen to thirty-six; and about a sixth are over fifty. At the time of the interview about two thirds were residents of southern or southwestern cities; about 6 percent were then in western or midwestern cities; and 29 percent were then in northern cities. In the sample, those in the South and Southwest are overrepresented relative to the U.S. black population, but in our chapter presentations we examine a large number of accounts from respondents in other regions. Wherever they reside now, many have lived in other regions, and their perspectives and comments on discrimination and related matters are often shaped by their travels and experiences in a variety of places. As we will see in the chapters that follow, racial discrimination is no respecter of region, age, gender, or socioeconomic status.[74]

Virtually all these respondents have occupied, currently occupy, or will likely soon occupy white-collar jobs and positions, or currently head their own businesses. Several are students at predominantly white colleges preparing for middle-class jobs. Most are managers, teachers, social service workers, doctors or other health care professionals, lawyers, electronics and computer professionals, government officials, college professors and administrators, journalists or others in the mass media, business owners, or clerical/sales workers. About 30 percent (including college students) reported household incomes of $35,000 or less; about a fifth, in the $36,000–$55,000 range; and about half, in the over $55,000 bracket.[75] As a whole, our sample is well educated. All have at least a high school degree, and almost all (95 percent) have done some college work. Nearly eight in ten have college degrees; and more than four in ten have done some graduate work. Practically all the respondents fall clearly into the black middle class, according to one or more of the socioeconomic criteria of "middle class" noted earlier, and many are in the upper middle class.

While we recognize that our sample is not random in the statistical sense, we have taken pains to insure that we have a broad group representing many subcategories and sectors of the black middle class. In Chapters 3 and 5 we also draw on two recent research studies by the first author that have examined the situations of other groups of African Americans, one a study of black businesspeople in a major southeastern metropolis and another of black college students and parents in an eastern state. In addition, we draw throughout the book on extensive discussions of our respondents' experiences with more than sixty

31

black middle-class informants across the nation, including journalists, administrators, graduate students, and scholars. Drawing on their own experiences, these African Americans have
often insisted on validating our respondents' accounts by telling
us about recent negative encounters they or their families have
had with white Americans.[76] Where possible, we also make use
of other recent research studies, including survey data, that relate to topics we examine in the in-depth interview data. Drawing on these multiple sources, we feel confident that the accounts of our respondents give an accurate picture of many of
the racial barriers and obstacles middle-class black Americans
face in their daily lives.

The main body of the interview schedule usually consisted of
open-ended questions on subjects related to life goals and recent
experiences with racial discrimination. Respondents were per-
mitted to discuss questions out of order and to digress to other
subjects they considered important.[77] One of the limitations of
brief surveys is that they do not let respondents assess issues in
their own terms. Our open-ended questions allowed our black
respondents to speak in their own terms and to present their
own accounts of everyday events, as well as to indicate much
about their social contexts and relationships. Many of our respondents' accounts have an important processual dimension,
that is, are narratives of events that have happened to them in
their daily rounds. The narratives are prisms revealing much
about the racial practices and structures of the United States.
Our interpretations of the black experience with discrimination
and other racial matters are profoundly shaped by being in
contact with the complexities of their everyday worlds.

We promised the respondents we would not reveal their
names and addresses and would keep interview responses anon-
ymous. Indeed, many talked with us only on condition of anonymity, perhaps fearing reprisals from some whites.[78] We usually opened the interview itself with a general break-the-ice

question probing what it means to be black in America these days, then asked about their personal goals, their recent experiences in employment, housing, and schooling, and their coping strategies and resources, both personal and familial. Most of the respondents' retrospective accounts relate experiences from the early 1980s to about 1989, with some references to an earlier period. Our other research accounts date from the mid-1980s to the early 1990s. We concluded the interviews with some other general questions, usually about social change and the future of racial relations in the United States.[79]

In the chapters that follow we quote from these interviews, with an emphasis on those with the most detail and insights about black experiences. We use numerous quotes to indicate what the barriers to achieving the American dream are for middle-class African Americans and to show how these respondents daily contend with obstacles. Each interview can be viewed as a "case study" in itself, since we usually listened at some length to our respondents' chronicles of discrimination and coping strategies. Moreover, like other qualitative researchers we have far more in-depth interview material on black-white interactions than we can possibly present in one book. We regret not being able to quote directly from all of those African Americans who kindly gave of their valuable time to be interviewed. Yet we do make indirect use of virtually all the interviews. The wealth of material on the daily lives, experiences, and perspectives of our entire sample, as well as other middle-class informants, constantly filters into our analysis at one point or another as we attempt to present a comprehensive portrait of what it means to be black and middle class in the United States today.

Conclusion

We have shown that the commonplace discussion of the declining significance of race and racism includes a singling out of middle-class African Americans as hard evidence that all blacks who "get it together" and work hard enough can "make it" in the United States. The black middle class reveals the great progress made in U.S. racial relations and proves, it is said, that black Americans, like white immigrant groups before them, can achieve the rags-to-riches Horatio Alger dream if they try hard enough. The premier measure of personal and group success in this society is upward mobility, and middle-class mobility and achievements are the chosen measures of black progress. No group has been more committed to achieving the American dream of equal opportunity and success through hard work than the black middle class. McClain, the prize-winning journalist cited earlier, commented in an October 1980 *Newsweek* column that middle-class blacks have the same American dream as whites: "These include the proverbial dream house, two cars, an above-average school and a vacation for the kids at Disneyland."[80] The behavior and achievements of middle-class African Americans demonstrate a strong commitment to the work ethic, to the belief that each American should work hard and strive to succeed in competition with others, and to the belief that those who work hard should have equal opportunity and be rewarded with a recognition of their achievements and with middle-class symbols and resources.

Yet our analysis suggests that racial hostility and discrimination make it impossible for any African American to achieve the full promise of the American dream. We can anticipate some of the later discussion with a few brief quotes from several respondents. Take the case of a once successful black executive in the North, now out of work and suing his employer for discrimination. He recounted his dream and his struggle: "So it's affected my life in a very profound way, and for one who has attempted all his life to achieve the American dream—and I say that in terms of having gone to school, done well in school, both in college and graduate school, served honorably in the military, given many years of outstanding service in a major corporation, and lesser useful service in several other organizations—to end up in a situation where you're having to go into the courts to have your basic rights reinforced, it's a real downer." Some material goods are secured; and personal achievements can be considerable, but racial barriers are routinely thrown up by the many whites who do not want blacks to succeed. The experience of middle-class African Americans on the street and in restaurants, neighborhoods, schools, and workplaces is quite different from the ideals of justice and equality, as a professor at a western university indicated: "It's a schizoid time. You have laws on the books that say that you, that there is no discrimination, that all men are treated equal. Yet every system that you encounter discriminates against you. It's very schizoid. You have to operate in two different spheres constantly." It seems likely that most African Americans with the income and occupational standing to be considered middle class sooner or later comprehend that they can never become truly middle class, at least in the ways available to white Americans. An anchorperson for a major TV station was adamant: "[There is] no black middle class, by the way. You know that's relevant. Every time I use 'middle class,' I know that. Because a black middle-class person is still not a middle-class person." And a government administrator put it another way: "Well, I heard somebody say, or I read once, that they were a middle class person trapped in a black body. And that's really the way I feel."

To be accepted as truly American, or not to be. To be allowed to be truly middle class, or not to be. These questions are forced on African Americans by a racist social system. Writing long ago in *The Souls of Black Folk*, Du Bois described a troubled black consciousness that is created by white racism: "It is a peculiar sensation, this double consciousness, this sense of always looking at one's self through the eyes of others. . . . One feels his two-ness—an American, a Negro; two souls, two thoughts, two unreconciled strivings; two warring ideals in one dark body, whose dogged strength alone keeps it from being torn asunder. The history of the American Negro is the history of this strife—this longing to attain self-conscious manhood, to merge his double self into a better and truer self."[81]

Chapter Two

Navigating Public Places

T ITLE II of the most important civil rights act of this century, the 1964 Civil Rights Act, stipulates that "all persons shall be entitled to the full and equal enjoyment of the goods, services, facilities, privileges, advantages, and accommodations of any place of public accommodation . . . without discrimination or segregation on the ground of race, color, religion, or national origin." Yet, as we approach the twenty-first century, this promise of full and equal enjoyment of the public places and accommodations of the United States is far from reality for African Americans.

Not long ago Debbie Allen, a movie star and television producer, recounted a painful experience with discrimination at a Beverly Hills jewelry store. A white clerk, possibly stereotyping Allen as poor or criminal, refused to show her some jewelry. Allen was so incensed that she used the incident as the basis for an episode on a television show. Across the country in Tamarac, Florida, a twenty-year-old black man, wearing a Syracuse University cap and hoping to invest his savings, visited a branch of Great Western Bank seeking information. After stopping at other banks, he returned to Great Western, got more information, and then went to his car to review the materials. There he was surrounded by sheriff's deputies with guns drawn, handcuffed, and read his rights. The deputies questioned him for some time before dismissing the report of white bank employees that the black man looked like a bank robber.[1]

Discrimination in Public Accommodations

In this chapter the middle-class respondents challenge us to reflect on their experiences with discrimination as they move into traditionally white public accommodations, such as upscale restaurants and department stores, and through public streets once the territory only of whites. They frequently report that their middle-class resources and status provide little protection against overt discrimination. Although there are, at least in principle, some social restraints on hostile white behavior in public accommodations, African Americans often experience hostility and mistreatment when they venture into spaces where many whites question the presence of a black person.

In the authors' experience many middle-class African Americans can relate several recent stories of being treated poorly by whites in public accommodations officially made hospitable by decades of civil rights laws. In our respondents' accounts restaurants are one site of hostile treatment, as are stores, hotels, and places of amusement. A black minister in a predominantly white denomination described his experience at a restaurant near a southern religious camp:

We were refused service, because they said they didn't serve black folk. It was suggested that if we stayed there any longer, that there was a possibility that our tires would be slashed. We finally stayed long enough for them to say,

"Well, I'll tell you what. We will serve you something to go, but you cannot come inside. We refuse that." And it was a situation that—I was not prepared for that. I was angry. I was humiliated, and I wanted to do something. I wanted to kick some ass.[2]

Given the threat of violence, he did not respond aggressively to this exclusion, but internalized his anger. Such encounters are not isolated events for many middle-class black Americans. The minister described yet another incident in a southern metropolis:

I was at this place called Joe's restaurant. I had to go into Joe's because I came up in that community. Joe's is a barbecue place that is right by the auto plant, so all of the executives from the plant would come there for lunch. I went there with a guy who was successful. [I] thought I was a decent black person, came in wearing a suit and tie, sat down, and I noticed that, you know, these white boys kept coming in, and the waitress kept on looking over me. And I eventually said to her, "Ma'am, I'd like to order." She said, "Well, you're going to have to wait." And I complained to the owner and he proceeded to cuss me out. Told me that I didn't have "no goddamn business" in that restaurant telling them who they ought to serve and when they ought to serve them. Told me that. I came up in the neighborhood, been eating there for years, and it suddenly dawned on me that white folk will take your money, but to them in their minds you're still a nigger. They're able to separate economics from dealing with relationships between them and black folk. He challenged me to a fight, and this was another source of humiliation. I said to myself, "If I fought this man in his restaurant with there being a hundred white boys that'll substantiate whatever story he told, they could

lynch me and say that I hung myself, you know." I left. I've
never gone back to that place. But I've always thought
about burning it down.

In spite of the 1964 Civil Rights Act black customers today
encounter poor service or are refused service. Even with the
growth of black economic resources, there seems to be some
conflict within many white business owners between taking the
dollars blacks can spend and recoiling from dealing with blacks.

In such events the person being rudely treated or ignored is
usually quite conscious of the historical context of the interaction, as can be seen in the minister's allusion of lynching. In
another account, a black news director at a television station
described an incident in which she and her boyfriend responded
very differently to an act of discrimination and the anger it
provoked in them:

> He was waiting to be seated. . . . he said, "you go to the
> bathroom and I'll get the table. . . ." He was standing there
> when I came back; he continued to stand there. The restau-
> rant was almost empty. There were waiters, waitresses, and
> no one seated. And when I got back to him, he was ready
> to leave, and said, "let's go." I said, "what happened to our
> table?" He wasn't seated. So I said, "no, we're not leaving,
> please." And he said, "no, I'm leaving." So we went out-
> side, and we talked about it. And what I said to him was,
> you have to be aware of the possibilities that this is not the
> first time that this has happened at this restaurant or at
> other restaurants, but this is the first time it has happened
> to a black news director here or someone who could make
> an issue of it, or someone who is prepared to make an issue
> of it.
>
> So we went back inside after I talked him into it and, to
> make a long story short, I had the manager come. I made
> most of the people who were there (while conducting my-

self professionally the whole time) aware that I was incensed at being treated this way. . . . "I said, why do you
think we weren't seated?" And the manager said, "well, I
don't really know." And I said, "guess." He said, "well I
don't know, because you're black?" I said, "bingo." "Now
isn't it funny that you didn't guess that I didn't have any
money (and I opened up my purse and I said, because I certainly have money). And isn't it odd that you didn't guess
that it's because I couldn't pay for it because I've got two
American Express cards and a Master Card right here. I
think it's just funny that you would have assumed that it's
because I'm black." . . . . And then I took out my [busi-
ness] card and gave it to him and said, "if this happens
again, or if I hear of this happening again, I will bring the
full wrath of an entire news department down on this restaurant." And he just kind of looked at me. "Not [just] because I am personally offended. I am. But because you have
no right to do what you did, and as a people we have lived
a long time with having our rights abridged."

There were probably three or four sets of diners in the
restaurant and maybe five waiters/waitresses. They watched
him [her boyfriend] standing there waiting to be seated. His
reaction to it was that he wanted to leave. I understood
why he would have reacted that way, because he felt that
he was in no condition to be civil. He was ready to take
the place apart and . . . sometimes it's appropriate to be-
have that way. We hadn't gone the first step before going
on to the next step. He didn't feel that he could comfort-
ably and calmly take the first step, and I did. So I just
asked him to please get back in the restaurant with me, and
then you don't have to say a word, and let me handle it
from there. It took some convincing, but I had to appeal to
his sense of, this is not just you, this is not just for you. We
are finally in a position as black people where there are

some of us who can genuinely get their attention. And if
they don't want to do this because it's right for them to do
it, then they'd better do it because they're afraid to do otherwise. If it's fear, then fine, instill the fear.

Discrimination here was not the "No Negroes" exclusion of the
recent past, but rejection in the form of poor service. Again a
black person's skin color took precedence over money. The
black response has changed too, since the 1950s and 1960s,
from deference to indignant, vigorous confrontation. Here the
assertive black response and the white backtracking are typical
of "negotiation" that can occur in racial confrontations today.

In recounting this incident this black professional mentions
black "rights" several times. Clearly imbedded in her response
is a theory of rights that she, like many African Americans,
holds as a part of her worldview. Her response signals the impact of the tradition of civil rights struggle, and civil rights laws,
on the life perspective of African Americans. Also of interest
here is her mention of her credit cards and other middle-class
resources. A quick reading of her statement, and that of other
black middle-class people who mention similar trappings of success, might lead to the conclusion that middle-class blacks expect to be treated better than poorer blacks because they have
worked hard and have money. But this does not seem to be the
meaning of such references. Instead, this woman is outraged
that the obvious evidence of hard work and achievements does
not protect her from racial discrimination. She has achieved
certain elements of the American dream, but they are not sufficient.

A close look at the experience of middle-class African Americans is important to understand the racial backwardness of contemporary U.S. society, for it confirms that no amount of hard
work, money, and success can protect a black person from the
destructive impact of racial stereotyping and discrimination. In

this book we show that middle-class black Americans, just like other black Americans, have terrible experiences with everyday racism. But we show much more than that. We also demonstrate that racial stereotyping and discrimination operate independently of the real identities and achievements of specifically targeted black individuals.

The ability of middle-class African Americans to act forcefully against discrimination by whites marks a change from a few decades ago when very few had the resources to fight back successfully. Black Americans have always fought against discrimination, but in earlier decades such fights were usually doomed to failure if not injury. In this account, the woman's ability as a professional to bring a television news team to the restaurant enabled her to take assertive action. This example also underscores the complexity of the interaction in some situations of discrimination, for not only is there a confrontation with a white manager over mistreatment but also a negotiation between the black individuals over how to respond.

It is an effective antidiscrimination strategy on the part of black Americans to make the confrontations public. An executive at a financial institution in an East Coast city recounted his experience with a pattern of poor service in a restaurant, explaining his decision to confront the discriminators:

> I took the staff here to a restaurant that had recently
> opened in the prestigious section of the city, and we waited
> while other people got waited on, and decided that after
> about a half hour that these people don't want to wait on
> us. I happened to have been in the same restaurant a couple
> of evenings earlier, and it took them about forty-five min-
> utes before they came to wait on me and my guest. So, on
> the second incident, I said, this is not an isolated incident,
> this is a pattern, because I had spoken with some other
> people who had not been warmly received in the restau-

43

rant. So, I wrote a letter to the owners . . . and sent copies to the city papers. That's my way of expressing myself and letting the world know. You have to let people, other than you and the owner know. You have to let others know you're expressing your dismay at the discrimination or the barrier that's presented to you. I met with the owners. Of course, they wanted to meet with their attorneys with me, because they wanted to sue me. I told them they're welcome to do so. I don't have a thing, but fine they can do it. It just happens that I knew their white attorney. And he more or less vouched that if I had some concern that it must have been legitimate in some form. When the principals came in, one of the people who didn't wait on me was one of the owners who happened to be waiting on everybody else. We resolved the issue by them inviting me to come again, and if I was fairly treated, or if I would come on several occasions and if I was fairly treated I would write a statement of retraction. I told them I would not write a retraction, I would write a statement with regard to how I was treated. Which I ultimately did. And I still go there today, and they speak to me, and I think the pattern is changed to a great degree.

The time- and energy-consuming aspects of publicly confronting discrimination are apparent in this account. The respondent invested much of himself in a considered response to a recurring problem. Forcing whites to renegotiate, especially by using negative publicity, can bring about changes. The arrival on the restaurant scene of middle-class black Americans with substantial resources has at least created situations that force whites into explicit negotiating.

Whites often enter into this "bargaining" situation with tacit assumptions and cultural expectations about black powerlessness. In the two previous examples we see the black profession-

44

als establishing "power credibility," as the whites decide that they are not bluffing. It is important to note that the whites here are not just the blue-collar whites often said to be the primary source of whatever bigotry remains in the United States. Those doing the discrimination include middle-class whites, a fact that signals the importance of race over class in much racial interaction.

That discrimination against black customers and employees in white-owned restaurants is widespread has become evident in several court suits filed since 1990 against national chains, including Denny's, Shoney's, and the International House of Pancakes (IHOP). In December 1991, for example, several groups of black college students were reportedly turned away from a Milwaukee IHOP restaurant and told that it was closed, while white customers were allowed in. In 1993 a federal judge ordered the restaurant to pay a settlement for the discrimination. Also in 1993, the Denny's chain, found to have a pattern of discrimination by the U.S. Justice Department, reached an agreement with the Department in which executives promised to train employees in nondiscriminatory behavior and to include more minorities in its advertising. This settlement did not affect a class-action discrimination suit by thirty-two black customers who reportedly had suffered discrimination in several Denny's restaurants in California. Moreover, in mid-1993 six black secret service agents also sued the chain, alleging discrimination at a Denny's in Annapolis, Maryland. The black agents reported that while they waited for service for nearly an hour, white agents and other white patrons were promptly served.[3] After much bad publicity, Denny's joined in an important agreement with the NAACP to work to end discrimination in its restaurants.[4]

As revealed in the court cases, restaurant discrimination has recently included long waits while whites are served, special cover fees applied only to blacks, and prepayment requirements only for black customers.[5] In the Shoney's case, the chain was sued over discrimination against black employees. According to the *St. Petersburg Times*, top officers in the white-run firm were well-known for their antiblack views, and local managers were discouraged from hiring black employees. In a 1992 landmark agreement the company agreed to pay $115 million, the most ever, to employees who could prove racial discrimination.[6]

Restaurants are only one site of discrimination. Daily life inevitably involves contact with clerks and managers in various retail and grocery stores. A utility company executive in an eastern city described how her family was treated in a small store:

> I can remember one time my husband had picked up our son . . . from camp; and he'd stopped at a little store in the neighborhood near the camp. It was hot, and he was going to buy him a snowball. . . . This was a very old, white neighborhood, and it was just a little sundry store. But the proprietor had a little window where people could come up and order things. Well, my husband and son had gone into the store. And he told them, "Well, I can't give it to you here, but if you go outside to the window, I'll give it to you." And there were other people in the store who'd been served [inside]. So, they just left and didn't buy anything.

The old white neighborhood in which this episode occurred exemplifies the racial-territorial character of many cities even today. The poor service here seems a throwback to the South of the 1950s, where deferential blacks were served only at the back of a store. This man chose not to confront the white person nor to acquiesce abjectly but rather to leave. Here the effect on the white man was probably inconsequential because there was no confrontation and interracial negotiation. The long-run importance of a service site may well affect a black person's choice of how to respond to such discrimination. The store in this exam-

46

ple was not important to the black family just passing through the area. The possibility of returning might have generated a more confrontational response.

Another problem that black shoppers face, especially in department and grocery stores, is the common white assumption that they are likely shoplifters. This is true in spite of the fact that national crime statistics show that most shoplifters are white. For several months in late 1991 a news team at KSTP-TV in Minneapolis conducted a field study of discrimination against black shoppers in several local department stores. Members of the team took jobs as security personnel in the stores, and black and white shoppers were sent into the stores in order to observe the reactions of white security personnel. The ensuring television report, "Who's Minding the Store?" showed how many black customers became the targets of intensive surveillance from white security guards, who neglected white shoppers when black shoppers were in the stores. As a result of the documentary, local black leaders called for a boycott of one of the store chains. Soon a number of the local stores changed their surveillance and security procedures.[7] Excessive surveillance of black customers in department and other stores was reported by some we interviewed. A black professional in the North commented on how she deals with whites who harass her with excessive surveillance and other acts of rejection:

> [I have faced] harassment in stores, being followed around, being questioned about what are you going to purchase here. . . . I was in an elite department store just this past Saturday and felt that I was being observed while I was window shopping. I in fact actually ended up purchasing something, but felt the entire time I was there—I was in blue jeans and sneakers, that's how I dress on a Saturday— I felt that I was being watched in the store as I was walking through the store—what business did I have there, what

was I going to purchase, that kind of thing. . . . There are a few of those white people that won't put change in your hand, touch your skin. That doesn't need to go on. [Do you tell them that?] Oh, I do, I do. That is just so obvious. I usually [speak to them] if they're rude in the manner in which they deal with people. [What do they say about that?] Oh, stuff like, "Oh, excuse me," and some who are really unconscious about it, say "Excuse me," and put the change in your hand. That's happened. But I've watched other people be rude, and I've been told to mind my own business. [But you still do it?] Oh, sure, because for the most part I think that people do have to learn to think for themselves, and demand respect for themselves. . . . I find my best weapon of defense is to educate them, whether it's in the store, in a line, at the bank, any situation, I teach them. And you take them by surprise because you tell them and show them what they should be doing, and what they should be saying, and how they should be thinking. And they look at you because they don't know how to process you. They can't process it because you've just shown them how they should be living, and the fact that they are cheating themselves, really, because the racism is from fear. The racism is from lack of education.

A number of racial stereotypes are evident in this account. Whites with images of black criminality engage in excessive surveillance, and whites with images of black dirtiness will not touch black hands or skin. Black shoppers at all income levels report being ignored when in need of service and the unwillingness of some whites even to touch their hands. Why such a reaction to black bodies? In a speculative Freudian analysis of white racism, Joel Kovel has argued that for centuries whites have irrationally connected blackness, and black bodies, with fecal matter and dirt. In his view, whites are somehow projecting onto the darkness of the black outgroup personal inclinations, desires, and fears that cannot be openly and honestly acknowledged.[8]

A common black response to contemporary discrimination is evident here. Rather than withdrawing when facing such discrimination, this professional sometimes protracts the interaction with verbal confrontation. She notes the surprise effect of calling whites on the carpet for discrimination, which she sees as grounded in fear and ignorance. Interrupting the normal flow of an interaction to change a one-way experience into a two-way experience forces whites into unaccustomed situations in which they are unsure how to respond.

Middle-class African Americans enter many settings where few blacks have been before. A news anchorperson for an East Coast television station reported on an incident at a luxury automobile dealer:

I knew I wanted to buy a Porsche, but I didn't know which model. So, on my day off, I went into a Porsche dealership in the city I used to work in. . . . And I was dressed like I normally do when I'm off. I'm into working out a lot, so I'm in sweatsuits, baseball caps, sunglasses quite a bit. So I dashed into this place dressed like that, and I must have walked around the show room floor for twenty minutes. No sales person ever walked up to me and asked me, "Can I help you? Can I give you some information?" Nothing. I got the impression, the opinion, that they generally thought that this person, being black, being dressed in a sweatsuit, cannot hardly afford to be in here buying a Porsche. He's wasting my time, so I'm not even going to bother. And I knew that. So I specifically, the next day on my lunch hour, dressed in my work clothes, having just come off the air, I walked into that showroom. And I said, "Can I see the general manager?" And they got the general manager for

me. And I said to the general manager, "I was in here yesterday." Well, I said, "First of all, I want to buy that Porsche
there, the most expensive one on the floor." And I also told
him, "Just yesterday I was in here, I was looking in, and I
was hoping I could get some information, and oddly none
of your sales people ever asked me if they could help me." . . .
And there is prejudice, discrimination and racism, and
things like that go on. Once they found out who I was,
they bent over backwards [to wait on me].

White salespeople apparently took the cue from this man's color
and clothing and stereotyped him as moneyless, an assumption
that the victim challenged the next day when he engaged in an
unexpected confrontation. This chronic mistreatment by white
salespeople, while white shoppers are generally treated with
greater respect, is infuriating for black customers. It is clear
from our interviews that African Americans must prepare themselves for this sort of encounter, for they never know when they
will be shown normal respect and courtesy as customers or
when they must "front" (dress in a certain way, talk in a certain
way) in order to receive the treatment accorded a comparable
white customer.

Among several respondents who discussed discrimination at
retail stores, the manager of a career development organization,
who found that discrimination by clerks is common, had a repertoire of responses for dealing with it:

If you're in a store—and let's say the person behind the
counter is white—and you walk up to the counter, and a
white person walks up to the counter, and you know you
were there before the white customer, the person behind the
counter knows you were there first, and it never fails, they
always go, "Who's next." Ok. And what I've done, if they
go ahead and serve the white person first, then I will imme-

diately say, "Excuse me, I was here first, and we both know
I was here first." . . . If they get away with it once, they're
going to get away with it more than once, and then it's
going to become something else. And you want to make
sure that folks know that you're not being naive, that you
really see through what's happening. Or if it's a job opportunity or something like that, too, same thing. You first try
to get a clear assessment of what's really going on and sift
through that information, and then . . . go from there.

In discussions with middle-class black Americans across the nation, both our respondents and a variety of informants and
journalists, we heard many similar accounts of white clerks
"looking through" black customers and only "seeing" whites
farther back in line. Such incidents suggest that much of the
hostility manifest in white actions is based on a deeplying, perhaps even subconscious or half-conscious, aversion to black
color and persona. This executive also spoke of her coping process, one that begins with sifting information before deciding on
action. Frequently choosing immediate action, she forces whites
to face the reality of their behavior.

The dean of a black college who travels in various parts of the
United States described the often complex process of evaluating
and responding to the mistreatment that has plagued him in
public accommodations:

When you're in a restaurant and . . . you notice that blacks
get seated near the kitchen. You notice that if it's a hotel,
your room is near the elevator, or your room is always way
down in a corner somewhere. You find that you are getting
the undesirable rooms. And you come there early in the day
and you don't see very many cars on the lot and they'll tell
you that this is all we've got. Or you get the room that's
got a bad television set. You know that you're being dis-

51

criminated against. And of course you have to act accordingly. You have to tell them, "Okay, the room is fine, [but] this television set has got to go. Bring me another television set." So in my personal experience, I simply cannot sit and let them get away with it and not let them know that I know that that's what they are doing. . . .

When I face discrimination, first I take a long look at myself and try to determine whether or not I am seeing what I think I'm seeing in 1989, and if it's something that I have an option [about]. In other words, if I'm at a store making a purchase, I'll simply walk away from it. If it's at a restaurant where I'm not getting good service, I first of all let the people know that I'm not getting good service, then I [may] walk away from it. But the thing that I have to do is to let people know that I know that I'm being singled out for separate treatment. And then I might react in any number of ways—depending on where I am and how badly I want whatever it is that I'm there for.

These recurring incidents in public accommodations illustrate the cumulative nature of discrimination. The dean first takes care to assess the incident and avoid jumping to conclusions. One must be constantly prepared on everyday excursions to assess accurately what is happening and then to decide on an appropriate response. What is less obvious here is the degree of pain and emotional drain that such a constant defensive stance involves.

Whether some of the incidents reported by the last two respondents are in fact discriminatory is a question raised by some whites to whom we have shown these commentaries. Several have said that accounts of not being served in turn or being assigned poor hotel rooms are not necessarily racial discrimination, for whites too occasionally suffer such treatment. This raises the issue of how black accounts of discrimination are credited by whites. When we have discussed these accounts with black informants and journalists, they credit them quickly because of their own similar experiences. Years of cumulative experience give these middle-class black Americans the "second eye" that one respondent described, the ability to sense prejudice or discrimination even in a tone of voice, a look, or a gesture. Having occasionally experienced poor service themselves, however, many whites accuse blacks of being paranoid in seeing racism in such incidents. Yet it is the consistent pattern of bad treatment, not only of oneself but of one's relatives and friends, by whites that is the basis for the black victims' interpretation of a particular incident as probable racial discrimination. Yet one more aspect of the burden of being black is having to defend one's understanding of events to white acquaintances without being labelled as racially paranoid.

Many incidents in public accommodations have no ambiguity whatever. In many a white mind a black person standing is certain places is assumed to be in a menial position. A physician in an eastern state described her feelings when she was staying in nice hotels: "I hate it when you go places and [white] people . . . think that we work in housekeeping. . . . A lot of white people think that blacks are just here to serve them. And we have not risen above the servant position." Middle-class blacks report this experience of being taken by whites to be in servile positions. Even Democratic party presidential candidate Jesse Jackson had such an experience. Elegantly dressed and standing by an elevator in an upscale New York hotel, right after a meeting with an African political leader, Jackson was approached by a white woman who said "I couldn't have made it downstairs without you." She put a dollar in his hand, mistaking Jackson for her black bellhop.[9]

Growing old does not eradicate the possibility of discrimination in public places. An eighty-year-old retired schoolteacher in a southwestern city recounted her experiences with whites at a drapery shop:

> The last time I had some draperies done and asked about them at the drapery shop, a young man at that shop— when they called [to him], he asked, and I heard him—he said, "the job for that nigger woman." And I said to the person who was serving me, "Oh my goodness, I feel so sorry for that young man. I didn't know people were still using that sort of language and saying those sorts of things." And that's the way I deal with it. I don't know what you call that. Is that sarcasm? Sarcasm is pretty good. . . . Well I've done that several times. . . . I'm surprised that I find it in this day and time.

Using "strategic indirection" in voicing her response not to the discriminator but to another white clerk within earshot of the insult, this teacher communicated the inappropriateness of racist remarks without giving whites the satisfaction of viewing her humiliation. With their long experience of blatant racism, older black Americans may be more likely to hurt in silence. When they do speak out, their response may often be measured and deliberate. Later this woman characterized such recurring racial incidents as the "little murders" that have daily made her long life so difficult.

Much creativity is demonstrated in the strategies for coping with whites in stores and other public accommodations. One such strategy was noted by a news anchorperson:

> And if I was seeking out a service, like renting a car, or buying something, I could get a wonderful, enthusiastic reaction to what I was doing. I would work that up to such a point that this person would probably shower me with roses once they got to see me. And then when I would show up, and they're surprised to see that I'm black, I sort of remind them in conversation how welcome my service was, to put the embarrassment on them, and I go through with my dealings. In fact, once my sister criticized me for

> putting [what] she calls my "white-on-white voice" on to
> get a rental car. But I needed a rental car and I knew that I
> could get it. I knew if I could get this guy to think that he
> was talking to some blonde, rather than, you know, so, but
> that's what he has to do deal with. I don't have to deal
> with that, I want to get the car.

The discrepancy between civility over the phone and discrimination in person is the acid test that proves the reality of everyday discrimination. Among the resources middle-class African Americans use to cope with bigotry is language. They often find themselves in situations where so-called "standard English" is required. They can code-switch as the situation demands it, speaking English without a distinguishable accent or grammatical variation that would make their racial identity known to whites. By erasing the so-called "black accent," which is often exaggerated in the white mind, they can sometimes avoid being victims. With creativity born of necessity this respondent uses her resources not only to secure services but also to bring some sense of her discomfort to whites caught red-handed. The idea of using artifice to get a positive outcome is an old strategy for African Americans, and here the psychological play seeks to educate rather than injure.

Some of the essential coping strategies are learned at an early age. One poignant example of discrimination took place at a suburban swimming pool, yet another type of public site. A manager at an electronics firm gave this account:

> I'm talking over two hundred kids in this pool; not *one*
> black. I don't think you can go anywhere in the world during the summertime and not find some black kids in the
> swimming pool. . . . Now what's the worst thing that can
> happen to a ten-year-old girl in a swimming pool with all
> white kids? What's the worst thing that could happen? It
> happened. This little white guy called her a "nigger." Then

called her a "motherfucker" and told her "to get out of the god-damn pool." . . . And what initiated that, they had these little inner tubes, they had about fifteen of them, and the pool owns them. So you just use them if they are vacant. So there was a tube sitting up on the bank. She got it, jumped in, and started playing in it. . . . And this little white guy decided he wanted it. But, he's supposed to get it, right? And he meant to get it. And she wouldn't give it to him, so out came all these racial slurs. So my action was first with the little boy. "You know you're not supposed to do that. Apologize right now. O.K., good. Now, Mr. Lifeguard, I want him out of this pool, and you're going to have to do better. You're going to have to do better, but he has to leave . . . this pool and let his parents know, okay?"

Taking his daughter back the next day, this father watched from behind a fence to make certain the lifeguard protected her. Apparently this was the first time his daughter had been the victim of such blatant racial slurs. She was not simply the victim of a rude child; she was the target of white rudeness and racist epithets that for this black father, as for other black adults, connote segregated institutions and antiblack violence. For father and daughter this incident was not trivial but took on the proportions of a painful and serious life crisis. For many African Americans one of the public places most redolent with historical memories of racism is the swimming pool, for in earlier decades many white communities closed pools rather than allow desegregation.

Discrimination in the Street

As middle-class African Americans move from public accommodations to less protected street sites, racial hostility can become even more severe. Encounters with whites in the streets can be dangerous, as in this report by a black man, now a television commentator, who was working during the mid-1980s for a media surveying firm in a southern city:

> I was parked in front of this guy's house. . . . This guy puts his hands on the window and says, "Get out of the car, nigger." . . . So I got out, and I thought, "Oh, this is what's going to happen here." And I'm talking fast. And they're, "What are you doing here?" And I'm, "This is who I am. I work with these people. This is the man we want to put in the survey." And I pointed to the house. And the guy said, "Well you have an out-of-state license tag, right?" "Yeah." And he said, "If something happened to you, your people at home wouldn't know for a long time, would they?" . . . I said, "Look, I deal with a company that deals with television. [If] something happens to me, it's going to be a national thing. . . . So, they grab me by the lapel of my coat, and put me in front of my car. They put the blade on my zipper. And now I'm thinking about this guy that's in the truck [behind me], because now I'm thinking that I'm going to have to run somewhere. Where am I going to run? Go to the police? [laughs] So, after a while they bash up my headlight. And I drove [away].

The discrimination in this account is part of a pattern of intimidation and threats whereby whites have kept most blacks from coming into this particular suburb. A consciousness of the history of lynchings and other antiblack violence in the South makes this violence and the threat of further violence even more frightening for this man. Drawing on his middle-class resources, he had the courage to tell the attackers that his death would bring television crews to the area. For most whites threatened by assailants on the street the police are a sought-after source of protection, but this is often not the case for black men.

A college graduate recounted a threatening experience near a predominantly white university he attended:

> One night I had gone to a midnight movie on campus. I was walking back to my dorm and this big four-wheeler, you know those huge trucks that white guys drive, with the big wheels, about six feet high? It came screeching around the corner. There were about six white guys in this truck and I could tell they were drunk, so I continued walking. And he slammed his brakes and started yelling and hollering racial slurs out the window, like "nigger go home," "blackie," "spade," all types of things. And my instant reaction was to spin around, you know, and get angry, which is what I did. And they saw that I did this, so they started in even more, started hurling even more epithets. But I noticed in the back of their window they had a big old hunting rifle back there and I didn't know if they'd use it or not; I wasn't about to stick around and find out. So I looked at them again with a real stern look like I didn't appreciate it, and I spun around and kept walking. Then they turned the truck around in my direction, and if they turned around just to go a different way on the street or if they turned around just to go after me, once again, I wasn't going to stick around to find out. And I started hauling for the nearest dorm because I knew I could lose them in the dorm.

Being a black student in a college town historically accustomed only to white students increases street vulnerability—and the possibility of intimidation and violence. This graduate student maintained his composure and figured out a way to escape a potentially deadly situation.

Racially motivated "hate crimes" have increased in the streets and neighborhoods of towns and cities since the 1970s. Mandated by the recent Hate Crime Statistics Act, the FBI's first hate crime report counted 4,558 attacks for the year 1991, with only 19 percent of law enforcement agencies sending in any data. The largest proportion (36 percent) of these were antiblack crimes, including property damage and serious personal assaults like the case above.[10] And this incomplete government report doubtless records but a very small proportion of the serious attacks on black individuals or homes in that year.

Racist epithets are a major problem for African Americans as they traverse streets and other public places. Such epithets are taken seriously because they may threaten action. They may also invoke in the black mind memories of past discrimination, including antiblack violence. A professor at a predominantly white university in the Southwest described a case of unforgettable street harassment:

> I was driving. This has [happened] so many times, but one night it was especially repugnant. I think it had to be, with my son being in the car, it was about nine-thirty at night. And as I've said, my car is old and very ugly, and I have been told by people shouting at intersections that it's the kind of car that people think of as a low-rider car, so they associate it with Mexican Americans, especially poor Mexican Americans. Well, we were sitting at an intersection waiting to make a turn, and a group of middle-class-looking white boys drives up in a nice car. And they start shouting things at us in a real fake-sounding Mexican American accent, and I realized that they thought we were Mexican Americans. And I turned to look at them, and they started making obscene gestures and laughing at the car. And then one of them realized that I was black, and said, "Oh, it's just a nigger." And [they] drove away.

This incident illustrates white hostility provoked by certain signals of minority group status, including an old car and dark skin; a black person suffered from hostility aimed at other people of color by whites unable to distinguish. The darkness assured the whites' anonymity and heightened the negative impact of the incident on this woman.

In research on street remarks Carol Brooks Gardner writes of women and blacks as "open persons," particularly vulnerable targets for harassment that violates the usual rules of courtesy in public places.[11] A health care professional who lives in an East Coast city described biking with his son near a shrine of American liberty:

> My son and I were riding bicycles and we were down
> around Fort McHenry. . . . And we'd gotten off the bikes
> and we were drinking out of this water fountain. And this
> car pulled up; these white kids drove by. And they said,
> "Hey, nigger!" You know? And we turned our heads and
> looked up, "Hey, niggers!" They never stopped, but they
> were just driving by slowly. And I said, "You're damn right
> I'm a nigger, and I'm proud of it!"

There is a deep irony here. Freedom from racially motivated street harassment is not yet a reality for this man and his son riding near Fort McHenry, whose bombardment by the British in the early 1800s inspired "The Star-Spangled Banner," memorializing "the land of the free." This man responded by turning the epithet into a badge of honor.

For younger middle-class African Americans, especially those who have been sheltered by their parents, racial harassment can generate shock and disbelief, as in the case of this student who reported a street encounter near her university:

> I don't remember in high school being called a "nigger" before, and I can remember here being called a nigger. [When was this?] In my freshman year, at a university student parade. There was a group of us, standing there, not knowing that this was not an event that a lot of black people went

to! [laughs] You know, our dorm was going, and this was something we were going to go to because we were students too! And we were standing out there and [there were] a group of white fraternity boys—I remember the southern flag—and a group of us, five or six of us, and they went past by us, before the parade had actually gotten underway. And one of them pointed and said, "Look at that bunch of niggers!" I remember thinking, "surely he's not talking to us!" We didn't even use the word nigger in my house. . . . [How did you feel?] I think I wanted to cry. And my friends . . . were ready to curse them, and I was just standing there with my mouth open. I think I wanted to cry. I could not believe it, because you get here and you think you're in an educated environment and you're dealing with educated people. And all of this backward country stuff. . . . You think that kind of stuff is not going on, but it is.

The desire to be accepted as an equal is strong in her comments: "We were students too!" We see a black student in pain, but who initially gave whites the benefit of the doubt. Her subsequent response was tearful acquiescence to the hostility, but her friends were ready to react aggressively, although the whites may have moved on before a considered response was possible. Note too the mention of the Confederate flag, a symbol that conjures up painful memories and associations for black Americans. This episode underscores the impact of racial coding on young people and hints at the difficulty parents face in socializing children for coping with white hostility.

Another white epithet is "welfare queen," often a thinly disguised derogatory reference to black women. Much white discussion of black women is rife with welfare stereotyping. A woman who runs a business in a southwestern city described her experience with such stereotyping in front of a grocery store:

We had a new car . . . and we stopped at 7–11 [convenience store]. We were going to go out that night, and we were taking my son to a babysitter. . . . And we pulled up, and my husband was inside at the time. And this person, this Anglo couple, drove up, and they hit our car. It was a brand new car. So my husband came out. And the first thing they told us was that we got our car *on welfare*. Here we are able-bodied. He was a corporate executive. I had a decent job. It was a professional job, but it wasn't paying anything. But they looked at the car we were driving, and they made the assumption that we got it from welfare. I completely snapped; I physically abused that lady. I did. And I was trying to keep my husband from arguing with her husband until the police could come. . . . And when the police came they interrogated them. They didn't arrest us, because there was an off-duty cop who had seen the whole incident, and said she provoked it.

Seeing only the blackness of the black couple, the whites here react on the basis of racial stereotypes. Like several previous respondents, this woman is outraged that her and her husband's hard work and achievements did not protect her from racial abuse. Seemingly no amount of success can counter the oppressiveness of white stereotyping. The angry response undoubtedly came as a surprise to the whites. If the off-duty officer was white, which is possible here, his intervention at least suggests that times have changed; in the recent past a white officer would very likely have taken the white side in the encounter.

Patience is a signal feature of many black middle-class responses to the pervasive discrimination they encounter in public places. The aggressiveness of the response varies with the situation and the resources at hand. A parole officer in a western city recounted how he dealt with a racial epithet in an determined manner:

I've been called "nigger" before, out in the streets when I was doing my job, and the individual went to jail. . . . [Ok, if he didn't call you a "nigger," would he have still gone to jail?] Probably not. [. . . . was the person white?] Yes, he was. And he had a partner with him, and his partner didn't say anything, and his partner jaywalked with him. However, since he uttered the racial slur, I stopped him and quizzed him about the laws, and jaywalking's against the law, so he went to jail.

In the social science literature on policing, the substantial street-level discretion available to police officers has been described in some detail.[12] Jaywalking is usually a winked-at violation, but this officer exercised his authoritative discretion to punish a racist epithet. (By "to jail" he may mean "to the police station.") Although this man was in a position of authority that might well have brought a violent retaliation to the verbal hostility if the colors of the men had been reversed, he restrained himself and used a measured but authoritative response to the negative treatment.

In addition to assault, threats of violence, and racist epithets, one commonly cited form of racial harassment in public places is the discourteous white "hate stare," an old problem for African Americans that dates back to at least the eighteenth century. This phenomenon was well described by white journalist John Howard Griffin in *Black Like Me*, his book about traveling as a black man in the South in the late 1950s. Even as a white man only temporarily dyed black, Griffin found the hate stares extremely disturbing and threatening. Hostile looks can occur anywhere blacks encounter whites; they illustrate the interstitial character of much hostile behavior.[13] One college student reported that on her way to her class she stopped at a bakery in a residential area where few blacks live. A young white couple sitting in front of the store stared intently and hatefully at her as she crossed the sidewalk in front of them and went into the bakery, and again as she returned to her car. She reported that in her experience this type of nonverbal expression of hostility was common. And a manager at a large company gave this account: "The first weekend we were here we went to have breakfast in this white neighborhood and we came out and got in our car. We got stared at until we got out of the parking lot and into the street. Noticeable stares—waitresses, patrons in the restaurant, two old guys standing outside in the parking lot. It was like, 'What are you doing here?'" Part of the story of racism is this racial coding of places, for some places are still more or less off limits to black Americans. A black person moving into these spheres learns, often immediately, that his or her presence is not wanted.

Hate stares might seem minor slights to most white observers, because again they have no history of such recurring experiences and are unaware of the historical implications. Yet for black Americans the intense stare often has a lasting impact. The last two respondents reported agonizing later over the stares. In his interview the man added that after they went home he and his wife became intensely focused on the incident and found themselves "talking about it too much." Numerous black respondents and informants have reported the difficulty of letting go of discriminatory incidents, for they can cause great pain and haunt the mind for months and years. Such unpleasant memories are potentially debilitating, interfering with performance in work and school.

Harassment by White Police Officers

Many black encounters with the police have unfavorable outcomes. Sociologist James Blackwell has reviewed research suggesting that three quarters of the white officers in certain mostly black precincts have some antipathy to black residents,[14] an antipathy that is reflected in the well-documented racist actions of some white police officers. A recent study of 130 police brutality incidents reported in regional and national newspapers across the nation found that blacks or Latinos were the victims in 97 percent of the assaults; there were only two cases in which the victim was a sole white citizen.[15] And 93 percent of the officers were white. It is clear from this and other studies that police brutality is not confined to southern cities but has been reported in most regions of the nation. Moreover, unwarranted police beatings of black men, such as the videotaped beating of Rodney King in Los Angeles in 1991, have directly or indirectly precipitated numerous riots in black communities from the 1930s to the 1990s. Given the history of police harassment and brutality, it is likely that most black men—including middle-class black men—see white police officers as a source of possible danger if not injury.

The television commentator quoted earlier described two cases of police harassment when he was working for a media surveying firm. In one incident in a southern city he was stopped by several white officers, one of whom asked, "What are you doing here?"

> I tell them what I'm doing here. . . . And so they had me
> spread on top of my car. [What had you done?] Because I
> was in the neighborhood. I left this note on these people's
> house: Here's who I am. You weren't here, and I will come
> back in thirty minutes. [Why were they searching you?]
> They don't know. To me, they're searching. I remember at
> that particular moment when this all was going down,
> there were a lot of reports about police crime on civil-
> ians. . . . It took four cops to shake me down, two police
> cars, so they had me up there spread out. I had a friend of
> mine with me who was making the call with me, because
> we were going to have dinner together, and he was black,

65

and they had me up, and they had him outside. . . . They said, "Well, let's check you out." . . . And I'm talking to myself, and I'm not thinking about being at attention, with my arms spread on my Ford [a company car], and I'm sitting there talking to myself, "Man, this is crazy, this is crazy." [How are you feeling inside?] Scared, I mean real scared. [What did you think was going to happen to you?] I was going to go to jail . . . just because they picked me. Why would they stop me? It's like, if they can stop me, why wouldn't I go to jail, and I could sit in there for ten days before the judge sees me. I'm thinking all this crazy stuff. . . . Again, I'm talking to myself. And the guy takes his stick. And he doesn't whack me hard, but he does it with enough authority to let me know they mean business. "I told you to stand still; now put your arms back out." And I've got this suit on, and the car's wet. And my friend's hysterical. He's outside the car. And they're checking him out. And he's like, "Man, just be cool, man." And he had tears in his eyes. And I'm like, oh, man, this is a nightmare. This is not supposed to happen to me. This is not my style! And so finally, this other cop comes up and says, "What have we got here, Charlie?" "Oh, we've got a guy here. He's running through the neighborhood, and he doesn't want to do what we tell him. We might have to run him in." [You're "running through" the neighborhood?] Yeah, exactly, in a suit in the rain?! After they got through doing their thing and harassing me, I just said, "Man, this has been a hell of a week."

And I had tears in my eyes, but it wasn't tears of upset. It was tears of anger; it was tears of wanting to lash back. . . . What I thought to myself was, man, blacks have it real hard down here. I don't care if they're a broadcaster; I don't care if they're a businessman or a banker. . . . They don't have it any easier than the persons on skid row who get harassed by the police on a Friday or Saturday night.

By the time they are in their twenties many black men in all income groups have been stopped by the police—often several times—simply because blackness is considered a sign of possible lawbreaking by police officers.[16] Officers in many police agencies are trained, either formally in classes or informally by other officers, to look for certain demographic cues that supposedly distinguish potential criminal offenders from other people, and high on the list are the classifications "black" and "male." This black experience with police harshness doubtless marks a dramatic contrast with the experiences of most middle-class white males. In the incident described above the respondent and his friend reacted to severe mistreatment with humiliating deference. We sense their anger that their personal achievements and symbols of success brought no protection from stigmatization and harassment.

Black women traveling the public streets may also be targets of police harassment. The professor quoted previously in regard to street harassment by white civilians spoke of her encounters with the police:

When the cops pull me over because my car is old and ugly, they assume I've just robbed a convenience store. Or that's the excuse they give: This car looks like a car used to rob a 7–11. And I've been pulled over six or seven times since I've been in this city—and I've been here two years now. Then I do what most black folks do. I try not to make any sudden moves so I'm not accidentally shot. Then I give them my identification. And I show them my university I.D. so they won't think that I'm someone that constitutes a threat, however they define it, so that I don't get arrested.

She then added this chilling comment:

> [One problem with] being black in America is that you have to spend so much time thinking about stuff that most white people just don't even have to think about. I worry when I get pulled over by a cop. I worry because the person that I live with is a black male, and I have a teen-aged son. I worry what some white cop is going to think when he walks over to our car, because he's holding on to a gun. And I'm very aware of how many black folks accidentally get shot by cops. I worry when I walk into a store, that someone's going to think I'm in there shoplifting. And I have to worry about that because I'm not free to ignore it. And so, that thing that's supposed to be guaranteed to all Americans, the freedom to just be yourself is a fallacious idea. And I get resentful that I have to think about things that a lot of people, even my very close white friends whose politics are similar to mine, simply don't have to worry about.

This statement underscores the pyramiding character of discrimination. This professor has been subjected to excessive surveillance repeatedly by white officers. She attempts to draw on her resources for protection; she asserts her status as a professor by pulling out her university I.D. This use of credentials in dealing with white police officers marks a difference from the days of legal segregation, when a black person announcing her achievements would have been considered arrogant and increased the danger. Yet it is still degrading for a black person to have to go through a rehearsed ritual to forestall being violently harassed by white authorities. She has to use the symbols of success that are recognized as such by whites. Note again the explicit theory of rights and justice. The tension in her mind between the deferential response required in dealing with white police officers and her sense of injustice is clear in her comments about the freedom of movement theoretically guaranteed by civil rights statutes.

These situations show the vulnerability of black men and women in encounters with white officers. Even black police officers have remarked on this sense of powerlessness. Quoted recently in *Essence* magazine, Ronald Hampton, executive director of the National Black Police Association, put it this way: "It sounds crazy for me to say that you can't defend yourself, but you can't defend yourself. Police have power over citizens." He added, "if there is going to be some abuse, there will be abuse." He advised black citizens that all they can do is to try to shield themselves.[17]

Black students at predominantly white colleges have regularly reported difficulties with white police officers. These problems occur on or near the campuses where they study, attend classes, and, often, reside. In an interview one college student who lives on a nearly all-white campus discussed how campus police officers had trained spotlights on her simply because she was black. Then she continued with this statement:

This past year there have been some incidents, some attacks on campus. And [my boyfriend] was at the gym playing basketball; and he was going to the gas station. He got out of the car at the gas station down the street. The [police] guy tells him to put his hands up, and he pulled a gun. It wasn't the campus police, but I feel they called him. Their reason was that they saw him leaving the gym, and they thought they heard a woman screaming at him. He said, "There was no woman." That doesn't make sense. I think they should be punished, it's just not right. But see, incidents happen to them, especially black men, incidents like this happen to them all the time. Have they written a letter? Have they done anything? No. They [the police] haven't bothered me but when they do, I will write a letter, and it will be publicized. I will make sure it is. I'm not going to take that. There's no reason that I should have to. Do you want to see my I.D.? Give me a reason. You can't just ask me for my I.D. when I'm just walking down the sidewalk. There are fifty billion other white people walking on the same sidewalk and you didn't ask them for their I.D. . . . You don't want to have your friends come here sometimes, because they'll be harassed. So, it's kind of bad. But I've heard a lot of campuses are like that, white campuses.

In recent years there have been numerous reports of local police harassing of black students at traditionally white colleges in all regions of the country. Black male students often become prime suspects for white officers investigating serious campus crimes. At the University of Nebraska (Lincoln), the campus police department photographed and interrogated five black men who were in the anthropology class of a white female student who had disappeared. Later two white men were charged with her killing.[18] Being unfairly interrogated or searched is a common occurrence for black male students. Even Harvard University's Divinity School advises its black students, during the initial fall orientation, to always carry papers of identification so that they will be prepared for the likely harassment from Harvard University and Cambridge police officers.[19]

The screening process used by a variety of police agencies to assess who is a likely criminal might be termed "stereotyped profile discrimination." When we related some of our respondents' accounts of police harassment to a black journalist at a major newspaper, she recounted a recent experience of her own. She was hustling through a major airport in a northern city on her way to an important assignment, when she was pursued by white drug enforcement officers. Rushing after her and stopping her at the door of her airport rental car bus, the agents asked who she was and where she was going. Although she showed her I.D., they persisted, getting on the bus with her. There the white agents stared at her and refused to answer her questions about what they were doing. Thinking back over the events later, she said they continued to cause her much pain: "I felt like ET, an alien in another world. I felt like I had been raped." She also remembered thinking hard about how she could prove her innocence to the agents. The only black person in a group of similarly dressed whites getting on the bus, she felt they stopped her because she fit the stereotyped police profile of a drug runner—young, black, and hurrying through an airport.[20]

It is not just police agents who operate on the basis of profiles grounded in stereotypes. A New England executive commented on the difficulty black men commonly face in getting taxi drivers to stop for them: "I traveled quite a bit during that time. You would hit the normal discriminatory actions of goings-away . . . being scrutinized very closely as to who you are and what your purposes are and so forth—the situations of trying to hail cabs in New York City, that's a classic one blacks face. No matter how businesslike they're dressed, there's a problem in that regard." The voice of this executive has a tone of resignation in it, as in his noting the "normality" of this street-level discrimination. Significantly, some middle-class informants with whom we have shared these public-place accounts have mentioned the strategies they use in street situations, such as taking pains to walk at a distance from whites or getting a white friend to hail a cab for them.

The Cumulative Impact

The cumulative impact of several of these types of street discrimination was underscored by a black student at a large, mostly white university in the Southwest. He described his experiences walking home at night from a campus job to his apartment located in a predominantly white residential area:[21]

> So, even if you wanted to, it's difficult just to live a life where you don't come into conflict with others. Because every day you walk the streets, it's not even like once a week, once a month. It's every day you walk the streets. Every day that you live as a black person you're reminded how you're perceived in society. You walk the streets at night; white people cross the streets. I've seen white couples and individuals dart in front of cars to not be on the same side of the street. Just the other day, I was walking down the street, and this white female with a child, I saw her pass a young white male about twenty yards ahead. When she saw me, she quickly dragged the child and herself across the busy street. What is so funny is that this area has had an unknown *white* rapist in the area for about four years. [When I pass] white men tighten their grip on their women. I've seen people turn around and seem like they're going to take blows from me. The police constantly make circles around me as I walk home, you know, for blocks. I'll walk, and they'll turn a block. And they'll come around me just to make sure, to find out where I'm going. So, every day you realize [you're black]. Even though you're not doing anything wrong; you're just existing. You're just a person. But you're a black person perceived in an unblack world.

In a subsequent comment this student described how white men had hurled objects and racist epithets at him as he walked home. Discrimination is every day and everywhere. This student's experience is an example of what Ralph Ellison meant when he wrote of the general white inability to "see" black Americans as individuals in *The Invisible Man*.[22] Unable to perceive this black male student's middle-class symbols of college dress and books, white individuals and couples have crossed the street, dodging cars, to avoid walking near this medium-stature black student. They are doubtless reacting to the negative image of black males. The student perceives such avoidance in a particular instance as racially motivated, because he and his male friends have often encountered whites taking similar "defensive" measures.

The common white view of black men as dangerous, held by police and civilian whites alike, is deeply rooted in the history and collective psyche of white Americans. In a pathbreaking book, *The Black Image in the White Mind*, historian George Fredrickson has demonstrated that long before the twentieth century whites had developed a view of black slaves and servants as fearful and dangerous "beasts," a stereotyped view that has often lain behind white violence such as lynchings of black men.[23] Still, this view persists. Today not just white police officers but many white media producers and commentators,[24] and a majority of whites generally, appear to view criminals who commit violent crimes against white individuals and property to be mostly black or minority males. Yet the world of crime is complex and for the most part does not fit this white image. Most (78–88 percent) of the whites who are assaulted, raped, or murdered are attacked by white assailants, according to the 1991 National Crime Victimization Survey and other government crime data. While black assailants do account for 44 percent of the assailants of white robbery victims, they account for only 17 percent of the assailants in all crimes of violence targeting white victims.[25]

In the white world black men, especially young black men, routinely suffer physical or psychological attacks from whites, yet such attacks get little publicity in the mass media, and then only when they are sensational. Attacks on whites by black men get much more media attention. For example, in a recent column about hate crimes and the First Amendment, nationally syndicated columnist James Kilpatrick focused only on one case, a racially motivated "get the white boy" attack on a white youth by some black teenagers. What is striking here is that such flagrant black-on-white cases are much less frequent than the reverse, today and even more so in the past, yet this prominent columnist did not find those white-on-black cases sufficiently newsworthy for his column.[26] The case of "Willie" Horton, a black man who raped a white woman, is a celebrated example of the same biased focus on black-on-white crime. In 1988 the George Bush campaign used Horton's image to frighten white voters. Although the overwhelming majority of the rapists who attack white women are white, the negative image of the black man as a rapist of white women is so exaggerated and commonplace among white Americans that the campaign could make use of it to attract white voters to a conservative cause.[27] Significantly, much media discussion and some scholarly dialogue have been devoted to white perceptions of black men as threatening and the justifiability of that perception. To our knowledge there has been no serious research or reporting on the very negative impact on the everyday lives of black men of white assumptions and the resulting avoidance and fear.[28]

Representing what appears to be a widely accepted view, one otherwise perceptive white analyst of discrimination has commented that whites' crossing the street to avoid black men is "a minimal slight."[29] This is far from the truth. The black student quoted above reported that repeatedly being treated as a pariah, in his own words a "criminal and a rapist," has caused him severe psychological problems. Similarly, after a phone interview with the first author on some of this research on public-place discrimination, one of the nation's leading black journalists reported that middle-class whites sometimes stop talking—and white women grab their purses—when he enters an office-building elevator in his New England city. Whereas the student said that he rarely had been able to respond to the street encounters, apart from the occasional quick curse, because they happened too quickly, the journalist noted that when possible he has reacted more assertively; he described how he turns to whites in elevators and informs them, often with a smile, that they can continue talking or that he is not interested in their purses.

Conclusion

The NRC report *A Common Destiny* found that by the late 1970s many whites believed that the Civil Rights Act of 1964 had brought a broad-scale elimination of racial discrimination in public accommodations.[30] Robert Lauer and Warren Handel have written that as black Americans get access to an outer circle "from which they had been previously excluded (such as eating at a public restaurant) they encounter inner circles from which they are still excluded (such as equal access to economic opportunities) and with an even greater hostility than that with which they were barred from the outer circles."[31] Unfortunately, our interviews and other sources indicate that deprivation of the full enjoyment of public facilities promised by the 1964 Civil Rights Act is not something of the past; attack, exclusion, rejection, and other types of antiblack discrimination persist in public accommodations today for African Americans, whatever their socioeconomic status. Streets and public accommodations are relatively unprotected sites, and African Americans are very vulnerable there to white maltreatment.

These accounts of encounters with whites in public places shaped the theoretical propositions we offered in Chapter 1. For middle-class black Americans white racism is not an abstraction generated by a militant ideology but rather a matter of ordinary experience. In these reports the emotional reaction to white hostility and discrimination in public places is explicit or just beneath the surface. Whether the incident took place in a restaurant, a store, or on the street, we usually can feel the humiliation, frustration, pain, and rage, as well as sense the stoicism and determination. The frustration and pain expressed in these accounts suggest that serious instances of hostility and discrimination can indeed be life crises. Even a single incident, such as the newscaster's encounter with knife-wielding white racists on the street, leaves painful memories that will never be forgotten. Even the hate stares, which may seem minor to whites, have a way of sticking in the mind's eye and tormenting a black person for a very long time.

Encounters with white hostility and discrimination shape the lives and perspectives of middle-class African Americans. A black person's life perspective—the personal assumptions about the world—may be shaped by discrimination to include a sense of lack of control over one's life. Research studies using the Rotter Introversion-Extroversion Scale, which measures whether an individual feels in control of his or her life, have found that black subjects tend to score differently from whites and to feel that their lives are controlled predominantly by outside forces. Reviewing this research, Mirowsky and Ross have underscored the importance of a sense of control for personal well-being and effectiveness. Without it, one feels a sense of powerlessness, creating a condition in which an individual may have difficulty in achieving desired goals.[32] For our respondents it appears that the steady dose of white racism creates a chronic dilemma of having to fight, sometimes successfully, sometimes unsuccessfully, against a realistic sense of powerlessness. One important aspect of the perspective these middle-class black Americans develop, however, is a deep commitment to securing equal rights.

The dilemma of how to deal with racism can be seen in the responses of the news director and her boyfriend to being pointedly ignored in a restaurant. The boyfriend, fearing he would lose his temper, wished to withdraw, but the news director pressed for a confrontation, asserting her professional status and her power as part of the media. Her strategy was clearly grounded in her reflection on previous experiences with racial discrimination and on her commitment to black rights. White discrimination is sometimes countered with a black comeback. In an August 31, 1981 column in the *Chicago Tribune* black columnist Leanita McClain described this situation as the "new racism": "The old racism wouldn't let blacks into some stores; the new racism assumes that any black person, no matter how well dressed, in a store is probably there to steal, not to buy. . . . The old racism didn't have to address black people; the new racism is left speechless when a black, approached condescendingly, has an eloquent comeback."[33]

Chapter Three

Seeking a Good Education

I N the spring of 1987 a white Columbia College student undertook a campaign of verbally and physically harassing black students. When asked by black students to stop the harassment, he replied, "Ah man, fuck you," and a fight between black and white students ensued. One black student was sent to a hospital, and another was chased by a white student yelling "Goddamn you fucking niggers." Black security guards trying to break up the conflict were attacked by whites. Black students said they feared for their lives. With the support of a few whites, black students organized against racist conditions on campus. Many white students reportedly viewed the black students as responsible for the problems, and Columbia's white administrators, although condemning the racial attacks, were unwilling to remedy the campus conditions cited by the black students as underlying the attacks. This episode of racial harassment and administrative insensitivity took place on a northern campus with an image of liberalism.[1]

There is not much information on the character and breadth of the discrimination faced by black youth in schools and colleges, but a few surveys are suggestive. A 1991 national survey of young people aged fifteen to twenty-four by Hart Research Associates found that 41 percent of the black youth said they themselves had been the victims of racial discrimination, but the survey did not ask where or how often that discrimination had occurred.[2] A few opinion surveys have asked general questions about discrimination in education. In a 1989 ABC News/*Washington Post* survey 37 percent of black respondents agreed that blacks generally face discrimination in getting a quality education. In an earlier 1986 survey, one quarter of the black respondents reported having personally faced discrimination in getting a quality education. Given that a significant proportion of those over the age of thirty had attended legally segregated schools, this proportion seems low. Neither in this survey nor in more recent surveys have questions been asked about the many aspects of public and private education, such as teacher-student interaction or extracurricular activities, in which racial discrimination could have occurred. And these surveys provide little information on specific patterns of educational discrimination faced by the black middle class.[3]

In this chapter middle-class African Americans discuss racially integrated or predominantly white educational institutions. At first glance, integrated schools and colleges might seem intrinsically more hospitable than the public settings we discussed previously, because many contacts with white students and teachers there occur in a context formally emphasizing collegiality and openness to learning, and because many of the whites with whom blacks interact are acquaintances, not strangers. Nonetheless, black students in substantially white schools face racial hostility in many facets of their educational experiences.

African Americans have long attached great importance to education for themselves and their children. Education has been seen as a way to be accepted, as the "great leveller" that should bring first-class citizenship. This emphasis on education can be seen in responses to a 1990 National Opinion Research Center survey in which blacks were more likely than whites to favor more government spending on preschool programs (76 percent versus 57 percent), slightly more likely than whites to feel that government was spending too little on education (72 percent versus 71 percent), and significantly more likely than whites to believe that a major cause of poverty was the failure to provide a good education for all (57 percent versus 33 percent).[4] Education still looms large in black dreams of opportunity and success.

Obstacles in Elementary and Secondary Schools

Where one lives can determine where one's children go to school and the quality of their schooling. In spite of housing laws banning discrimination, our towns and cities remain bastions of racial segregation. In most towns and cities people can tell you "where blacks live" and "where whites live." Black residential areas often have poor government services. In central cities many black middle-class residential areas are adjacent to other black neighborhoods (see Chapter 6).

Black parents' decisions to live in a predominantly black or black middle-class community can give their children social support in the form of black friends and black organizations, yet the public schools available may not be as well equipped or staffed as those in white suburban areas. Black middle-class parents are aware that living in historically white areas can often provide their children public schools with better resources. Some research, such as a Hartford, Connecticut study that followed 318 black students at predominantly white suburban schools and 343 black students at predominantly black central city schools, has touted the advantages of white schools. In this Hartford study black students who attended white high schools were more likely to graduate from high school, to go to college, to complete more years of college, and later to live in integrated residential areas than those who attended the central city high schools.[5] However, this case seems to be exceptional. Other studies have reported on the subtle and blatant racism, including hate crimes, that black students at predominantly white public schools have encountered.[6] Such hostility affects school performance, and some students drop out. The short term and long term damage that discriminatory white actions in desegregated schools can often do to black children puts this Hartford study into a more critical perspective.

Black parents who put their children into historically white schools soon become aware of the racial obstacles their children face. White administrators, teachers, students, and parents can create hurdles, as a counsellor at a western university explained in discussing her daughter's school:

[We had] to enroll my daughter in school after we moved into a different school [district]. And this particular location was pretty much white; there was some integration going on. And I knew there was something wrong when I walked into the school, because there was this hush as I walked in. I thought, OK, whatever. I mean, everyone turned to look. And this woman wanted to know if I lived in their school district. And I said, "Yes, otherwise I wouldn't be here." And she wanted me to go home and get my deed to the property, and some other documents, and not thinking, I was like, "Oh, sure, yes." And then I thought, what is this? And once again, I found myself on the phone, calling the superintendent of schools. And when I went back the next day to enroll my daughter, the woman said that I didn't have to go over her head to her superiors. And I said, "Obviously I did." And I said, "Let me tell you one other thing. If my children experience any form of retaliation because of what I did, then I'll be back."

Once again a respondent mentions subtle racial cues, the strange looks or the familiar "hush" noted by many blacks entering traditionally white spaces. Like the "hate stare" noted in Chapter 2 they are part of the fabric of everyday life. This black parent did not respond directly to these racial cues until they were confirmed when she was pressured for excessive documentation. Her aggressive response signals again the insistence on civil rights that is part of the black repertoire for fighting discrimination.

The school curriculum in both predominantly white and integrated schools often presents additional obstacles to black students. A black professional in a northern city explained what she objected to in the integrated schools her children attended:

> [The school was] expecting that my children will not be achievers, therefore not offering them challenges in their schooling. And I as a parent have to [check] with regard to reading lists, making sure that my children have the opportunity to choose books by and about black people. When they talk about classics, there are black classics, so I want my children, and other children, to be able to read those classics as well. So, I've offered additional books for the reading lists, with some struggle. [What do they say about that?] "Oh, I didn't know, I didn't know about those books," or, "Oh, that's a good idea," or "These are the books that the colleges want young people to have read, so we have to use these." And my response is "Still, you can put all of those books on the list, that shouldn't stop you from adding additional books to the list." And they recognize that the population that they are educating has other races and nationalities and languages, and so they have to put other things on the list. But it's a struggle.

Across the nation, school desegregation as it has actually been implemented mainly mixes together children and teachers of

82

different racial backgrounds. Much else remains as before. The curriculum is often not desegregated, but continues to reflect the topical interests of the white parents. A black parent may have to fight to bring new materials on African Americans into the instruction process. Punctuating her comments with some biting laughter, the same respondent reflected on other changes she has sought:

> And then, Columbus Day holidays, we had a discussion around that—helping teachers expand the discussion, frame the questions appropriately. Not "What did Columbus discover?" But how he accidentally, when he got lost, ran aground and he was discovered! Framing history in a different way, demanding that when you talk about African Americans and their contribution to society, that we were not just slaves. And looking at the inventions and the contributions of African Americans in a much broader way.

Like many other African Americans, several respondents suggested the need for expanded multicultural courses and programs in schools, including educating all children about the contributions of Africans and African Americans to the development of the United States. In recent years prominent white critics of multicultural programs in schools and colleges have been forthright about their white Eurocentric bias. Historian and presidential adviser Arthur Schlesinger, Jr., has called the multiculturalism perspective "an astonishing repudiation" of the idea of the melting pot: "The contemporary ideal is not assimilation but ethnicity. We used to say 'e pluribus unum.' Now we glorify 'pluribus' and belittle 'unum.' The melting pot yields to the Tower of Babel."[7] Schlesinger and other white observers worry that the United States cannot survive with a vibrant pluralism of racial and ethnic groups and argue that an integrated society requires all groups to adopt "Western culture" as their rudder. These whites usually oppose most of the modest cultural diversity courses and programs proposed for or implemented in some public schools around the nation, although often without any direct experience with the schools or their programs. In contrast, much criticism of school curricula by black parents is grounded in everyday experience with cultural bias and racism in the public school system.

In assessing the current state of public schools, black parents are also critical of how their children are tracked. The negative psychological impact of tracking black and white children into separate schools was at the heart of the 1954 *Brown* school desegregation decision, yet within desegregated schools testing procedures, administered under the guidance of school counsellors and teachers, have often been used to place black children into special tracks. Conventional tracking procedures can create serious difficulties, as a social services administrator in an eastern city illustrated:

> I get a sense that often my children, as well as other black
> children, have been steered into vocational type subjects
> and given to believe that that's "best for them," quote, un-
> quote, "best for them." And I have certainly encouraged
> my children that I would like [them] to take the academic
> courses and to do well in them. I believe that their testing
> and that sort of thing shows that they are able to do it.
> And it takes a lot to stay in there with them, and try to
> make sure that nobody's undermining my goals for them.

Interestingly, the stratification of schools into vocational and academic tracks, begun in the early twentieth century with the support of U.S. educational reformers, initially segregated white children by class within their racially segregated schools. Since the 1920s, children from higher-income white families have tended to be placed in college-oriented tracks; those from moderate-income and working-class backgrounds have been more likely to be assigned to a vocational track. With the great increase in racially integrated schools since the 1960s, black and other minority students have been overrepresented in the lowest tracks.[8]

The tracking decisions of white teachers and counsellors can shape the educational career of a student. A teacher in a northern city discussed her son's attempt to get into a more demanding high school:

> He went to the public schools here in the city, and he had in his mind to go to Smith Tech. But his guidance counselor had in his mind that he should go to Jones High. Of course Jones—there's this mentality that white folks seem to have about us sometime. And that mentality basically deals with the fact that, it's something that was started back in slavery days, pre-slavery days, the fact that the black man should be taught to be productive with his hands and how to behave himself in society. So, the point is that they seem to feel that black folks, instead of becoming intellectual, being able to function in jobs that require some intellectual ability, they seem to think that we're better off being mechanics and whatever else, floor sweepers or whatever type of job that seems appropriate for us as long as we behave ourselves. Anyway, this guidance counselor, she tried to push the boy—the fact that the boy had merit roll and honor roll [was neglected]—she tried to stress the fact that he should go to Jones High. And of course that's just to train mechanics. And my son wanted to go to Tech. And what I had to do, I called her up on the phone to remind her that one of the main objectives of the city public schools is for every student to attain an education and become all that he can become capable of. And therefore, since he had the frame of mind to want to enter Tech, I wanted him to take the test for Tech.

The counsellor's decision forced him to take the test late, and although he passed, he went on the waiting list for Tech. She

85

added: "So, consequently he did go to Jones High. But at Jones, he did very well, and wound up one of the winners, out of all of the students, one of two students to win scholarships. And he's presently attending a local college in the technical engineering program."

Contending with White Prejudices and Stereotypes

The interaction of black parents and children with white teachers, parents, and children can involve contending with common antiblack stereotypes. A black teacher discussed her integrated school:

Another example—I was STOP sponsor, these are kids who are on the verge of dropping out. So at school we can volunteer to sponsor a couple of kids, or one kid. One little girl I sponsored is very dark, very huge lips, very short hair, pleasant personality, pretty to me. Well, I went to talk to her biology teacher because she was not doing well, and she said, "Oh, I know Aunt Jemima! Was she a STOP student? Aunt Jemima! You know, she's always chewing that gum and got all that red lipstick." I called her aside. I said, "I need to talk to you." I said, "Do you call her Aunt Jemima in class?" She just smiled, "She's such a sweet child." I told her, "Now, maybe you don't know what connotation Aunt Jemima has for blacks. Maybe you don't mean any harm, but *please* don't call her that. It's very offensive to blacks." Well, I talked to the student and I asked her, "How do you feel when she calls you Aunt Jemima?" "Well, I'm trying to get out of that class because I don't like it."

The racial slur by the white teacher may not have been fully conscious; her "sweet child" comment suggests a maternalistic orientation. A best-selling pancake product made by a major

U.S. corporation still uses the Aunt Jemima image, and antique shops across the nation feature racist memorabilia of this type for sale, so it is not surprising that some white teachers can be extremely insensitive to the deeper meaning of these symbols for African Americans. Clearly, insulting remarks by teachers affect the way children think about themselves and how they perform in class.

With some resignation in her voice a professor at a northern university commented on white parents' images of her children at a mostly white private school:

> Both of our sons went to high school here in this city, and everybody, every other parent in the school, *always* assumed that our children had full scholarships. And they didn't. My husband and I struggled and paid their tuition, you know. But they assumed, because they were black, that they had full scholarships. And there were some students in the school who *did* have some scholarship help, and I think there were some black students who had had some full scholarships. So that often assumptions are made about you just because you are a minority.

Reflecting on events some years before, this woman perceives questions about scholarships not to be favorable comments on her children's performance but rather to reflect white assumptions about their income. The white public's furor over affirmative action and equal opportunity programs from the 1970s to the present has been fed by the assumption that blacks in educational institutions are there substantially because of minority scholarships.

As the minority in predominantly white schools, black children are often set apart. Apparently white children learn their prejudices at an early age. A television news manager in the North described his children's experience in a white school:

They go to white schools and some of the kids make fun of them because my son's nose is big, or his hair is different, or skin color. They tease him about his nose. He has a big nose. He is eight and not at a stage where he can even begin to try to ignore that kind of stuff, but kids are kids I guess, and they learn that from their parents; because you take great pains in trying to teach our kids to share with other people and not call people names and to try and treat everybody as you would want to be treated, but they have a hard time. My son was concerned enough to make me concerned. He just said that the kids at school were teasing him because his nose was big, and how come we had to have a nose like that, and why was this happening. Of course, we've tried to teach our children about the differences between blacks and whites and Indians and Mexicans and Chinese, and what have you. . . . And my daughter, who really hasn't been faced with that problem, but I notice that she doesn't want to wear [braids]. We tried to put the braids on her hair at one time. "No, no, no." She gave me an indication that she didn't want to be labeled that. She wanted to fit in more than she wanted to stand out. You see, I would look at that as a way of being different and she didn't want to be different, she wanted to be the same. It just made us more aware of our jobs in trying to teach our kids who they are, what they have to do.

We feel the anguish of a father, who has given lessons about respecting racial and ethnic differences, over his children being taunted about their physical characteristics. The serious psychological impact on the children can be seen in their discomfort with their physical differences. Although most children are self-conscious about their physical appearance, at least by the time they are adolescents, African American children in desegregated settings *at a very early age* bear the extra burden of dealing with

88

comments and taunts about their skin color, hair, and other physical characteristics. Here we can also sense the early age at which some white children have learned to abhor and racialize the distinctive physical characteristics of black children.

An administrator at an East Coast law school discussed the trials of his seven-year-old daughter in a private school where she was the only child of conspicuously African American heritage:

> So my daughter was having real [hard] times adjusting, and I couldn't understand it because she wasn't the type of child to have an adjustment problem. So I sat her down and talked to her one day, and she says, "You know, they treat me differently, and the teacher treats me differently." And she said, "All I want to do is be in a place where everybody is the same or would think of me as the same." We're talking about, this was a seven-year-old telling me. So I asked her what would she want to do? Would she want to go to an all-black school? She said, "Yes, if everybody's going to treat me like I'm just one of them." [How did they treat her?] Well, the way I got it is that she couldn't do anything right, although her grades sometimes were pretty good, and then they wouldn't include her in some of the playtime activities, and made it as though that she's the odd person out in the activities. And that tended to make her feel that she was different. She knew she looked different, but then they rubbed it in. The students did it, and then the instructor was not discouraging it and in some ways encouraging that sort of behavior. So, we have a friend of ours that's a child psychologist and she's pretty well known in her field and she'd studied this instance. And she went by the school and talked to them and also talked to my child just to see what the problem was, and she helped us get to the root of it. So it wasn't something we just thought of; we had somebody

look into it. [Is she still there?] No! No. Absolutely not. I'm not going to pay anybody that treats me bad, or my child.

This parent tells us that the failure of the teachers to discourage the harassment gave the black child the impression of collusion. Exclusion from some playtime activities breeds a sense of quarantine and isolation. At a very young age a black child may wish for a strong solution, such as an all-black school.

Schools that are predominantly white develop their own cultures, often with a certain tolerance for conventional white prejudices and even racist symbols, as can be observed in this dentist's story about his son:

> Well, just recently in the last year, he experienced a phenomenon called PUNISH, which is a penal system that they use in the school district for children that violate certain school laws. When these infractions are made they are sent to PUNISH, which is a prison-type setting, for so many days. He became a victim of this because he got into a verbal confrontation with a young man who . . . had on a swastika pin, he had on a KKK pin, and my son and this young man got into a few words, and my son told him to go to hell. The teacher heard him and therefore sent him to the principal, and because he used profanity, my son was assigned to a PUNISH detention. I confronted the teacher in front of the principal, and it was only after a very, very heated and emotional debate was I able to get my point across.

From the early 1980s to the early 1990s the nation witnessed increasing tolerance for the symbols of the Ku Klux Klan and the neo-Nazis in many white communities across the country. Membership in these organizations grew. In this account the symbols of these groups precipitated a heated exchange, and the black youngster was the one punished. Several research studies have found that black children in desegregated schools are more likely to be punished for their infractions of the rules than are whites. One important study found that black children were more likely than whites to be suspended for subjective offenses such as personal appearance, disobedience, and disrespect for teachers.[9] This study and our vignettes suggest an ongoing clash of worlds, a conflict of values and cultures, between black children and white school authorities. Later in our interview, this father stated that the white school authorities had defended the punishment and the white child's free-speech right to wear racially offensive pins, even though the school's policy did not extend a similar right to boys wearing other expressive decorations such as earrings.

One might wonder how a white teacher or an administrator could ignore the impact on the black psyche of these flagrant symbols of racial and ethnic violence. At the heart of what Gunnar Myrdal called "the American dilemma" is the contradiction between white American ideals and the reality of discriminatory actions.[10] Black children often learn about this contradiction at an early age. In desegregated schools black children are taught "The Star-Spangled Banner" and Pledge of Allegiance along with white children, and they read many stories about freedom, liberty, and justice. But degrading experiences with whites in the same schools doubtless raise serious questions about the meaning of these ideals.

Black Students in Predominantly White Colleges

In the late 1980s a report of the National Commission on Minority Participation in Education and American Life, *One Third of a Nation*, found a significant decline in black participation in higher education.[11] The proportion of black high school graduates going to college grew during the 1960s and 1970s to a high of about 48 percent in 1977, about the same as that for whites, then decreased to 37 percent in 1986, while white rates were still rising.[12] By the late 1980s the proportion of black students attending college had increased slightly but was still a minority of high school graduates and below the comparable proportion for whites. Some analysts have attributed the problems of black participation in higher education to the rising costs of a college education and the significant decline in financial aid. Others point to the alternative of good jobs in the military. Yet others emphasize the allegedly anti-educational values of black individuals and families. As we noted in an earlier chapter, white scholars like George Keller have argued that the reasons for black educational problems lie primarily within the black family or community.[13] In recent years many white analysts have minimized the relevance of white-controlled schools and white racism within those schools to the problems of black students. Yet, as we have just seen, the obstacles placed in the way of black elementary and secondary students by white counsellors, teachers, students, and parents—and their impact on achievement, motivation, and self-concept—explain in part the troubling statistics on the scarcity of blacks in institutions of higher education. Moreover, once black students make it past elementary and secondary school, they will confront similar hurdles as they enter the halls of historically white colleges and universities.

Most assessments of the state of African American students in predominantly white colleges and universities have relied heavily on numbers, such as enrollment rates, grade point averages, and graduation rates. Yet a deeper examination of the experiences of black students in these places requires something more than numbers gathered in school records and surveys or in classroom testing. We need to listen closely to what black American students tell us about what happens to them and how they feel, act, and think. In the rest of this chapter we examine the black educational experience from the point of view of black undergraduate and graduate students on majority-white campuses. Whatever their class backgrounds, all aspire to middle-class occupations and positions. We also draw on interviews with college graduates about their experiences as students at predominantly white colleges and universities. In addition, we quote occasionally from the observations of black faculty and staff members at these colleges and universities about the barriers black students face.

On entering predominantly white colleges and universities black students soon become aware of an essentially white campus culture. An honors student at a university in the Southwest discussed her feelings about being a black person in a predominantly white institution: "Everything, everywhere I look, everywhere I turn, right, left, is white." Revealing the historical context for her evaluation, she continued:

> I'm not saying that white people are all out to get us, because I don't think they think about us that much, where they sit down and actually plot, in some dark smoke-filled room, how they're going [to] stomp on black people. They don't have to because it's ingrained in the system. So things are like that. And white people call me paranoid and stuff, because I guess they look at things in regards to like the sixties when black people were like being beaten up every damn day, and crosses [were burned] in front of yards, and it was so blatant. But now it's changed. And just because it's not blatant any more doesn't mean it's not there. In fact, I think it's worse.

Discrimination is not less burdensome because it is subtly imbedded in the values, rules, and other institutional patterns of a college or other traditionally white setting and is less violent than cross-burnings. Black students are pressured to give up their identities and to adapt to the surrounding white culture, with its distinctive white middle-class ways of talking, dressing, and acting—to become, as another black student put it, "Afro-Saxon." We see here another modern variation on the double consciousness of which Du Bois spoke in *The Souls of Black Folk*.[14]

This honors student also reported on her trip to an Ivy League university as part of the process of choosing a college:

> I applied to a lot of different schools besides here, and I got accepted to this Ivy League school. And I went up there, checked it out. And a lot of people at home were like, well, you only got in because you're black. You don't deserve to be there, or you don't deserve to go, which may be true. I may have gotten in on affirmative action, but I deserve to be there, simply because of my merit. And I felt bad; I felt out of place. One reason I didn't go there, besides the money (I couldn't afford it), one reason I didn't go was because it reeked of whiteness. And that is no joke. And I am not exaggerating. I was only there for two days, and after one day I wanted to leave. And I mean, really, it just reeked, everywhere I went, reeked of old white men, just lily whiteness, oozing from the corners! [laughs] I wanted to leave. And I knew that socially I would just be miserable. And I talked to other black students; I talked to all of them because there aren't a lot. And so I said, "do you like it here?" And they were like, "No, we're miserable." I'm like, "Well then, why are you here?" And they said, "Because I'm black; it's Ivy League. I need everything I possibly could get." So, I said, "You're willing to be miserable for this?" They were like, "Yes." And then they asked me where else I was going. And one black female told me, Mary, go to the state university, "Don't come here." Really she did; and she was dead serious!

The students reported being alienated and miserable, yet because an Ivy League degree would give them a boost in the

94

outside white world, they were resigned to the indignities of that milieu. Surveys at several predominantly white universities suggest that the campus culture is alienating to students of color. One study of students at a California campus found black and Latino students were more isolated and alienated than the white students.[15] Another study at a midwestern campus likewise found that black students scored higher on an alienation scale and dropped out more often than white students.[16] One reason for this alienating environment is that college desegregation since the 1960s has not brought fundamental changes in the character and cultural norms of white institutions. For the most part white regents, administrators, faculty members, staff, and students have shown little willingness to incorporate black values, interests, or history into the core of campus culture.[17]

At predominantly white colleges most campus activities reflect white student and faculty interests and traditions. In a study of black students at predominantly black and predominantly white colleges Walter Allen found that 62 percent of black students on white campuses, but just one third on black campuses, felt that the campus activities there did not relate to their interests.[18] This situation encourages black students to congregate in their own groups and plan their own activities, a reaction that often brings white condemnation. An undergraduate explained how this can be problematic:

It's a constant battle dealing with racism. It is so much a part of everything. To integrate means simply to be white. It doesn't mean fusing the two cultures; it simply means to be white, that's all. And we spend so much effort in passing into the mainstream of American society. They have no reason to know our culture. But we must, in order to survive, know everything about their culture. Racism is simply preferring straight hair to an Afro; that's certainly more acceptable in our society today. Black vernacular, it's not seen

95

as a cultural expression, it's seen as a speech problem. When you look at something as simple as just a group of people talking, black people are given much more, a much higher, regard if they are seen in an all-white group than they would if they were to be seen in an all-black group. If you're seen in an all-white group laughing and talking, you're seen as respectable, and probably taking care of something important. You're not wasting time. You're all right. But if you're in an all-black group, regardless if they can even hear your conversation, white people think you're trying to, you're congregated to take over the world. It's just that basic. . . . You're just punished for expressing your black culture. . . . You're just constantly forced to take on the culture of white America.

Black students not only must learn the white culture but face whites' rejection of their personal values and preferences.

For some first-year students the encounter with a white campus brings significant culture shock. A black community leader who speaks at first-year student orientations charged that many black parents do not prepare their children adequately for what a white college setting will be like:

Kids come to this university with blinders on, that their parents put on them. . . . They've been through the university, they've been through corporate America, because a lot of the kids who've made it to the university are coming from "middle class America," suburbia, [from] racist, white suburban high schools, which is minor league compared to what they're going to face on these campuses. If parents don't do a better job of preparing their children to come to these universities—and it will have to start before they come on campus, because once they get on campus, it's a little bit too late—they've already got this preconceived idea of what campus life is about. They think they've watched TV, and they're falling for some b.s. that they show on TV. And that's not real life. So when the culture shock hits them, parents need to be very up front. A lot of the parents have gone to this university. They need to relate their experiences, because the university has not changed. It has not changed.

Why do some black parents fail to prepare their children fully for racism in the outside world? Some blacks suggest that it is because black parents, like white parents, try to protect their children from pain and particularly from the pain that they have experienced themselves. Perhaps too some black parents keep hoping that the situation has improved since they were in college.

Problems with White Students

The pervasiveness of white culture on campus brings not only subtle pressures to conform to white standards of dress, language, and group behavior but also blatant discrimination. According to the National Institute against Prejudice and Violence, there were published reports of at least 250 racial incidents involving physical violence or psychological assault on college campuses between 1986 and 1990.[19] At the Citadel in South Carolina, white students dressed like Ku Klux Klan members in white sheets and hoods threatened a black student with a burnt cross. The white students were not expelled. At the University of Massachusetts a group of white students severely attacked a black student during a celebration following the World Series. Racist graffiti, fraternity and sorority parties and parades with racist themes, the distribution of racist literature on campus, and violent attacks on black students have continued into the 1990s.[20] For example, at the University of Alabama in the fall of 1991 a white sorority had a party at which pledges blackened

97

their faces and dressed as pregnant women on welfare. And in 1993 a white fraternity at Rider College in New York reportedly had its pledges talk in "black speech" as they carried out cleaning chores.[21]

Several respondents discussed how they became fully aware of what it meant to be black in the United States when they encountered flagrant hostility and discrimination on campus. One young woman, a college graduate now working in administration for a state agency, reported on racist joking:

> I have to say that I've gotten bitter. . . . Last summer, I can remember people telling jokes, that's what I remember most, everyday there was a racial joke. And they found it necessary to tell me. It might be funny and then I'd laugh, and then I thought about it while reading that book [*Black Power*]. Even if they didn't mean any harm, how can they not mean any harm? How can they not, these people who are your classmates. And supposedly some of them are your friends. How can they not mean any harm? What do you mean they don't mean any harm? Why am I making excuses for their actions? I think that's what I was doing a lot of times was making excuses. [Why do you think you were doing that?] I think probably that's just the kind of person I am, just really very passive. [Do you think it's necessary to be that way as a black person?] No, I don't think so. Before I did: Don't make too many waves. And I still think sometimes there's a right way and a wrong way to get certain things accomplished. But if we're talking about [racism] . . . how do I deal with it, let me think, on a day-to-day basis? I don't wake up and give myself a pep talk, "You're black, you're proud!" [laughs] I don't do that, but I think that. . . . I feel it now. Maybe there was a time when I didn't feel it, but I feel it now. And yes, I never thought about it, but I don't have to say it because I feel it.

[What makes you feel black and proud?] This university! Every time I had to go across some kind of barrier, whether it was white-America-related or not, then that made me stronger, and strengthened one area. This is it. This is the learning tree.

White students may not realize how offensive and troubling racist jokes can be; others may tell such jokes intentionally because they know the jokes cause pain. For the latter, racist humor may be an outlet for passive aggression. Half a century ago Gunnar Myrdal pointed out that white jokes, stories, and popular fiction about blacks act as a "sounding board for and as a magnifier of popular prejudices" about black inferiority.[22] A striking feature of racist joking on campus is that black students and faculty with whom we have talked about such matters have reported no comparable incidence of antiwhite jokes among black students. Racist joking on campuses appears to be one-sided.

Many white college students hold firmly to negative stereotypes about black youngsters, views they probably learned before they came to college. An administrator at a western university discussed the attitudes of some white students about "dirty" black high school students who came there for summer college preparation and athletic programs:

Somebody will have the idea that the dorm is exclusively theirs, so therefore we can't have these "germy, diseasey, dirty, filthy" black kids live in their dormitory. So that's one obstacle that we have to deal with every year, that our kids don't belong there. The dorms rent rooms out all summer long to all different kinds of groups. But, if anything goes wrong, our group gets blamed for it. If anything . . . gets broken, it's always our group. Whether it's our group, or a black basketball team, or a baseball team, it's always the black group [that] was far worse than the other group. But

99

yet, we know that other groups have destroyed the place, torn it up, but you hear, "Oh, well, they were just being kids." . . . . Black kids are seen as a gang now. They must be on drugs, or crazy or something. They perceive it as a fantastic problem rather than, they broke a door knob or something, "Oh, OK, it's no big deal." . . . When the kids eat food in the cafeteria, at first, until the college kids get used to them being there, [they say] "What are they doing here? Why don't they have a separate time and sit somewhere else? We don't want to mix and mingle with them."

A student at a university in the South also reported encountering stereotypical assumptions about black students: "That's the first question they'll ask you: 'Are you an athlete?' Professors, students, everybody here will ask you, 'Are you an athlete?' When you say, 'No,' they're like, 'Oh!' And it's like you got here because you're black." Much of the discrimination we have seen discussed so far seems blatant and motivated by malevolent intentions. However, middle-class African Americans also encounter what John Calmore has termed "subtle discrimination" resulting from a tendency to relate most easily to people like ourselves. There is an "unconscious failure to extend to a minority the same recognition of humanity, and hence the same sympathy and care, given as a matter of course to one's own group."[23] A college student gave a common example:

Here in my dorm, there are four black girls. Me and my roommates look nothing alike. And the other two are short, and I'm tall. They [white students] called me by my roommate's name the whole semester, and I didn't understand that. [Maybe] I understood it, but I didn't want to have to deal with that whole thing. That's really upsetting. It's like they put their shutters on when they see a black person coming. And the few black people that do get along

with the other students, they seem to sort of put on a fa-
cade. They pretend to be something they're not.

Whether the differential treatment is subtle or unconscious discrimination does not matter; it is still painful and enervating.
One reaction is to confront it verbally. Another is to be resigned
to it and to put on a mask that hides one's true feelings.

A young lawyer in an eastern city noted some of the other
assumptions white students make about black students: "In law
school, there were some whites who were offended because I
was smart. The teacher would ask the question and point to me,
and they didn't think I should have an answer. And I would have
a correct answer. But then they started to respect me for it, and
they would tell me that: 'Hey, you beat us on that; we knew you
would have known that,' or 'What happened? Did you study all
night?'" Like others in our study this respondent spoke about
the personal testing, competency testing, that black Americans
must pass to receive any degree of white acceptance. Once accepted, moreover, a new problem may kick in. Certain black
students may be put in a bind if they become the measuring rods
for other black students. Because black students are often in a
small statistical minority on historically white campuses, some
of them may come to accept white views of their accomplishments and even white views of how they should see themselves
in regard to other black Americans. A graduate student at a
predominantly white university in the South recently noted the
pain of accomplishment in a discussion with the senior author:
"One problem that you often face as a 'smart' black person is that
whites have a tendency to overemphasize their admiration of your
success, as if you are a strange bird among your own people."

And, as always, black students have to face the assumption
that they have momentous advantages over comparable white
students because of government programs like "affirmative ac-

tion." A professor at a northern university commented on an incident that occurred right after she finished her Ph.D., in the 1980s:

I was mentioning to friends in the church that finally I [had] finished my Ph.D. And most people were very congratulatory, and there were both black and white people in this group, and generally they were happy. And then one white male, whom I've known for over twenty years, who, by the way, has never finished his Ph.D., even though he started one probably twenty years ago, said, when I was speaking to, there were about three of us in a group standing there, "Yes, but now that you're, because you're a black female, now that you've finished yours, the world is open for you. You can have any job that you wish." And I quickly said to him, "Well, you know, it's very interesting that you say that, because one of the things that's true is that I've never stopped working. I've been working all along while I've been working on that Ph.D., and I'm not sure that getting it's going to change my job status or even my paycheck at all.". . . He makes this assumption that because I'm a black woman, that my getting it now means that the whole world opens up to me, and it's not going to be. And . . . I've known many blacks, specifically in academic circles, who have that thrown at them *all* the time. . . . I think it's the assumption. It's part of the racist attitude, and I think it's one of the things that blacks cope with all the time. And I think it's part of the whole business that, "What with affirmative action, you get all the breaks and we get none."

Not only do the signs of black achievement not diminish whites' racist assumptions and actions, as we saw in the last chapter, many whites question whether middle-class blacks should even be credited with their achievements. The stereotypical notion about blacks' unfair advantages is widespread. In a 1990 National Opinion Research Center nationwide opinion survey 69 percent of white Americans said it was likely that today "a white person won't get a job or promotion while an equally or less qualified black person gets one instead." Yet two thirds of the black respondents said this situation was *not* likely.[24] Conservative commentators often cite the stigma of affirmative action programs in both educational and job settings as the reason why such programs should be abolished, yet they miss the essential point that the stigma is not in the programs themselves but in the prejudices of the *whites* making the evaluations. This white stigmatization of black achievements causes black Americans much pain and frustration.

Most white students on traditionally white campuses, even those who do not engage in openly racist behavior, seem insensitive to the many negative aspects of campus culture for black and other minority students. One survey at the University of Maryland found that about one in five minority students had been the victim of at least one incident of racial harassment and that the overwhelming majority of black students felt they were potential targets. Yet two thirds of the white students were unaware that harassment ever occurred; most did not perceive antiminority prejudice to be part of the campus culture.[25] Moreover, a leading expert on racism in higher education, Jacqueline Fleming, has argued that white students are taught to ignore race as a subject, and thus "the average student does not feel responsible for the racial climate or civil rights."[26]

The stereotyping and insensitivity of many white students makes relationships with them a problem for black students. Social isolation can create a quandary, as one undergraduate student suggested in response the question, "Do you feel that you can trust white people?"

I'm sure you could. But I just haven't been in a situation where I could find out, because most of the white people that I've met here at college all seem to be reacting on a superficial basis. . . . People that I've met living in the dorm—you know most of the time there's a majority of people who are white in the dorm, and most of the people who really develop a close friendship are just white. People I start out knowing, though, I usually get phased out with towards the end of the year. I still don't know why. I've tried to figure it out. But lately I try not to bother with it, because it will just cause me mental anguish, and I don't want to do that to myself. Now when I was in high school, it was different. We hung out with a lot of different people. We had a lot of Orientals, Mexicans—it was just a whole rainbow of friends I had in high school. I didn't think much of it, but when I came to this university, it seemed to change. I don't know if it was just me, or the environment, but somehow my view of intimacy with other people, especially white people, has soured since then.

Past experience with cultural diversity did not prepare this young man for white students reacting to him on a superficial basis. His "I don't know if it was just me" reaction signals some denial and self-blame. We sense his resigned acceptance of his fate.

Punctuating her comments with occasional laughter, a young attorney in an East Coast city reflected on her college experience a few years back:

I lived in the dorms for a couple of years, and you sit around in the dorms and eat food with the girls, eat popcorn and watch the soaps when you didn't have classes. And I remember this particular incident, this girl, we had just socialized the night before, watching TV, having popcorn, et cetera. And I saw her on campus the next day, and she turned her head to make sure she didn't have to speak to me. And I had that happen more than once. And I think that was a bout with discrimination which just slapped me in the face, because it doesn't feel real good to be a friend to someone, or an associate to someone at seven o'clock, and then at eight o'clock, or eight-thirty, when they're around friends of the other race, they don't know who you are or what you are, and don't even give you the consideration of acknowledging your presence or speaking to you. I think that happens a lot. Even now, I see people that I've gone to law school with in court, and sometimes they just say, "hi." Or sometimes they just don't speak. Or, they'll look at you like, oh, you made it too, I can't believe you made it. And I'll just say, yeah, just watch me, I'll even go further!

Difficulties in making same-sex friendships are just one type of isolation black students face on campus. Several black students and informants touched on the issue of cross-sex friendships and interracial dating. One black female student talked about a liberal white male student whom she had dated. It took her a while to realize that he saw her as a "sexual object, something to try, something new or different." Here sexism mixes with racism in white stereotypes of black women, another example of "gendered racism."[27] Indeed, interracial dating has been one of the underlying issues in white-black conflict at a number of U.S. colleges and universities in the early 1990s. To take just one example, it was one of the factors leading up to verbal and other attacks by white students on black students at Olivet College in Michigan during the spring of 1992. As a result of the white hostility, most of the black students left this predominantly white college campus before the end of the spring semester.[28]

In the last few quotes we see black students uncertain whether or not they can trust white students. The reason for this uncertainty may lie in the two-faced character of some whites' behavior to black students. For example, in a 1992 study at a predominantly white eastern university, Joe R. Feagin conducted group interviews with several dozen black students. In one interview a light-skinned black student reported that he had gotten a glimpse of how some white students talk behind the scenes:

> I can hear them going, "Those black people, this." And it's like the time—it's amazing, you sit there, and they think I'm Hispanic. . . . You'd be amazed what people are saying when they don't think there are black people in the room. They're like, "Oh I can't stand that black guy." And they'll be saying "nigger this, nigger that." But when the black people are around it's like, "Hey Bob. What's up, bro?" And they play like this nice little role. . . . I'm kind of like weird in the sense that I can sit in between, and I can see all this happening.

Mainstream white analysts, including many in the media, often associate the use of racial epithets with white extremists openly committed to racial oppression. Certainly, one of the conventions of polite society is not to use racist epithets in mixed-race groups. However, accounts like this suggest that there is much overt racism being expressed backstage, when black people are not present, and even among white college students. Such racist attitudes could account for some of the ambiguous or inconsistent behavior of white students in their interactions with black students.[29]

Professors as Obstacles
White Stereotypes and White Models

Analyses of the difficulties of black students in white colleges and universities have often neglected the role of white faculty members and administrators. The research reports reviewed by Keller, for example, rarely consider how white professors create racial obstacles for black students.[30] Many observers would expect a university setting, in the North, South, Midwest, or West, to be a cosmopolitan place generally free of overt racial discrimination. The fact that professors in a particular university are drawn from many different graduate schools and regions of the country reinforces this assumption of cosmopolitanism. Yet the reality in all parts of the country seems to be that some white and other nonblack professors can create major hurdles. A student at a western university commented on her graduate school:

> And the conversation is so stiff that it just comes down to racially motivated thoughts or activities at that point. Well, I've heard different things that have happened to different students. . . . I had a professor that treated me so badly during this particular quarter in school that several white students came to the assumption—not that they said [it] to me, but they said [it] to another student that relayed it to me—that they thought that the professor was a racist. Because it had been so obvious that the treatment that I had received in the class was unfair.

Again, this student's account reveals the careful evaluation many middle-class black Americans make before coming to a conclusion of racial discrimination.

One frustrating aspect of being black on a predominantly white campus is the chronic inability of many white faculty members and administrators to "see" black students as individuals, rather than as "representatives" of their racial group, thereby failing to give them the kind of academic and professional advice they are due as students. One graduate student described a black undergraduate's experiences with the chair of her department:

107

A black undergraduate in my department is doing some research on black and white achievement in college, and one of her advisers was once the head of a rather prestigious organization in my field, not to mention chair of the department. Apparently she assumed that this one undergraduate somehow spoke for all black people. And this professor would ask her things like, "Well, I don't know what you people want. First you want to be called Negro, then you want to be called black. Now you want to be called African American. What do you people want anyway? And why don't black people show up in class more? Why is it that I can't get enough blacks to sit in on my classes?" So every now and then that sort of racist mentality comes out.

In one form or another we have seen this lack of white sensitivity to black individuality in previous quotes. Again we observe an example of Ralph Ellison's point about the inability of whites to see African Americans as individuals. When looking at blacks, many whites tend to see "figments of their imagination —indeed, everything and anything except me."[31] Several students suggest in their interviews that they have had to be assertive with whites to get their uniqueness recognized.

Some white professors question the competence and potential of black students, failing to give a black student the same benefit of the doubt that they might give a white student, or assuming a student's work will be inferior. A sales manager at an East Coast company described the problems she faced as an undergraduate in a predominantly white college. She noted that discrimination often came in "borderline" grading decisions by white faculty members:

Early in my undergraduate career . . . instructors were less inclined to give me, or other blacks, the benefits of the positive side. I mean, you were like borderline in the grading situation. And you would talk to some of your white fellow

students who you knew had the exact same average that
you had going into, you know, after completing final
courses, when you get your grades, and you would find out
that they had an 88 or 89. And they got an A, and you got
a B plus. That happened more earlier, [but] less frequently
as I continued in the program. Because I also understand
that the game you have to play is making yourself known
to your professors, where they feel like they know that you
are a good student. And they had perceptions that blacks
are not going to achieve as much or to be as good a student as the white students, particularly at a predominately
white institution which I attended.

We heard this metaphor of a rigged game again and again in our
interviews and in many black middle-class discussions of everyday coping with whites, not only in schools and colleges but
also in employment and business settings. For middle-class African Americans the institutional game is usually controlled by
whites, and in addition to the regular norms (for example, expectations of grading) there are racialized norms (for example,
expectations of black incompetence), which can be changed as
whites see fit. Until the student proved herself and learned to
play by the rules of the white game, she had great difficulty.

Even in graduate school, a black student's work often has to
be better than average to head off the assumption of incompetence, particularly in writing, as a recent Ph.D. from a northeastern university noted:

I would say that occasionally with individual professors
that I've had along the way . . . there are the kind of racist
assumptions that come. They're surprised if you've done a
good piece of work, especially when it comes to writing. I
think there are a lot of stereotypes about blacks not being
good writers, so that there's a surprise if you've done this.
And *that*, I've met. And the person will compliment you,

109

but they don't know that underneath that is this racist assumption.

Such stereotyping can lead to action, as a teacher in a northern school system reported:

So, what happened one time in graduate school, I had this professor, and I didn't talk much in class, so when I did a paper, a final paper, he refused to accept the fact that I did the paper on my own ability. So, what he told me in essence, he would not accept the paper, and I wouldn't get another grade until I redid the paper, which I refused to do. I thought that was basically a discriminatory act. What he was saying was that black folks can't write this good. He didn't know my ability, what I was capable of. I didn't talk much in class, the class was boring. [So, did you do the paper over?] No, I didn't. I took the incomplete. And I talked to the head of the department and I think he put a withdrawal on it. [So you didn't get any credit for the class?] No. I refused to do it. But I didn't like that. I thought if it had been a white student who kept their mouth shut in class, and did a paper that was above what he thought, I'm quite sure that he wouldn't have challenged them.

In reaction to the commonplace white doubting of black proficiency, many black people develop a wary watchfulness.

Another common assumption among white professors and administrators is that students from black communities are not able to handle the difficult course loads and educational requirements that white, or white male, students can. A black professional in a northern city recounted her sister's reaction to this assumption:

My sister is a surgical technician, and she's just completed getting her master's degree in nursing. And she's talked about as an older student—again the expectation, being

110

from a black community in the inner city, that she would
not be able to sit in the classroom with younger white students and do as well as they could. But she's proven differently. [I talked] . . . to her about her struggles with her
professors, about what she is capable of doing, the course
load she is capable of handling, and [her] trying to convince
them that she can take on this course load, as opposed to
them being supportive and saying, "Whatever you think
you can do is fine, and I'll see that you get the kind of
guidance and support that you need." [What exactly did
they do?] Well, limit her course work. . . . They said, "You
can't take this course," and she got into a fight with the
dean.

White misconceptions about black competence may be magni-
fied when the student is an older black woman, as in this case, in
which her struggle to succeed against white barriers required the
determination to overcome whatever obstacle she encountered.

The pervasive whiteness of the historically white college environment is conspicuous in the role models typically encountered
by black students. Few, if any, of their professors will be black
or provide a black perspective. A talented student at a predominantly white university in the Southwest described how an English professor evaluated her essays about the black experience:

[He told me that] if a white person, for example, picked up
one of my stories he would not understand what the hell
was going on. So therefore I shouldn't write about these
things. But I should write about [other] things, and he
quoted William Faulkner quite liberally. I should write
about things that appeal to the human heart, that everybody can appeal to and can relate to. And, see me, in my
nice trusting self, I said "No, he's not saying that black
people aren't people enough to be termed as universal. He's
not saying that, he's meaning something else. He couldn't

111

possibly be saying this to my face." I was very, very confused. I did not understand what the hell he meant by it,
not just the racial implications, but the whole statement.

The professor, who was Asian American, regarded her accounts
of the black experience as hard for whites to understand and not
as universal as stories by a white author. By citing Faulkner
he suggested to a young black woman that the relevant model
for excellent writing was not only white but also male and
southern.

Similarly, in Feagin's 1992 study at an eastern university, one
black student observed a bias in white professors' reactions to
papers on black or African issues, explaining, "It can get kind of
bad when you bring up certain issues," and giving as an example a paper he wrote in an English class about how African
civilization antedated other civilizations: "If it's controversial,
it's not good. . . . I mean you can see it when . . . you get, you
know, B's, B+'s, A's and then all the sudden you write this paper
on Africa and you get a C−." In his experience and that of other
students, some white professors do not respond well to papers
on such topics of concern to the black students and do not grade
them fairly.[32] In her work on gender issues Catharine MacKinnon has pointed out that the leading doctrine of equality in the
United States has been: Be the same as the dominant group.
Paraphrasing MacKinnon for racial matters we can say this:
Concealed in many white evaluations of the black middle class
is the substantive way in which the white standard has become
the measure of things.[33] We see most of our black respondents
caught in the dilemma of resisting this white middle-class standard at the same time that they must accept it to some degree in
order to survive in a white world.

Some white teachers of black students have difficulty not
only with the substance of their writing but also with their

language and style. In an eastern city a young male banker reported an experience he had had in an English course:

> The only thing that hurt me was certain white institutions. Instead of helping you and educating you, they will browbeat [you] and downplay the educational level that you have. I turned in a paper one time at a college, and I had an instructor tell me that I was speaking black English. I was the only black in the class, and it was a freshman writing class. And she told me that I was speaking black English. And it kind of, in one sense, made me not want to be black, and, in another sense, wonder what was black English. Because I had gone to white schools from the sixth grade on, and I had been speaking—not speaking but writing—white English all my life. I couldn't understand what she was talking about. . . . If I remember right, she gave me a D in the course. She had given me D's and C's on all my papers. And I know for a fact that certain people did less research, less work than me, but she was very hard on me. That really woke me up, because that really taught me to take a lot of English writing workshops. Where now, I guess you could say, my writing skills are above average. And that's great because by her hurting me, and telling me that I was speaking black English, now I'm able to speak black English in a white format, where I can get my point across and be understood.

Another aspect of being black in a white institution can be seen in the sense of inferiority the student felt when a white teacher stereotyped his writing as "black English." The teacher's harsh evaluation of his work hurt and embarrassed him but also made him determined to become more expert in the English language and to prove himself. With his "made me not want to be black" statement this young man revealed the life-crisis character of

113

these events. One of the most serious reactions to white insensitivity and misunderstanding is the rejection of one's own group, and thus of one's self.

Yet another aspect of using white experience as the norm is the heavy use of white-oriented screening tests, such as the Scholastic Aptitude Test (SAT) and the Graduate Record Examination (GRE), at most historically white colleges. Black parents, teachers, and students often complain about the alien character of this testing. The SAT and GRE are educational tests created by whites and are reflective in a number of ways of white culture. One study by Allan Nairn and his associates examined the SAT and the GRE and found that both the tests and their administration were biased against students from minority and blue-collar backgrounds. The language and situations used in test items generally favor those from middle-income white families.[34] Percy Bates has noted that a "test-wiseness" curriculum has not been added to most central city schools and that "predominantly white high schools are more likely to offer their students special courses on how to take tests, and white parents are more likely to invest in private coaching to improve their children's college education test scores."[35] As a result, the standardized test scores are often inadequate measures of black students' potential for future achievement.

A student at a historically white private university commented on her experiences with her SAT scores and a white professor:

> When I got here it was an ignorance, a closed-minded igno-
> rance that I didn't know how to handle. One of my
> professors—I went to him as a freshman asking for help,
> and he asked me my SAT scores. And I told him. And [he
> said], "I don't know why they let you in, you're not ex-
> pected to do well. There are so many people like you here

that aren't qualified, and I can try to help you and find a tutor."

The professor assumed that because her scores were lower than the very high average for incoming students at this elite university that she was not qualified. In her interview the student continued by noting that the professor asked her about the high school she had attended. When she told him that she had graduated from a prestigious private school, "his face just went every which way, [his] eyes went big, and then he said, 'Well, I'll help you get a tutor, and we'll study, because I know you're prepared for this.'" Black students are often well aware of the views of black competence and capability that many white educators hold. Here the relatively low SAT score at first confirmed the professor's assumption of her inferiority. However, the fact that she had graduated from a tough private, and mostly white, high school made him reevaluate his estimation of her potential and offer assistance. This student reported she had similar experiences with other white professors.

Restriction and Rejection

Some white instructors seem to go out of their way to make the educational agenda of black students more difficult, as a registered nurse in an East Coast city suggested:

It was extremely hard, when we did our clinical practice at some of the hospitals with the white instructors who always gave the black students the harder patients to do. You really, really, really got the harder patients to do. . . . I think that's been demonstrated in that, of the ten or fifteen teachers that were at that school, they had one black instructor. She was a Ph.D. psychiatric nurse. Our class grad-

115

uated 115 students; ten of them were black. So, you have to make a conclusion from that. It was rough.

Black health professionals with whom we talked often reported having a difficult time in school or in the early years of practice, in that they were tested in unfair ways or were expected to fail.

In most historically white medical schools and hospitals, faculties are still composed mostly of white males, so that empathy for female students and those from different racial and cultural backgrounds is often lacking. Indeed, it was not until the late 1970s that women and minority students began to penetrate many medical schools and teaching hospitals in significant numbers. A doctor in an East Coast city reported on her internship problems in the late 1970s: "About twelve years ago, when I started my internship, I was the first black to ever train at that hospital. And at that time the discrimination was, 'So you're here to train, I hope you make it' type of thing, but they were not going to help you. You were going to have to do it all on your own. That was a rough time, but I made through it."

African Americans are often pioneers in predominantly white institutions and may be resented as interlopers. The resentment may stem from difficulty with a black person's style or perspective. A nurse commented on her recent experience at a northern university:

Well, it was just an instructor . . . a young white male who was teaching; health care industry was a part of his curriculum. And I'd been a nurse and in the health care arena for almost thirty years; I pretty well knew a lot of things. However, it was as if he made it, instead of letting me understand his concept, he went to the extreme of making me feel somewhat uncomfortable about being in his class. It's kind of hard to explain, it really is. I knew it was happening, something very subtle was happening, but you can't pinpoint it, you can't put your finger on all of it. And as a

116

matter of fact, I got the worst grade from this guy. And in all my years at this university I have *never*—now can you imagine a nurse of almost thirty years who had made A's and B's in all of her other classes and the *one* class, the one area that I have expertise in, was the area where I made a C.

An experienced white nurse might also have made this young professor uncomfortable, but, as an older black female facing a young white male, this woman concluded from subtle situational cues that the instructor treated her as he did because of her gender and her color.

Professors' discomfort with black students can be caused by the difficult questions they sometimes ask, as an accounting officer recalled:

Looking back over the last five years of my attendance in college, I feel very strongly that I have not been given an equal opportunity in seeking my educational goals. I face constant discrimination by white students and the all-white faculty members. Once it is known that you have the knowledge they have, or your knowledge surpasses theirs, then you are watched, feared, and kept back. The students have no real control, but the professors will see to it that you fail or are given a low passing grade. Three summers ago I took a writing class. The instructor was white. From the start she did not like me because I kept questioning the things that she was teaching. She also could not give answers to some of the questions that the students would ask. To make things worse my own style of writing was very different from what she was used to. I made a D plus on my final paper and was told I would get a C for my final grade. After a long and nasty conversation between us, and no resolution, I got my grade report in the mail with a C plus for my final grade. Other instructors have tried to lower my self esteem, but after experiencing a few episodes of what is outright discrimination I have learned to "play the game."

Some readers might consider this respondent's sense of persecution to be exaggerated, for she is quite strong in her view of her college years as a struggle against constant discrimination. Yet if her sense of persecution is more acute or dramatically stated than some other students', it nonetheless communicates well the embattled character of the black student's experience at mostly white universities.

A problem that many college students, black or white, have with college professors is the lack of feedback on course performance. But a lack of feedback and reinforcement is doubly difficult for a black student already at sea in a white world and facing other negative reactions from white faculty members. One university student described a white professor's response to an inquiry about grading:

I can think of several courses where I honestly feel that I was very much discriminated against. One class was an honors course in social science. And it just so happened that the criteria for getting in the course was to have made a certain grade in a previous social science course, which I did. So I took the course. . . . But when it came time for grades, the grade that I got was not the grade I earned . . . and the professor actually never even respected me enough to sit down and talk to me about my grades. The only feedback I got from the guy was when I approached him after I got the grade. And he talked to me only the amount of time that it took him to walk out of his office and go to where he had to go, and I stood there as he walked through his door. And except for that he wouldn't even give me any feedback. And essentially what he told me was that, first of all, my attendance was poor in class. And secondly he told me that some work which he

118

gave as optional work—that I had done—was . . . poor work. So what I understood him to say was that he took off of my regular grade for extra credit work. And as far as attendance goes, he said that I never attended class. But in fact I only missed two classes the entire semester, and the only reason I missed those two classes was because I was required by the military to be out of town on those two days.

An important aspect of life on a white campus is the tone of the place, the sense of being welcome or unwelcome. Joseph Katz, a pioneer in research on white faculty and black students, found that black students "consistently report that white professors avoid eye contact with them and engage in other forms of behavior that limit contact and recognition of the contributions and thoughts of black students."[36] According to the account above, the white professor, incommunicative, did not fairly evaluate the student. Conceivably, he might have acted the same way with white students. However, on a student already assaulted by the many slights of racism, such insensitivity and lack of feedback, whether intentional or not, can have a very negative impact.

As we have already seen, the poor treatment of black students can result from assumptions about both racial group and class. An academic advisor at an eastern university noted the difficulty some white faculty members have in relating to black students:

Some of the white faculty, they really don't understand the problems of students, they don't understand black students. Some of them just don't care about them. You have a group of faculty in the school of business. They're not looking at those students who are working full time with children, single mothers who have lost husbands, or maybe who never had a husband. They have kids, one woman has a kid with spina bifida, and she's trying to work hard to get

119

herself educated so she can make her family one where she can support them. Faculty don't look at this, they don't care about these situations sometimes that black students have.

They're paying their hard-earned money to take one course at a time. Some of them are not eligible for other kinds of financial assistance. But faculty, some of the faculty, don't even think about that. And if you're black, they think you're full of excuses. And they already have a mindset, before you get into that class, that I don't deal with you because you're black. They don't want to hear that you can't be here for class because you have an appointment with your child's doctor that you've been waiting for two months to get. . . . They tend to listen to their white students more than they would listen to black students. I had one girl come in and say a faculty member slammed a door in her face because she didn't have time for her. And all she wanted to do was ask about one problem, one question. The student is a good student, strong grade point average. The faculty member didn't even have time to talk with that girl, she wouldn't even talk to her. And then she saw some whites go into her office later and the woman let them in. . . . So, these are the kinds of things that I know that are here, because I hear them all the time. And they're not just from blacks, I've had white students come in with black students, and say, that's right, these things happen.

A few black college students with whom we have talked in informal settings have noted a counterpart to the problems of neglect mentioned here, the situation of some white professors being too solicitous and giving too much attention to a black student. While this may reflect a genuine desire on the part of a white professor to help, it can also make black students feel

120

"different" or inferior. The racist world of the white campus brings dilemmas for all.

At the core of most predominantly white colleges is the Euro-American bias in courses, curricula, and research agendas. Several students explained that some white professors call on black students primarily to give the "black side of the story" or, conversely, avoid calling on black students who have questioned a professor's excessively Eurocentric viewpoint. One black student, noting the bias in classroom discussions on non-European cultures, described her Jamaican roommate's reaction to their American studies professor in a class on cultural and mental disorders:

> She becomes really, really irritated because he'll talk about . . . a Jamaican medium. And she tried to explain to him that some of the things that he thought were abnormal, were very normal for her culture. And he just kind of like dismissed everything, and . . . I have to like push her to go to the class because she is really, really irritated with the class. She usually doesn't say anything anymore, and she is very intelligent, I mean she has a lot to contribute to the class.[37]

The white professor's harsh normative judgments of an Afro-Caribbean culture not only irritate a Jamaican student and her black roommate but also alienate them from the class. Such incidents suggest that much in the traditionally white university environment condones stereotyped interpretations of non-European cultures.

A career counsellor, now employed in a southwestern firm, reported on a recent college experience:

> I had an incident with a professor, and he and I got into a heated argument. He was giving a lecture and he was saying that the reason that there're so many [crazy people] in

121

Louisiana is because black people have polluted the white
Louisiana blood. The professor said this in class and he and
I got into a heated verbal exchange. And he apologized
subsequently, but my rationale was, you know, "What basis
do you have for saying that? You have no proof of that."
But that was just his ideology; that blacks had contami-
nated white Louisiana blood.

The pseudo-biological thinking of "race and blood" is obviously still part of some whites' thinking about racial relations. It
is significant that here the reference is to Louisiana, a state from
which one of the nation's foremost white supremacy politicians,
David Duke, emerged in the late 1980s. Note again that an
important dimension of this encounter was the aggressive response of the black student and the backing down of the white
professor.

Ironically, the subject of U.S. racial history is such a charged
one for many black students that some professors avoid candid
presentations of the worst abuses that occurred. One college
student commented on this dilemma:

A friend of mine was telling me that he's taking a history
class. He was telling me that he was talking to some of the
things that went on during slavery. His professor said that
there are certain things that he simply cannot talk about in
class because black people would get upset. And what
makes me angry about that, I have to blame the education
system on that, because that is such an example of self-
denial, of shame. What I hate so much is that if this was
taught on the junior high level, on the high school level, we
wouldn't be running from that kind of education. We could
sit through it. My friend was saying how he used to talk
about the rape of black women in slavery. And he said
black women would leave his class, they would be so upset
they wouldn't want to hear about it.

Then she turned to whites' ignorance of this Afro-American history:

It's because we don't share that kind of knowledge, that white people can walk around [uninformed] today. The white people who don't take any other social science classes besides history or government, if they're business students or engineering or whatever, they can walk around and still ask, "How come black people are so far behind? How come black people are so poor? How come the illegitimacy rate is so high? What's happening to them?" If [public school teachers] would talk about those things, white people could not get away with being so ignorant. The way the high school system is set up, they're not going to talk about the concrete things that happened during slavery, so when you come to college, you find yourself running out of the class, not being able to hear certain things.

This account brings to mind George Santayana's famous comment that "those who cannot remember the past are condemned to repeat it." In this student's view white students badly need to learn about U.S. racial history, especially before college. She is also critical of the schools for not teaching black students about their history earlier, for encounters with this history in college can cause great distress. She implies that one solution would be much more candid education about slavery and racism in primary and secondary school for all students.

This interview excerpt raises the issue of how African-American history has been transmitted in this country. Much African-American experience, past and present, has been carried as oral history in black families and communities because most white authors have written only from their own narrow or unenlightened perspectives, and because black scholars have rarely been able to get major white publishers to print unexpurgated accounts of that history. Often white editors see critical black

123

writings as "too emotional" or "too pessimistic."[38] Moreover, some black writers cannot write the true history of the black experience because it is too emotionally draining. In the account above we have evidence of how that history arouses intense emotion in African Americans. When an accurate version of Afro-American history is presented, many vicariously relive the experience, including the accompanying pain and rage.

Another important aspect of the whiteness of the traditionally white campus world is the assumption about what is valid and serious research. Like members of white immigrant groups in the early 1900s, black students often see the university as a place for learning and research that can be of help to their struggling communities. A graduate student at a southwestern university noted that he has had to go outside the university to pursue his research goals; then he commented on the experiences of some friends:

> I know of people who have been in my department who have left. I can think of a black woman, who I never actually met, who left the year before I got there, who felt that the department was so constricting in terms of not only the types of research that she could do, but in terms of attitudes. Apparently, she was told at one point [that] she wasn't thought of as a black person, largely because she was doing so well. She was outperforming the white students in a class. And apparently a faculty member told her something like, "Well, we don't think of you as one of them any more." And I also know someone who was in my department, who received a very cold reception, not only in terms of the type of research he wanted to do, but also in terms of basic politeness. . . . That individual ended up switching departments. He got his doctorate but never felt at home in that department.

One reason for the black attrition at many historically white graduate schools is the attitude of some white professors to many black students' concern with research that will benefit black communities.

An assistant professor recounted her recent experience at a major West Coast graduate school. Her white adviser pressured her to specialize in a certain period of white literature, not in Afro-American literature, because she would thus be

doing something he didn't consider most black people did. And that job offers would come in for that reason. And, further, that doing Afro-American literature was not in and of itself important intellectual work. Well, I insisted . . . and he finally gave in and gave me permission. He never stopped thinking that it was important for me not to do Afro-American literature as evidence that I was a real scholar. You couldn't do Afro-American lit and be a real scholar at the same time. And I ran into that attitude when I was on the job market.

One signal that historically white college cultures are not racially integrated is in the downplaying of humanities and social science research on African Americans, not only at the undergraduate and graduate levels, but also in college hiring practices.

One black counter to obstacles on mostly white campuses has been to organize black support groups. Although such organizing may be necessary for survival, it can result in black students being labelled as separatists or militants by white students, faculty members, and administrators. Discussing effective ways to deal with discrimination, one graduate student commented,

When I was involved in efforts to integrate the department more fully, I did receive a rather cold reception from several faculty members. . . . [We] set up a meeting of grad students to discuss the recruitment and retention of minorities

125

in the department. And a few of the faculty members there
who were pretty much of the old school. . . . We had
agreed that the meeting would be open and candid. Their
idea of open and candid was that it would be closed to everyone else except those who had been invited to be part of
the discussion. So, in that sense, the department has been
quite reactionary. It seems to be acting in good faith now in
terms of recruitment, but only because it has been pressured to do so. . . . But it is frustrating to realize how, not
only insensitive, but ignorant, a lot of supposedly intelligent
white people are. I think [of] the faculty especially in that
regard. There seems to be an attitude that things are well
enough now for blacks and other minorities that there's no
need to rock the boat. I've certainly seen that in my own
department, but I think it extends beyond that department.
Indifference to a variety of issues, whether it's investment in
South Africa, or faculty recruitment. . . . And when people
come along who want to set things right, so to speak,
they're the ones that are confronted, they're the ones that
are met with . . . excuses, such as [that] divesting from
South Africa would be making a political statement, where
obviously remaining invested is a political statement in
itself.

With the rise of successful South African political movements,
race-related issues on campus have included not only localized
issues such as black faculty and student recruitment but also
international issues such as black empowerment in South Africa. The South African liberation movement, with its so far successful political struggle and its visible leaders, has captured the
political imagination not only of black students but also of
African Americans generally (see Chapter 8).

Whether as undergraduates, graduate students, or professional students, blacks have organized both for protective pur-

poses and for larger protest and political objectives. A physician in a northern city described his medical school days:

> For me it's been a very, very hard struggle. First, to begin with, I was the first one of seven, as a group of black students entering medical school. The whites at this university were very opposed to the seven of us being admitted into medical school. There was a lot of strife around that. The white students were very rebellious. Openly rebellious to the extent that that propelled me into the forefront of fighting racism on campus. Thus, I became involved in black Students Association, Student Medical Association. . . . And we became more intensely interested in teaching . . . in the black community. For example, [we] started the black sickle cell program here and various other things like that. But it was a real struggle. I don't think at any point, during our education, we were accepted. It was always fight hard to make the grade.

The black student organization here went beyond student protection to organizing for the health interests of the black community. Over the past decade we have discussed these concerns with a number of black graduate students and faculty members who made it clear that for them the larger context of their institutions was the black community, to which, as educated Americans who have succeeded, they felt a great responsibility.

The campus climate at historically white colleges and universities is also shaped by the prejudices and discriminatory actions of white administrators, staff, and alumni. The last two accounts both allude to the role of white administrators in restricting the progress and organization of black students. And in Chapter 2 we observed the physical harassment that some black students encounter from campus police officers. In Feagin's 1992 study, one black student described the blatant difference between how white students' and black students' social events are policed by campus security personnel.

> I know when you go to a black party, and if you notice how all the police are around, you know what I'm saying. And that's the thing: you have eight police there, plus a police car outside, plus student aides right there at the party. But yet you go down to the [white] frat row, and they've got no type of security there, . . . and they end up having a big 300-people fight, and something like that. And then they are so wild. Me and my friends went to one of those white frat parties, and they are so wild it's ridiculous. And black people do not act anything like that at their parties. . . . But it's funny how you have all the security at the black functions and nothing at the white functions.[39]

He continued by describing this observed pattern as "subtle racism," for the singling out of black students for special surveillance is discriminatory. Here again the excessive policing may be motivated by the white image of black people, especially young black men, as prone to violence.

Other white staff members play a role in creating a campus bureaucracy oriented to white students. Reviewing graduate education, sociologist James Blackwell has proposed that the factors contributing to the low black attendance include the scarcity of financial aid, as well as the general character of college climates and mentoring programs.[40] The difficulty of obtaining financial aid was aggravated in the 1980s and early 1990s by the conservative Republican administrations' major cutbacks. A nurse commented on her experiences at an East Coast university:

> I worked hard at it, nobody gave me anything. I mean, I struggled as a mother of three children and then a divorced mother of three kids to put myself through an associate de-

gree program, a baccalaureate degree and a master's. So no one really gave me anything at all in any aspect. As a matter of fact, I . . . did encounter some racism in that aspect because I found out that some monies were more available to white students than was in fact available to black students to finish the graduate program at this university. . . . I had to stand my ground and say, "I want to finish this program, I have this time frame to finish this program. I can do this program, but I need some help." And so, not that they gave me the help, but they were able to extend my payments so that I was able to still take the courses and still manage to pay the tuition. But it was not easy; they didn't just offer it to me, I had to fight to get it.

Struggles with college bureaucracies, many of which are oriented to the needs of white middle-class students, become serious when daily survival is in the balance. There is a widespread notion in this country that African American and other minority college students receive large numbers of race-exclusive financial aid packages. Indeed, during the Bush administration in the early 1990s the U.S. Department of Education targeted these race-exclusive aid programs as a major problem, thereby communicating to the nation the false impression that a large proportion, if not the majority, of minority students benefit from them. However, the Department of Education's own statistics show how inaccurate this impression is. In one recent year only 45,000 minority students benefited from race-exclusive scholarship aid. And these students constituted about 3.5 percent of all minority college students. To put it another way, less than .8 percent of all aid students are minority students receiving help from race-conscious programs. The real problem is not the one so widely discussed, but rather, as the student in the previous quote suggests, the lack of funds to assist minority students to achieve their educational goals.[41]

An Agonizing Dilemma:
Black Colleges or White Colleges?

Most black parents work hard for their children to succeed, and many see advanced education as a way up for their children. In a 1992 study in an eastern state Joe R. Feagin conducted group interviews with a number of college-oriented black parents with children of college age or children old enough for them to be considering a nearby university.[42] Significantly, when the black parents were asked about this predominantly white university, many did not see it as a strongly welcoming milieu for black students. Drawing on their own experience and that of relatives and acquaintances with this university, as well as on media accounts, many portrayed black students there as facing racial barriers set up by white students, faculty, staff, and administrators. Racial barriers are not discussed by black parents just to be argumentative, for such obstacles are at the heart of an agonizing dilemma many black parents and students face: that of choosing between a predominantly white and a predominantly black college. Black parents themselves, such as this mother in one group, talked about this choice for their children specifically as a "dilemma":

> I have a seventeen-year-old daughter who's looking at college now. . . . [She] was very set on a major black university, where many members of my family have gone. And I wanted her to go there. But I also knew that she was going to make connections in college that will last for her life. And [at a white university] the people you spend your undergrad with very often are the CEO's of tomorrow. So it was a dilemma. Do I want her to identify with who she is ethnically, or do I want her to start the groundwork for her future career?

In choosing a college, few white parents or students must con-

130

sider racial discrimination, the loss of faculty and other social support, or the greater difficulty of participating in campus life that the choice of a white college frequently involves for black parents and students.

Once in a predominantly white university, many black students consider dropping out, often because of the constant questioning of their capabilities. In our national middle-class sample a business executive commented on his daughter's experience at two predominantly white universities and at a black university:

> My daughter, who graduated from a predominantly black southern university, initially began her college training at a [white] midwestern university. . . . [Later] she moved back to the southern city to be with us, with my wife, and went to a white university there. [She] then decided she needed a little more exposure and went to the black university. The thing that was so interesting to her was that at the midwestern university and the white southern university, both good schools, there was a night and day difference in how you were treated by the faculty. The faculty at the black southern university were interested in you as a person, wanted to insure that you were successful in completing courses and getting your degree. And at the midwestern university and the white southern university they could care less about you as an individual; you're more or less a number. . . . She decided in a number of instances that there were some assumptions made by her faculty at these universities that she would not be able to comprehend some of the information they were giving her. Just on an assumption! Of course, she was able to do that, had no problem. But it was just that "Well, I know the university is here, and black students are competing with the white students, and we're really not going to expect you to do too well."

Many middle-class African Americans such as this executive

131

and his family must constantly debate the virtues of black and white colleges. Business researcher John Butler, himself African American, has noted that for many middle-class black professionals and business people "there is a general feeling that these [black] schools prepare them well for participation in society" and that simply "because a school is attended and operated by whites, it is not automatically superior."[43]

Conclusion

Many white commentators on the crisis in black education blame the victim in their assessments of elementary and secondary education, and especially of higher education. George Keller has argued that middle-class blacks bear the greatest responsibility for the problems of black youth, arguing that

> educators and do-gooders outside academe must move beyond their naive pieties onto the treacherous, unknown ground of new realities. Petulant and accusatory black spokespersons will need to climb off their soapboxes and walk through the unpleasant brambles of their young people's new preferences and look at their young honestly. . . . They will need to encourage, lift up, and argue with those youths who do not see the urgency of education in a scientific, international, and information-choked world. . . . Critics will need to stop the fashionable practice of lambasting the colleges as if they were the central problem.[44]

In this analysis Keller provides a window into the mind of many influential whites, including policymakers, as we approach the twenty-first century. Many whites feel that the burden is on middle-class black leaders to quit being "accusatory" and to work harder to encourage black youth to view education as the main way to overcome poverty and inferiority.

132

These white critics are oblivious to the influence of the contemporary racial climate at traditionally white schools and colleges and fail to see white-run institutions as a source of serious problems for black students. Yet life for black students in mostly white schools often means daily struggle and recurring crises. They struggle to find out what the rules of the game are, officially and unofficially. When black students say "whiteness" is an omnipresent problem, they are not just talking about color or racial identification. They are reporting being at sea in a hostile environment. Painful difficulties with teachers, fellow students, and curricula not only accumulate year after year for black children as individuals and as a group but also regularly bring to mind the collective memory of past discrimination.

We have observed numerous ways in which encounters with white hostility shape the perspectives of students and their parents. Life perspectives and identities are challenged constantly, and some students seem to walk on the edge of denial of their own blackness. Yet most maintain their balance and meet the recurring pain and anger with a determination to excel and conquer. As we observed in Chapter 2, the array of responses to discrimination that becomes part of one's repertoire is great, ranging from resignation to open confrontation. A black professor who has worked in various parts of the country eloquently summed up the impact of white racism in creating a defensive lifestyle and life perspective:

When a black student walks into a predominantly white environment, that student gets the same feeling that I get when I walk into a predominantly white situation. I immediately become fearful and defensive: fearful that someone will openly show hostility, that someone will openly show that I'm not wanted there; defensive, trying to set myself up so that if I face that I can deal with it. Students don't have all of the kinds of coping mechanisms held by adults and

133

professional adults; therefore this is more difficult for them. I still find myself uncomfortable if I walk into a strange environment where there are only whites and I'm the only black. And unfortunately, usually someone, at least one person in that environment or in that situation, will say or do something that's negative, if it's no more than just ignore you.

So, you come in defensive. . . . your fear is reinforced. That's what happens to so many of these youngsters on these campuses, they're dealing with kids who are sons and daughters of bigots. And as soon as they find a friend who accepts them, and they feel real good and start to relax, they run into this young bigot who brings back all the pain, all of the hurt, and it almost erases all of the good that's there. So, they're constantly in a state of stress. There's not a time when they feel that they can afford to let down. And when they let down, they're hurt.

Chapter Four

Navigating the Middle-Class Workplace

O N May 29, 1984, one of America's most talented journalists, Leanita McClain, committed suicide. Only thirty-two years old, she had won numerous major journalism awards. She was the first African American to serve on the editorial board of the *Chicago Tribune* in its long history. Two months prior to her suicide *Glamour* magazine had acclaimed her as one of the outstanding women working in corporate America. Why did such a talented woman commit suicide? Reviewing McClain's life, Bebe Moore Campbell has assessed the culture shock blacks face having to cope with a culturally different, often discriminatory white world. In the white-normed corporate environment, "Black women consciously choose their speech, their laughter, their walk, their mode of dress and car. They trim and straighten their hair. . . . They learn to wear a mask."[1] In addition to facing particular experiences of poor treatment by whites, black employees in corporate America are under constant pressure to adapt, unidirectionally, to the values and ways of the white world.

In this chapter we examine the world faced by those African Americans who work in thousands of white-collar workplaces. Employment as white-collar workers in very large numbers in historically white workplaces is a relatively new experience for African Americans. The black middle class of professionals, managers, sales workers, clerical workers, and entrepreneurs has increased dramatically since the 1960s. In 1988 approximately 9 percent of clerical workers were black; about 6 percent of sales workers were black. The professional-technical category was 8 percent black, and the managerial category was approximately 6 percent black.[2] Black employees make up about 11 percent of the labor force, so it is evident they are still underrepresented in these white-collar categories. Furthermore, as we discussed in Chapter 1, these broad categorical data give a misleading impression of how much progress has occurred, for white-collar blacks are disproportionately concentrated in lower status sectors within each category. Moreover, these statistical data do not tell us how individuals are actually treated in the workplace. Indeed, in the three decades that have elapsed since the 1964 federal anti-discrimination law, *no* research group has to our knowledge undertaken a major national study of day-to-day discrimination faced by black men and women in the workplace.[3]

Discrimination at the Entry Stage

Black professional, managerial, and clerical employees typically work in establishments that were until recently, at least in their white-collar ranks, exclusively white. Black employees in a white-collar work milieu, unlike in public accommodations, might be expected to be somewhat sheltered from racial hostility because the workaday cast of characters is relatively constant and the workers often know one another. In addition, fair employment laws are well known, and one might conclude—

erroneously—from media discussions, well enforced. Yet the probability of experiencing discrimination and intolerance in such a workplace environment is still great.

Job discrimination questions have totalled perhaps half of the survey questions asked of national samples of black Americans on the subject of discrimination. In a 1988 *Business Week* poll 80 percent of the black respondents, but only 32 percent of the whites, felt that if an equally well-qualified black person and white person were competing for the same job, the black applicant would be less likely to be hired.[4] In a 1989 ABC News/ *Washington Post* survey, a bit more than half of the black respondents were certain that black workers generally faced discrimination in getting skilled jobs; 61 percent replied in a similar way in regard to managerial jobs. On the same survey question whites generally saw far less discrimination than blacks. An earlier 1986 ABC News/*Washington Post* poll, one of very few to ask about personal discrimination, found 39 percent reporting experience with discrimination in getting a job and 41 percent reporting discrimination in getting equal wages.[5] We suspect these latter figures are low estimates of the actual proportion of black workers encountering discrimination, because the questions are very brief and do not examine the many dimensions and conditions of employment settings. In addition, the data were not reported by income level. It is possible that in the workplace middle-class black employees face an even greater range of instances of everyday discrimination than working class black employees because they are pioneers in many formerly all-white settings.[6]

Most of our respondents hold positions in the better-paying professional, managerial, technical, sales, and clerical categories. Like the business people we discuss in the next chapter, these Americans have adopted the ethic of hard work and have taken the promises of the American dream very seriously. In conventional middle-class terms they represent the most successful group of African Americans, those thought by most white Americans to "have arrived."

Hiring is the first stage in the employment process. The 1964 Civil Rights law bars differential treatment in employment, and the "equal opportunity employer" phrase used in advertising suggests that there is indeed equal job opportunity. But legal statements of rights are not necessarily statements of reality. Several respondents reported being rejected because of their race as they sought employment. One well-educated, experienced legal secretary in a southern city recounted her experience:

> Exactly five years ago I ran into an employment barrier when I first came here. The employment office sent me around to legal offices that had openings. And since I've been a legal secretary for at least fifteen years—that's my specialty in the clerical field—I've never had trouble getting a job until I came here. And when they talked to me over the telephone, they were real nice, you know, "Come on down, yes, we have an opening." But when I got there—I went to two different law offices—when I got there, I didn't get an interview. They came, they saw me, they were shocked. They went into their office and buzzed the secretary and said, "Tell her to leave her application and we'll call later; we're too busy to do it now."

Neither firm called her back. Choosing not to challenge this discriminatory behavior, she found another job. It is important to note that the whites here, as in many similar workplaces, are not the Archie Bunker hard-hat whites whom many whites think of when the term "racist" is mentioned, but rather are educated professionals or managers. Again we observe a middle-class black American who sounds "white" over the telephone to white ears initially receiving the same treatment as a white applicant.

138

Although the poor treatment of this respondent was relatively overt, its character makes conclusive proof of discrimination difficult. In our discussions with whites, some have raised questions about the ambiguity in certain black reports of discrimination. The question some whites might ask of this black woman, "How do you know that the rejection was on the basis of discrimination?" would likely be received as a hard blow. Whites questioning her interpretation of a situation that for her is clearly exclusionary is painful, because she, an older black woman, is experienced in the ways of white restrictions in many organizational arenas.

Stereotypes, conscious or unconscious, about the skills of black workers may cause some white personnel officers to see a middle-class black applicant either as a menial worker or a poor risk regardless of qualifications. A college graduate working for a telephone company in a western city discussed the hiring experience of a friend: "A good friend of mine was being interviewed about the jobs that are being offered at a large hotel-casino that's just opening up. A black woman was applying for a job as a manager, or a higher-skilled job. She was then told: Wouldn't you be more comfortable being a waitress? Wouldn't you rather be a maid? This happens all the time."

Race-related factors have blocked the entry of African Americans into almost every category of workplace. A director of library services gave this account of her son's attempt to achieve his dream of becoming a professional driver in auto racing:

He has a goal; he wants to be a professional automobile racer. There are no black . . . professional automobile racers. And he's been training. He's finished three different schools for automobile racing. But he can't break into the professional ranks of that because it takes a large corporate sponsor. It takes a lot of money to do that. And he has written proposals and he has made presentations to a lot of

139

large corporations. And he hasn't been successful in getting the funding, we feel mainly because he's black. He has the skills, we've been and we've seen him race, and he's been critiqued by professional racers and instructors. And they say that he has high-level skills, and he could break into professional racing, but because he's black [he cannot]— that is a white society's sport. So he can't get corporate sponsorship.

Every day, reports in the mass media support the impression that black sports figures are very successful in many different sports. Yet some major sports, such as tennis, golf, and auto racing, are off-limits to more than a token number of African Americans. The internationally famous Indianapolis 500 has so far had only one black driver, Wally T. Ribbs, who was allowed to participate beginning in 1991. Although praised by local professionals in his sport, the young black man described in the quote learned that the views of blacks by whites in corporate suites were more powerful than the views of professionals at the track.

What little recent research has been done on racial discrimination in hiring has focused on less-skilled jobs. Thus, in a 1990 study of discrimination in hiring in Washington, D.C. and Chicago, the Urban Institute sent pairs of black and white men, matched in terms of biographical characteristics, to apply for low-skilled entry-level jobs in service, retail sales, and manufacturing jobs that would typically be filled by high school graduates. Twenty percent of the black men received unfavorable and differential treatment; they did not advance as far in the hiring process as their matched white counterpart. Although it focused on less-skilled positions, this study showed that discrimination in hiring is still a serious problem for black men in major cities.[7]

Subtle forms of exclusion in the workplace can bar blacks from professional and other white-collar positions. A law professor at an East Coast university commented on the preparation necessary for being hired in law firms:

> You may move into an environment and not know the rules, and therefore not know how to play the game, and not know how to succeed. What happens, the barriers and obstacles are often that people will not allow you into the inner circle. Well, for example, let me try to be as concrete as possible. In law school, as a law professor and as a former law student myself, one of the things I recognized was that the students who get the best grades are the students who know how to talk to the law professors. They know how to take a look outside of the legal profession and see what things they'll be doing. They know how to call on their fathers and brothers and uncles to introduce them into the profession. And that's the way they approach the law, and therefore they learn legal analysis, the proper approach, the methodology, and so on. Therefore, they're ready. They also understand the social professional aspects, how to dress, how to approach people and so and so forth. . . . But the barriers [for blacks] are often that people will simply avoid talking to you. Or, they won't let you into the little social circles where you learn the tone, the tenor, the manner, the little techniques, the appearance, the dress, and so on.

The grooming game and the informal social learning that begin in law school, he continued, extend directly into the law firms in the large city where he practiced law for a time:

> What I saw was that people simply didn't share the rules. They would simply observe you, or watch you, but they wouldn't talk about the real deal, as I call it. Therefore, you don't have the opportunity to groom yourself, to be able to go into the upper echelons. You can often get an in-

terview, and sometimes they're willing to take a few blacks.
But so many times you just don't know what you need to
do, how to act, how to carry yourself. Those are the obstacles. One obvious obstacle is just people simply decide not
to hire you; they decide not to invite you into their social
circles. But they can't make the barriers as hard and fast.
There are certain [circumstances]—because the job has an
opening, and because you have a right to interview, and because they want to say that they've interviewed so many
blacks, and because they may want to hire a few—that
may soften up the old absolute barrier of eliminating
blacks. But what happens is, they might decide they really
don't quite want to hire you, and often they simply don't
say anything. And if you've gone through your graduate
school, through your training and preparation, even though
you get the degree, the certification, you often haven't
learned the real social rules, the real professional rules, and
that's just so key. And those in my mind are the obstacles,
in addition to simply the reluctance to hire, the reluctance
to accept, the reluctance to invite—somewhat similar to the
old, hard fast rules of exclusion. These days, it's the more
subtle rules, where they don't discuss the real rules around
you. They just look at you, or they discuss superficial
things, so that you never really discover what it takes.
Therefore, when judgment time comes, when the decision
time comes whether to hire, whether to promote, well, you
just don't quite have what it takes.

The lack of proper connections and of access to social knowledge is a major employment barrier subtly or overtly linked to
differential treatment later on in the professional workplace.
Many white employers may not even realize that a black candidate has been excluded from the cultural socialization necessary
to make it in the legal profession. Like the business networks we

will examine in the next chapter, the preparatory grooming and networking that are obvious in this account provide clear examples of institutionalized discrimination.

Discrimination in Salary, Evaluations, and Promotions

A large proportion of black employees in white-collar positions are pioneers, and many have been hired as racial tokens. For the most part, their superiors are white, which means that their success or failure is being judged by whites who as a rule have little or no experience with blacks as colleagues or supervisors. In the aforementioned *Business Week* survey, 62 percent of blacks interviewed felt chances for blacks to be promoted to supervisory jobs were not as good as those for whites; and 41 percent of the whites polled agreed.[8] In the early 1980s, researcher Ed Jones, a former corporate executive himself, conducted the first survey of black managers with top business school degrees who were working in white firms. In this pioneering research Jones found that nearly all the black managers felt that blacks had not achieved equal opportunity with whites in corporate workplaces, and more than 90 percent felt that black managers had less opportunity than whites, or no chance compared with whites, to succeed in their firms on the basis of ability. In addition, two thirds felt that many whites in corporations believe blacks are intellectually inferior and that the racial climate had a negative impact on the performance evaluations, assignments, and promotions of black managers.[9] Not surprisingly, a 1989 survey by Korn Ferry International found that only .6 percent of top corporate executives were black.[10]

In a variety of workplaces wage and salary inequities have been a reality for blacks for decades. In the *Business Week* opinion survey over half the black respondents felt that most blacks are paid less than whites "doing the same job." In contrast, less than a fifth of whites agreed; most felt there was equal pay for equal work, revealing little awareness of the continuing problem for many black employees. The pattern of answers was similar in the 1989 ABC News/*Washington Post* poll.[11] Moreover, United States Census Bureau data make it clear that there is substantial and continuing inequality at all income levels. For example, in 1990 black households headed by people with four or more years of college had incomes that were still only 78 percent of those of comparable whites.[12]

One of our respondents, a social science professor, reported an unfair evaluation of her work experience when she was hired at a western university:

> I sued the university on salary equity, and I won. My salary was less than three other people who were hired at the same time that I was hired with the same degree. And the points that they gave—and none of us had taught at universities prior to that, we had only worked for agencies—and they were counting their agency experience toward giving them a higher salary and denying it [to me]. . . . And the university did not agree with my point of view in our discussions, so I sued them, and I won.

This framing of discrimination again underscores the critical impact of civil rights laws on black thinking. Going to court won her the proper salary, but she incurred significant personal losses. Later in her discussion she described relations between her colleagues and herself as one of antipathy, of "no love lost." Relations with higher administrators may also have been difficult and strained. Sometimes it appears that some top administrators, as well as chief executives in the private sector, fight a clear case of salary inequity involving a black employee just to protect the principle of white authority.

The experiences of our middle-class respondents confirm and extend the opinion survey findings about evaluations and pro-

144

motions discussed above. In their white-collar workplaces they have been subjected to inappropriate negative evaluations, deliberate attempts to restrict their advancement, and exclusion from mobility ladders and mentoring networks. While employee tracking is considered necessary in many U.S. workplaces, it can become a type of racial discrimination. A young manager in an eastern city described his experiences:

> When I first started working for the bank, I went into the bank with a degree, and I had a white friend. We graduated from the same college. We both started at the bank at the same time. We both went in for management training. They put him in management training, and put me on the teller line, and told me it would be better for me to start off as a teller and work my way up from the bottom, whereas they automatically put him on the management training. Where management training automatically goes through two weeks of teller training, I had to go through a whole year of teller training.

This manager also described instances of overt hostility from fellow white employees. His cumulative experience lends credence to his sense of injustice and his perception of the discriminatory nature of tracking. Nonetheless, this man indicated elsewhere in his interview that, in spite of the racial hurdles, he has steeled himself and become even more determined to succeed in the white world.

Prior knowledge of a white supervisor's prejudices has enabled some black employees to prepare a counterstrategy. A sales account manger at a communications company discussed a performance evaluation process involving her white supervisor:

> We had a five scale rating, starting with outstanding, then very good, then good, then fair, and then less than satisfactory. I had gone into my evaluation interview anticipating

that he would give me a "VG" (very good), feeling that I deserved an "outstanding" and prepared to fight for my outstanding rating, knowing my past experience with him and more his way toward females. But even beyond female, I happened to be the only black in my position within my branch. So the racial issue would also come into play. And he and I had had some very frank discussions about race specifically. About females, but more about race when he and I talked. So I certainly knew that he had a lot of prejudices in terms of blacks. And [he] had some very strong feelings based on his upbringing about the abilities of blacks. He said to me on numerous occasions that he considered me to be an exception, that [mine] certainly [were] not what he felt the abilities of an average black person [to be]. I was of course appalled and made it perfectly clear to him. . . . But, when I went into the evaluation interview, he gave me glowing comments that cited numerous achievements and accomplishments for me during the year, and then concluded it with, "So I've given you a G," which of course just floored me. . . . [I] maintained my emotions and basically just said, as unemotionally as I possibly could, that I found that unacceptable, I thought it was inconsistent with his remarks in terms of my performance, and I would not accept it. I think I kind of shocked him, because he sort of said, "Well I don't know what that means" when I said I wouldn't accept it. I said, "I'm not signing the evaluation." And at that point, here again knowing that the best way to deal with most issues is with facts and specifics, I had already come in prepared. . . . I had my list of objectives for the year where I was able to show him that I had achieved every objective and I exceeded all of them. I also had my sales performance: the dollar amount, the products, both in total dollar sales and also a product mix. I sold every product in the line that we offered to our customers. I had exceeded all of my sales objectives. As far as I was concerned, it was outstanding performance. . . . So he basically said, "Well, we don't have to agree to agree," and that was the end of the session. I got up and left. Fifteen minutes later he called me back in and said, "I've thought about what you said, and you're right, you do have an O." So it's interesting how in fifteen minutes I went from a G to an O. But the interesting point is, had I not fought it, had I just accepted it, I would have gotten a G rating for that year, which has many implications.

In a recent survey of black professional and managerial women, Elizabeth Higginbotham and Lynn Weber found that 42 percent had personally experienced discriminatory treatment, especially in regard to promotions and wages.[13] In the quote we see how these black women have to contend with sexism and racism. So ingrained were the male executive's negative attitudes that only after the respondent forced the issue did he award her the rating she deserved. Like similar managers in corporate and government workplaces, he was forced to negotiate with his black employee. Noteworthy too is the extra effort this black manager exerted to check her emotions, so as not to play into the stereotypes of women and blacks being too emotional and out of control.

A service manager in an electronics company explained how a white salesperson had sold an oil company the wrong computer equipment and had promised services that the service department could not deliver:

Everything that this sales rep promised had to come from me, a black field service manager. . . . [I said] "I cannot deliver this, Mr. Customer, because of these reasons. And some of those reasons included: the sales rep sold you the wrong equipment. This will not make your computer work. So no, I cannot deliver." And so the sales guy came back to the office and told my boss that I was out on site airing the company's dirty laundry in front of the customer. Hence, [my] performance appraisal: "I don't think Jack has the oomph or the go-for-it to be a field service manager." . . . [This white manager] has been the most prejudiced, the most discriminating manager that I have ever worked for, and I identified every instance that I could think of. . . . So I told *his* boss: "I don't feel that I could be successful working for this guy, and I solicit your support in helping me identify new employment and new career opportunities, since this guy said that I'm not, you know." So it got to the point where it was escalated to the vice-president of field service on the East Coast.

After discussing the rejection and pain associated with his negative performance rating, this black manager proceeded in his interview to explain that in a meeting with the vice president and other high-level managers of his company, all white, he was asked to prepare an action plan that would satisfy the customer who was alienated through no fault of his own. Though hurt deeply, he did not give up but prepared, on short notice, a plan that was accepted and successful. After the incident, however, this manger was moved by higher-level white executives to a more difficult position in another city, a position he believed he was assigned to in order that he would fail. The "promotion" was not in his view to be taken at face value.

Many workers, black or white, may face some struggles related to promotions over the course of their careers. Yet for black employees the normal pressures of seeking a promotion tend to be exacerbated by restrictive racial barriers. A researcher at a major university described his frustration: "And I did an exceptional job at that; however, I never really got a decent promotion out of that. But I did all those things that they

148

said they wanted [you] to do, and in fact, a couple of my managers wanted to promote me but they told me they were stopped, literally they just said no. . . . A white guy told me, he said, 'Listen, you're black. They're never going to promote you.'" For many middle-class black employees time spent in a white organization brings the realization that there is a "glass ceiling"—some say a "concrete ceiling"—beyond which they cannot be promoted. Indeed, this is one reason that some quit their jobs and start their own businesses, "free from 'glass ceilings' and racial tensions in white corporations."[14]

A striking feature of our interviews was that not one respondent expressed an open and generalized hostility toward all whites. Given the prevalence of white discrimination this seems somewhat surprising. Perhaps one reason is blacks' awareness —expressed in our interviews—that some whites support their quest for equal treatment. From the Underground Railroad of the nineteenth century to white support for civil rights movements and organizations since the 1950s, white support has been important to black empowerment. The situation today was described this way by a professor at a New England university: "[what] blacks have to learn to do is to find whites in the system who are supportive and helpful to them, and there are such whites. I think that you can. Even though racism is a big factor in the world . . . there are people who are white who are not racists and who are willing [to help]."

There is evidence that some whites in desegregated workplaces resent a black employee daring to do the same job as a white or to do better in performing that job. Whites often squander corporate resources by putting personal prejudices above company profits in decisions regarding black employees. An executive for a large corporation reported on what he had learned from recent company personnel decisions. He has seen evidence that white salespeople in the company have been promoted even when their sales are far less than their sales objectives ("budgets"). He gives the example of a successful black salesperson:

> [He] had a budget of six [million]; he brought in eight. The next year they gave him a budget of eleven; he brought in more than eleven million. This same black could not have aspired to a management role, and the reasons that I got when I said, "Well, why is it that this guy is not being promoted? Why does he have to fight for it? Why aren't you seeking him out? Giving him the mentorship that he needs? Because he's demonstrated his sales skills; he's brought you the money. What are you doing for him?" . . . I get these real thin, veiled excuses about, "Well, there's a perception that Jim is not sales executive or management material." I said, "What's the perception? *Whose* perception? The customer doesn't give a damn, because they're buying the product. The peers that come to him for help in order to close this business on their accounts don't seem to have a problem, because they *know* that he can help himself. So who's got the perception? *You* have the perception."

The incongruity between the outstanding performance of this salesperson and the way he was perceived by higher-up executives suggests that such white perceptions deny blacks access to positions of greater power within a corporation. This manager continued with an account of a black woman with an outstanding sales record:

> Five years, almost six, without a promotion. Company Elite Sales is a status that says you have met your sales budget every quarter in the fiscal year, and if you make this, that means you made your budget every quarter and you made your budget for the end of the year. So for five years, the lady made Company Elite Sales. That's extraordinary, okay.

150

That means that you are 110 percent hitting consistently. Now if you do that over a certain number of months, you can win what's called Top Gun. Such people go on vacation overseas for two weeks with their spouses, all expenses paid. . . . Now, these same people [higher management] did not put her in for a promotion *again* because of some perception that they say exists about her, her follow-up skills and her attention to detail and a bunch of other stuff. Perception. There's a perception that she's not able to communicate effectively with senior-level management because one senior-level person at an account wanted her off. Said that he didn't want to work with her anymore, supposedly for some issue that probably was created. They wouldn't give me a lot of details. For that reason I said, "Okay, well, there may be a valid reason why she had a problem with that account. But what I'm asking you is how you make a determination about a person who is a winner by every other management standard? You say she has one problem with one account. She *still* made her Company Elite Sales. She still made her budget, and she still made Top Gun, and she is two grade levels below your turkeys that are just half making it."

An extraordinary salesperson, this black woman was not promoted because of conflict with one white executive and because of the white perception that she was not "management material." We observe here the ghostly and elusive character of some workplace discrimination. Since no one took personal responsibility for the discriminatory judgment about this black woman, there was no specific discriminator to be challenged. The presence of civil rights laws was important in this case, for the respondent relates later in the interview that he pointed out to senior management they might be facing a lawsuit because of the discrepancy between her performance and her corporate rewards. In his account the senior executives did not seem to comprehend that they were squandering corporate resources in restricting the advancement of a talented black woman. The limited opportunity for this salesperson belies the conviction of many whites that blacks now have the same or better opportunities as whites.[15]

In her research on a large industrial corporation, Rosabeth Moss Kanter found extensive discrimination against women, most of whom were white. Citing other studies that have found criteria such as the "right" class and racial background as highly important in promotions, Kanter concluded that the replacement of old white males by new white males in an organization's promotional system provides "an important form of reassurance in the face of uncertainty about performance measurement in high-reward, high-prestige positions" and that management positions "become easily closed to people who are 'different.'"[16] A human services manager in a northeastern city described the following problem in trying to get promoted to middle management:

> I did work for eight years for a private company. . . . I wanted to move up into middle management, and I had to prove myself. It was an obstacle course. There were many white males who did not have the experience that I did who were sitting in higher positions, and I fought that. Well, I got very loud about it. I threatened to go to the State Commission Against Discrimination, and they didn't want to see that happen, so they placated me by creating new positions [so] that they could eventually say, "Oh, we don't need that position anymore." That's when I knew I had to leave there. [What was the problem with you moving into one of those management positions?] Well, I wasn't necessarily the showpiece that they wanted to have in some of the front office positions. Just a year ago I started to

152

press my hair, so from the time I was fifteen until a year
ago, I wore my hair in its natural state. I wasn't necessarily
your picture of the budding executive! . . . I think part of
it, too, was that I haven't always been one who minced my
words, and I've been pretty open about my thinking and
thoughts and so forth, which again can be a drawback.
They like us to be quiet and reserved and speak when spoken to.

A 1991 black business study, "A Blueprint for Success," found
that black managers faced a concrete ceiling when it came to
moving into higher management positions in corporations.[17] As
a *Black Enterprise* journalist assessing this study put it, "Unwilling to bet the success of their department or pet project on a
black colleague, white managers 'play it safe' putting white
males into the visible positions of their companies."[18] Image is
perhaps more important than performance in this corporate
"cloning" of white managers in corporate and other workplaces. With her Afro hairstyle and outspoken ways, this talented woman was not the picture, for key whites, of the "the
budding executive." Middle class African Americans risk punishment when they step out of the invisible "place" that they
occupy in many corporate settings. When the respondent was
forced to became aggressive, her superiors responded by creating what she saw as a temporary position.

In some situations one motivation for exclusion and restriction may be white employers' ignorance about or lack of experience with African Americans. Many white managers and supervisors have had little contact with blacks; they may never have
seen a black executive or may have only seen blacks in menial
positions or as entertainers, athletes, or criminals in the mass
media. Many live in exclusively, or almost exclusively, white
suburbs. A white manager with this limited experience, drawing
on his or her images of blacks only from stereotypes, may select

another white person over an equally or better qualified black person because of deep-lying, even unconscious, feelings that the white candidate is more compatible or competent.

Moving up the corporate ladder usually requires good mentors. All too often, however, there are few (or no) senior white managers willing to be effective mentors for black employees. And the aforementioned cloning process means there are few blacks in higher positions who can be mentors for other blacks. An assistant vice president at an East Coast bank commented on her struggle against discrimination and the absence of mentors:

> I have a constant battle. As a matter of fact, I have an ongoing discrimination suit now. It has been more or less settled, and we signed a consent decree. . . . I guess that's how, why I learned that you have to be able to know white America, and white corporate America in order to deal with them. With me, coming into an organization such as this, I didn't have any mentors, any black mentors. And the few that you have, let's face it, they didn't have to share their knowledge. I'm not going to be that way. I do it now, so that's why I feel that I can help other people, by teaching them, telling them things that I had to learn the really hard way on how to cope with some of the different problems.

This manager suggests that she would like to be more of a mentor than white executives and a few higher-level black executives she has known. However, one should not underestimate the problems blacks in higher positions face in trying to mentor. In his pioneering research, former top executive Ed Jones described a black manager (called "Charlie") who had met with other black employees seeking his advice on coping with discrimination. Feeling the problems should be brought to senior white management, Charlie arranged a meeting. However, before that scheduled meeting he encountered the company president at an informal gathering and was reprimanded with these

154

words: "Charlie I am disappointed that you met with those black managers. I thought we could trust you."[19]

One reaction to social "cloning" in the workplace is resignation, a reaction that can lead to a cross-generational lowering of expectations. The president of a credit fund described the impact of his experience at a major corporation in an eastern city:

> As I told the senior personnel person once, blacks in the
> company had jobs, and whites had careers. And that is still
> true in most corporations today. We're employees, we're
> not on the fast track to the executive suite. We are needed
> for statistical purposes, but going to the top of the organi-
> zation is not truly there. So, within that framework, I de-
> cided the job was nice, the money was delightful, and I
> coexisted. I did my job, but I did not do it with the intent
> of looking toward a goal and being frustrated, that I would
> be an executive of the company one day. Where some peo-
> ple do get involved in the American dream—thinking that
> they will be there—[they] become totally frustrated and dis-
> enchanted with the system. The system was wonderful to
> me. . . . I have a son now who just completed his first year
> at an Ivy League university, and one of the things I've
> shared with him over the years, particularly since he was in
> high school, is that he has to face reality in the society, no
> matter if he went to A&T or whether he went to Princeton,
> or Harvard or Stanford. This is the kind of thing he has to
> understand who he is. He cannot think for a moment that
> he's totally equal, because he's not.

Typically, whites on favored tracks can not only think in terms of careers but also secure the special in-house training that facilitates moving up.[20] This respondent lowered his expectations for corporate advancement and passed on to his son his pessimistic, yet realistic, view of real-world equality. There is no clearer example in this book of the cumulative impact of discrimination. Racism in his employment experience seems to have shaped his life perspective in basic ways. Writing about psychological costs, Mirowsky and Ross have suggested that minority status is associated "with a reduced sense of control . . . partly because for members of minority groups, any given level of achievement requires greater effort and provides fewer opportunities."[21]

Advancement in government can also be very difficult, as one southern state legislator forcefully asserted:

It's not easy for a black woman . . . to get good committee assignments, unless you have been what is considered to be a team player. A team player is a person who normally votes and adheres very closely to the leadership. . . . I face discrimination by whites all the time, all the time. [Could you be specific?] Committee assignments is one [area]. I had been here about fourteen years before I got a committee chairmanship. It was a little do-nothing chairmanship, the chairman of rules and resolutions. Nothing but you have to watch the rules and resolutions of what people sent out, either congratulating somebody, or memorializing somebody in their district. That's what that was. [Do you think they see it as a danger by putting you in as a chairperson, or do you think it's primarily because you're black?] I think it's probably because I'm black, period. They don't want to put us in really powerful positions. I'm the chairman of the judiciary committee, and even [as] chairman of the judiciary committee, they moved out a whole lot of things that normally the judiciary committee would control. And they put it in other committees. When somebody else was the chair—of course a white had it— they had better control. They had more powers. When they made a black chairman, they reduced those powers and took them away.

A common accusation against black managers in corporate workplaces is that they are not "team players."[22] Here we see the same accusation made against a black legislator. In her detailed interview this woman gave several examples of having been excluded by the white elite in the legislature from key meetings and political advancement. With anger in her voice she explained that she protested and forced white colleagues into interracial negotiation. However, she has kept her public criticism of these influential whites within bounds lest she become even more restricted. After the tape recorder was turned off she presented an even more negative view of the white leadership than she was willing to put on the tape. For most of this nation's history, state legislative positions were off limits to African Americans, especially in the South. As recently as 1940 only 90,000 of the 3.7 million adult blacks in the South, where most then resided, voted in the general election, and in 1942 only a dozen black state legislators served the nation, not one in the South. A major enlargement of voting power came after the passage of the 1965 Voting Rights Act, and by the early 1990s the number of black elected officials in the nation as a whole had increased significantly, to about 7,400, with more than half serving in the South.[23] Yet these numbers are still far from proportionally representative. Moreover, as the account above shows, they signal only the beginning of the struggle for real organizational power. Some scholarly debate has focused on the effectiveness of black elected officials, much of it on their characteristics and performance, but to our knowledge no significant research has been done on discrimination they face within state and federal legislatures.

Marginalized in the White-Collar Workplace

In some middle-class workplaces there seem to be positions reserved just for black employees. Social psychologist Kenneth

Clark has observed that black employees in corporate America frequently find themselves tracked into "ghettos" within companies, such as departments of "affirmative action," "community affairs," or "special markets." In many firms, professional and managerial blacks "are rarely found in line positions concerned with developing or controlling production, supervising the work of large numbers of whites or competing with their white 'peers' for significant positions."[24] Among our respondents, a salesperson working for a Fortune 500 company in an eastern city gave this account:

> Even though they say you're given territories blindly, the contrary is true. It seems as though blacks are always given the least productive territory, and it's been a recurring thing too. Again, people seem to be comfortable with giving majority people the best territories because there's a fear there that white people will get mad. . . . Therefore, you find that a black is given a territory that might be identified as a "growth" area, but really [it is] one that has not really produced to the level that the other territories have.

This segregative tracking involves hiring blacks for nontraditional jobs and putting them in less desirable or powerless positions. Similarly, Kanter found that minority and female white-collar workers were often put into special or low-mobility "staff" positions, such as those in personnel or Equal Employment Opportunity (EEO) offices, where there were fewer chances for mobility and where they had to rely on white male "line" managers to implement important policies.[25]

Another example of tokenism in traditionally white institutions is the hiring of black professors for the Black Studies programs inaugurated at more than five hundred historically white colleges since the 1960s, often in response to pressure from black students and black communities. It is one thing to

158

set up a such a program; it is another for senior white administrators and professors to support it with adequate funding and to respect it as a legitimate and major academic enterprise. The presence of black professors has helped to make white institutions seem progressive on racial matters, but the veneer of legitimacy is often not desesrved. A professor and administrator in a Black Studies program commented on his position:

> [I have] tried to speak to the administration about blacks. The way they look at it, they're not paying you to do that. They're paying you as administrators to stay in line and help them. In that sense, you're kind of a fire insurance against black people. And I've never been able to do that. I mean, whether we like it or not, we legitimatize the institution, quite frankly, just by being in it. It's an undeserved legitimatizing in some cases. It's not doing as much as our presence might connote. . . . I think that we have to raise the contradiction; we have to raise the accountability of institutions like this one for our continual push. We have to do that. I'm just not prepared to sit here and say everything's all right because they help me feed my family. I just can't do it. What's the dues? You don't get as much money, you don't get the positions, the goodies. But I've got other kinds of goodies, and other kinds of things I value. I sleep at night, because I feel I've done the best I could. But it's not easy, you swim upstream a lot.

Many colleges and universities have responded to some degree to pressure from black communities to hire more black faculty members. Still, one survey of more than 400 black faculty members at white colleges found that 41 percent thought that racism was the important barrier to black employment in their institutions, an obstacle much more important than the limited supply.[26] Moreover, black faculty members who are hired in white colleges often find themselves to be among a small number of black representatives in a mostly white world, sometimes with little chance of longterm survival there.

Tokenism as "fire insurance" can also be seen in this news anchor's account of a previous position in the Midwest:

I was working for one of the networks in a major, major city. . . . I was the *first* primary black anchor that they had hired. Keep in mind, prior to that I was working for a [non-network] station in a midwestern city, and this network had a station in that city. I helped my station knock the network out of number one into a number three position. Plus, [at] the network's other station (that I eventually went to work for) civil rights groups were picketing in front of the station. You don't have any blacks on the air. So, my being hired by that station in that major market was a result of, number one, beating their pants off in the market I left, and helping get civil rights leaders off their front steps so to speak. But once I got there, I realized that, I think, to a large degree the only reason why I was hired was so they could say, "See, o.k., we did something about it. We did hire a minority, and black leaders you can go home now." And once the pickets stopped, and what have you, my personal services contract I felt was reneged on. I don't think I was used as I negotiated to do, and as I indicated I was going to do. Otherwise I would have never taken the job. And I can't add anything else to that happening except for the fact that I was black. And once you reach a situation like that in whatever you do, you have a choice to make. Either you can deal with it, or you can change it. And I decided to change it. I left. I quit. I decided, if you're not going to treat me fairly, I'm not interested in being a puppet for you, or someone to make you look good.

Note the multidimensional character of discrimination. There are the surface events and the hidden meanings as he saw them. This black pioneer helped one television station beat out a network's station; then that network hired him, primarily to get civil rights protestors off the third station's doorstep. He describes a racial "bait and switch" episode, rife with frustration, illustrative of the black limbo experience often overlooked by white observers. Hired under one set of rules and confident of his professional abilities, he quickly comes to realize that he is working under a new set of rules.

Tokenism and ghettoized tracking can even be seen in historically white church groups that officially profess the values of justice and brotherhood. A black minister in a predominantly white Protestant denomination explained:

There is a great difference between being a black minister and being a white minister. One is that if you're a white minister, you have any number of career moves that you can make just based on the personal ambition. If you are a minister who is prepared, who is on the ball, more or less, has got things going for yourself, you can move within a particular conference. You can move intra-conferences and advance. If you're a black minister—and I'll use this conference as an example, we have eight black churches . . . until someone dies or someone moves to another conference, there is no mobility for me. We have not reached the sophistication where a black minister can be assigned to a white church. . . . There are people within the systems who would use the system against other folk in an oppressive manner. . . . The system is set to perpetuate racism. A black minister ran for bishop last year and withdrew his name in the first or second round, because whites just won't be supportive. There's a whole area of the conference who said, "We don't want this man, because we don't feel like a black man can handle our conference, so he can become bishop here, but we don't want him here."

There is support here for the old saying that "11 o'clock on Sunday is the most segregated hour of the week." Within some desegregated denominations a type of internal segregation can reappear. (In contrast to the often negative role of the white church in U.S. racial relations, the black church has been a mainstay for black survival in a racist society.)

Marginalization within a private or public institution can have other consequences as well. Commenting on the current situation of some black professionals who had been hired into corporations some time ago, a senior secretary underscored the fragile nature of their positions:

> They're tokens. Given the era that I grew up in . . . there were certain black professionals—people that I know and have been associated with—that have held certain positions and certain jobs with certain companies, large companies like IBM, Xerox. They were successful in obtaining [a job as] the manager of a certain district or a supervisor of this or that, and for whatever reasons, those jobs became surplus or were done away with. And they were not able to just walk out and walk right into another position, not paying those same salaries. And I think several of those people—just here recently—that back then in the '60s or '70s who had their heads up in the air and thinking that they owned the world and they were turning over the world, now they're not doing that. They're out there in the unemployment lines.

In her work on corporate executives, researcher Sharon Collins has argued that the black middle class is in a very vulnerable economic position. One problem is that much black advancement since the 1960s was substantially the result of federal policy pressures, which lessened in the 1980s and early 1990s. In addition, black managers and professionals hired into corporate America in the 1960s and 1970s were often new "tokens," many of whom were ghettoized in positions oriented to affirmative action, special markets, or minority communities. The withdrawal of federal supervision of private sector employment practices during the Republican administrations in the 1980s and early 1990s eroded the positions of many middle-class blacks.[27] The weakening of civil rights enforcement encouraged many firms to abandon or neglect their (typically modest) programs to diversify workforces along racial and ethnic lines, and, as the executive director of one black management group put it, the ranks of black executives were "decimated."[28] In addition, most middle-class black employees who lose their positions do not have the parental or family resources that a large proportion of middle-class whites have to fall back on.

The marginalized position of many black managers and professionals can also be seen in their daily struggles against pressures to think or become "white." White workplaces rarely accommodate basic black interests and values. Instead, black employees are expected to assimilate. Drawing on interviews with seventy-one black female managers and professionals, researcher Ella Bell has described the everyday experience of having a foot in both the black and the white worlds as a "bicultural life experience." Her respondents reported they were constantly working to prove that they were competent and that they fit into the white world, while at the same time they had to exert an equal amount of energy in maintaining their black identities and "maintaining ties to the black community."[29] The minister quoted above commented on these bicultural challenges:

> They [white coworkers] don't see you or me and say this is a talented human being. . . . No, they say "He's black, but"

163

or "She's black, but." There's an exception. So to be black and be [a] successful contributor is to be an exception to what white folks see in other black folks. The temptation is that we begin to think that we are an exception to other black folks. And most of the time when we step out on that, we get burned, because we would become coopted into the white community, into the white world, and to the white value system, and to the white frame of thinking. We excise ourselves from the black community, or we stay with our Afro-Americanness and take the risk of offending our white friends.

Caught between his white denomination and his Afro-Americanness, this minister described what might be seen as a contemporary variation of the "double" black consciousness about which William E. B. Du Bois wrote so eloquently.[30]

White Supervisors, Coworkers, and Associates

Acting on their racist prejudices and assumptions, both white supervisors and white colleagues can create a hostile workplace climate. A detention officer in a southwestern police department made this clear in describing her first days on the job:

When I was hired I was told, and I quote, "I hope *you* make it." Emphasis on *you*. And I told my new supervisor right then and there, I stopped her right in her tracks and I said, "What do you mean? I detect some sort of implication here regarding the pronoun *you*. I don't feel that you're addressing it singularly, but plural. And there's nobody here but me and you." She said, "Yeah, yeah, no black's ever made it. We never had a black person make it." So that makes you feel really good, like you've got this black cloud [laughs] coming over your head through the probation period. They don't think I'm going to make it anyway. . . .

Now if she had said, "It's a hard position. Not many people have what it takes." If she had said something objective,
I wouldn't have felt anything. But to single something
about me, you know, that confused me, and I didn't know
if I'd make it or not. And subsequently, I had to go the entire nine yards of my probation. People that were hired after me, which happened to be white, didn't have to go
through their [full] probation.

Her white boss's admonition signalled to her that she would not
be treated fairly. Whites in charge of hostile work environments
create, often intentionally, conditions that contribute to poor
performance and failure.

A college-educated secretary and civil rights activist working
at a large corporation described discrimination in the informal
rules for employee behavior:

Across this nation millions of [non-job-related]
things . . . are achieved on the job by whites. And it's done
during the day on the job, with paid salaries or what not.
My example would be, even just like the use of a telephone. . . . Last year I was a delegate for Jesse Jackson to
the Democratic Convention in Atlanta in which there was a
lot of media—television, newspaper and all of this—saying
you're a national delegate. They'd come to the job, and
somebody would want to take pictures of me. Many companies would have been proud to know they had somebody; and my company would have too, except that I was
a delegate for a black person, Jesse Jackson. Then they call
me in the office and say, "Okay, we don't want any
NAACP work done on the job. We don't want any democratic [political activity]." Because part of this time I had
said let's launch a voter registration drive for every employee. . . . Then they will say, "it's time for your review. Now,
your outside work does not have anything to do [with your

165

work here]. We don't care what you do outside, but we just
don't want you to do it here. . . . The personnel manager
went to a Chamber of Commerce meeting and had to come
back to our plant and xerox 'x' number of copies. The
Chamber of Commerce had nothing to do with them [our
company]. But if I go back to the machine to run just a
copy of maybe one letter, then that's personal (and I have a
dime). But why do I need to give them a dime for one copy
when here is a man running twenty-five or thirty-five copies. And they worry about what the little people are doing,
blacks and other minorities, but it's the big company people
who are ripping them off.

The company is an international firm headquartered in Europe,
but this city is in the South, a part of the nation that a few
years back had seen whites violently intimidating, sometimes
killing, civil rights activists such as this woman. Racial discrimination can involve the intentional creation of anomie, as a black
person goes beyond formal rules of fairness to discover the
informal rules applied unfairly. Here a double standard is explicit in the overly close supervision of blacks by white superiors
and the latter's inconsistent evaluations of civic activities by
black and white employees. One gathers from the rest of her
interview that in spite of her substantial qualifications, including a college education and administrative experience, she has
not been considered for promotion to a higher-level white-collar
position.

A registered nurse in an eastern city described her indignation
at excessively close supervision by a white administrator:

That was probably the last straw . . . I resigned and gave
my resignation and left because I would not let him have
the opportunity to think that he could—after I had been
functioning autonomously for twelve years—all of a sudden
[there] is this white male who's going to tell me when I can

166

go, what I have to do. And I have to ask him permission for everything—and the manner in which he stated it. I just wrote in my resignation and left before I had to deal with him, because I was *not* going to be subservient to him in any way, shape, or form. So, of course, white skin, it has played a role, and I'm convinced that if the color of my skin was different from black I would have been treated differently by that white manager. . . . who did not bother to deal with half the problems that I was saying that was occurring within that particular organization. And I've always felt that if you work for a man, speak well of him, and when you no longer can speak well of him it's time to go.

One senses here the weariness common in black accounts of coping with mistreatment. Resigning in protest can improve the situation of the victim of discrimination and, sometimes, can force whites to reconsider their actions. On occasion, the "I'm tired" feeling has motivated dramatic protest actions like that of civil rights activist Rosa Parks, whose refusal to give up her seat to a white person on a bus in Montgomery, Alabama helped to spark the civil rights movement in the 1950s.

Research on complex organizations has shown that older workers are sometimes antagonistic to new workers, in part because of their jealousy or uncertainty about the new workers' outlooks on life and work, or moral values.[31] The resentment faced by new black workers in a historically all-white milieu may be particularly intense. The director of a midwestern drug abuse program described his frustration as the lone black working with middle-class whites:

I was working in a predominantly white hospital. And I feel as though the way I was discriminated against was I always got considered or got identified as "that black counselor up

167

on that unit." . . . That always qualified my experience, it always qualified my expertise, or either it discredited it, I should say. "Well, that's John, that black guy upstairs on that unit." So I had to always fight through that, and, as a result, I ended up always having to deal with people being able to accept my credibility. I mean, I was running a unit that was 99, 100 percent white, minus myself. And predominantly white middle-class females. And no offense to females in the world, but they had a hard time being able to accept leadership or orders or direction from a young black man who had some experience in some of this.

Being constantly identified as "the black whatever" is an inescapable problem for many black workers desegregating traditionally white institutions. As a result of his experience and authority being questioned, the director left the hospital to take his current position, in which his abilities have also been questioned, this time not by coworkers but by whites running a funding agency:

The middle-management funding agency for our program was run by white males. And they sort of tried to underestimate that I, as a young black man, knew what I was able to do. . . . They try to play those little word games and try to play that little intellect game. But see, the difference is, we as black men can become as intelligent as, if not more intelligent than, them. But we've got one other thing going for us; we've learned how to survive, from a street sense.

He added that his "street" sense enabled him to sit down at the table with them and "throw things in their faces that they can't deal with." By keeping them off balance, he suggested, he not only was effective in his negotiations but also maintained his

168

dignity. Quite evident here is the intensity of the daily struggle that black managers face.

Alliances with coworkers are critical to success for white-collar employees, especially in large firms, and black employees may have a difficult time breaking into them, making for a chilly office climate. A human services manager discussed the difficulties she encountered in her office:

> White staff may meet together to discuss a particular pro-
> gram and think that they may not need to discuss it with
> me until after they've gotten it together. [Are you the only
> black?] No, there's another black woman, and often times
> she hasn't been in that circle either, and we've been pretty
> vocal about bringing it to their attention. [Why did they
> think that you didn't need to be there?] "Oh well, we just
> thought we would sit down and discuss this together and
> get what we thought, and we'd bring it to all of us." And
> "we've known each other a really long time, and we're per-
> sonal friends and so forth." And this is their explanation,
> and clearly it's like, let's get our act together before we take
> it to the body. . . . Oh, I confront that. I don't let it slide. I
> let them know I know they've met and the issues need to
> be put on the table, and the executive director is pretty
> good about nipping that kind of thing in the bud.

Informal workplace groups often form along racial lines, with whites who have been there for a time setting the informal norms. Yet in this account there are not only racist whites but also a supportive white executive.

A young lawyer in an East Coast law firm commented about the presumptions many of her coworkers make:

> They look at me as a young black, and they can't believe
> I'm an attorney. They still open their mouths like, "Oh,

that's who the new attorney is!" And then it's, "I didn't
know you were a [pause] woman." Well, my name is Judy,
how many men named Judy do you know? So, that's not
the surprise. I've had more than a number of them submit
reports to my office and then call to ask me if I understand.
And my response to that is, "I understand English. Did you
write what you meant? Well then, yes, I understand." And I
know, like with my predecessor, that did not happen. . . .
By the same token, it's presumed that I can't read a clear
sentence, or interpret a clear sentence, or I need some extra
help. They also want to have a lot of meetings to make
sure I understand. They don't like my making decisions. If I
tell them that I don't think their case will win in court, or it
doesn't meet the legal standard, then they tell me I don't
understand law. . . . I think that a lot of white people are
very intimidated by black people, especially black men who
are successful, and who have degrees and goals and
strength about them, and know who they are, and don't try
to abuse their identity. I think it's known throughout the
agency that I'm [aggressive]. One of the problems that I
have is I'll say, "How ya doin'?" If I'm in the mood to say,
"How ya doin'?" instead of, "Good morning, how are
you?" that's part of who I am, and who I grew up to be.
And I don't want to change that. By the same token, I play
my music in my office, whether it insults them or
not. . . . They see a problem with that.

Research has shown that high-level (usually white) women employees must carry out their jobs under greater corporate scrutiny than their male counterparts.[32] In addition to being pa-
tronized, this attorney is quite conscious of the prevailing
notions of propriety in the white corporate culture, which she
resists.

In the late 1980s the *National Law Journal* reported that

blacks accounted for less than 2 percent of the lawyers and less than 1 percent of the partners of the nation's 250 largest law firms. Black lawyers and judges are rare in most courtrooms. For those whose workplace is the courtroom, however, discrimination can still be a problem, as a law professor at an eastern university explained:

> I was an attorney with the justice department. And I tried cases; I met judges [who] were incredulous that a black man could try a case before them, or be a lawyer even, and certainly be one that represented the United States government in court. And often the discrimination took the form of their trying to get me to do things that would compromise my case: "Well, counselor, you don't need to interview any witnesses, do you? We can just move on; you can just chat with them; you don't have to interview them under oath do you?" [I said] "Well, your honor, you have to have them under oath because that way they may be more likely to tell the truth. Or if they don't, then we have some way of having sanctions apply." Well, that's one example. As a lawyer, I dealt with judges a lot, and some of their discrimination was relatively overt.

This lawyer displayed considerable patience while standing his ground vis-a-vis the harassment of a white judge.

Coworkers' and associates' discrimination can be blatant. A young manager of a service firm recounted numerous experiences with racial hostility:

> Probably the most racism I've ever felt has been in the workplace. One company that I worked for, I was the regional manager for five of their branches. I traveled back and forth to the different branches to make sure that everything was OK. This one particular branch that I got was in a southwestern city. The demographics for this branch were

bad. . . . When I went to the branch, the branch manager, his face dropped as soon as he saw me, he didn't know that I was black. The other people in the office couldn't deal with the fact that they would have to take instructions from a black person. I think that I was probably one of two black people in that city, because I never saw any black people there. I remember one time, one supervisor, we became fast friends. He was white. We got along very well. And he would always tell me all the horrible things said about me, and they were primarily because I was black. I remember the second day that I was there he told me that the installation manager, of all people—he has absolutely nothing to do with my job—told him [that] he didn't understand why he was so attentive to me, so concerned about what I thought about his job. And he said, "Well, she's my supervisor. I should be concerned about what she thinks." He said, "Well, I wouldn't worry about it. Don't worry about it. She's just a black woman. It's no big deal. I'm sure they're going to get her out of here soon. It's no problem. Don't worry about it." But that was just one of so many crazy things. . . . Everybody was so conscious of the fact that I was black, and they just couldn't deal with me being somebody that they had to take instructions from. I guess if I had been the maid I would've gotten more respect. But it was just that constant struggle, constantly dealing with those people.

As the first black person to hold a supervisory position in this local firm, she was treated as a temporary aberration by whites who were unwilling to abandon their stereotypes and feelings of racial superiority. In her interview she also discussed how she learned that one of her subordinates kept racially derogatory cartoons in her desk, then added: "Our secretary at work just didn't want to do any of my reports. I mean, that's her job, and she didn't want to do any of my reports. So I had to call the divisional manager just to get her to do her job." For a long time this respondent continued with her job, but suffered much internally. She also assessed the steeling effect of the hostility she encountered: "I just really feel that going through that I could get through anything in this world. This country cannot be nearly as evil as that environment was."

One way that whites show hostility to blacks in the workplace is by making racist jokes, sometimes quite publicly, as the manager of human resources in an East Coast office of a large corporation recounted:

> I was in the auditorium doing a presentation to about a hundred and fifty people here; basically most of them were white. There were maybe five or seven blacks in the audience out of a hundred and fifty people. And I had to put a "vu-graph" up for a visual aid, and it wasn't a very clear vu-graph. In fact it was a poor vu-graph. It had been copied here at the company, and I was talking about, the subject was, minority business and the reporting we have to do as far as the government's requirements. And one of the people in the back hollered out, "It probably was done by a minority vendor." And here I am at the front of the room, microphone and everything, and it was a matter of hey, quick thinking on your feet. You know, do you blow it here and say what you really want to say, or how do you handle this? And I just smiled and said, "No, unfortunately it was done by this corporation."

The insinuation by whites that incompetence is a peculiar characteristic of minority individuals is a feature of racism that we have seen before in many workplaces. The comment was insulting both in its content and in the speaker's attempt to humiliate a black manager making an important presentation to a predominantly white audience. This incident is also an example of a point that came up repeatedly in black discussions of differential treatment: one has to be prepared constantly to assess what is happening and then to decide, often quickly, on the appropriate response.

A young project administrator for an East Coast company commented on the office climate in a firm for which he previously had worked:

> I was the only black in the company. And me, I can take a lot of ridicule and all, and there were black jokes here and there, and I can go along with it. I'm the kind of guy who's an easy target in a sense, but they just went overboard. And I was looking to stay with one of these companies for a long period of time, but they just really overlooked that, hey, I'm [an] individual. And like I said, I was eighteen or nineteen, and hey, I'm a young guy. And in a way I was reaching out for help, because I had these other guys who had experience and what have you, but they didn't really look at me, I mean, a young black man. Everything was "black this" and "black that" and "Joe black" this and that—jokes and ridicule. And at the time, like I say, I went along with it and all, and I didn't get an attitude until after hours. I wouldn't speak up. I wouldn't speak my mind because I knew how much rage it would have been. And I would just get to my car and just sit back, and talk to myself.

In a white-male-dominated workplace, masculine posturing may take a certain racial force when a black male is present. Even though the respondent was seeking help, his coworkers ignored his needs and made his work experience more miserable with racial joking. Gunnar Myrdal pointed out in *An American Dilemma* that such joking about blacks acts as a sounding board for popular white prejudices, especially notions about racial inferiority.[33] Such racist humor is made all the more painful by its coupling to other racist actions and often can, as here, create great psychological damage.

Racist insults such as barbed joking often seem to be motivated by a desire to drive out a black employee. A college-educated clerk in a parts department of a large international corporation described the persistent harassment she has faced:

> In fact for the past twelve years I've faced discrimination
> on my job because I work with all men. They feel that the
> job I do is a man's job. They've often told me, "Go home,
> you don't belong here. This is not the place for you." (I'm
> suing the company now because of that.) When I refused to
> leave, they started to [put up] . . . racial photographs, pic-
> tures, drawings, writings on a calendar and things of that
> nature to try to intimidate me into leaving. But I stayed.
> I'm still there. They refused to fire me and I refused to quit,
> but still I'm in the process of suing the company. . . . I filed
> with EEOC first, over a year ago. And when nothing could
> be settled with them, I asked for no money at that time,
> when nothing could be settled with them, in fact, they re-
> taliated against me. They called me incompetent, even
> though I run the place alone, and had to have someone sit
> in while I went to listen to them call me incompetent. And
> I'm still running the place alone now. In fact, I replaced
> three men. . . . They refused to give me an increase in sal-
> ary, even though my work increased. For two years, it had
> increased. They managed to give me $.33 an hour in two
> years for a tremendous amount of work that I
> do. . . . There are maybe two or three who don't feel
> threatened by my presence. Yeah, it's sexism, racism, be-
> cause I've heard the Mexican-American guys called "wet-
> backs," "Olympic swimmers," "taco benders." I've heard
> the blacks called "niggers" and "boys" and "spooks."

She continued:

> The calendar was hanging on the door in the parts room
> where I work—the truck parts room. It was the 19th of
> January. . . . Somebody wrote in that square, "Dr. Martin
> Luther King's Birthday." And in the square next to it they
> wrote, "Nigger Day Off." So I showed a couple of white
> guys the calendar and a couple of black guys the calendar,
> then I took it down and took it home. . . . So I started col-
> lecting evidence and keeping a notebook and all the little
> drawings and pictures, and some of the pictures were ridic-
> ulous. They had lips on these people so big it looked like
> turtleneck sweaters. These I found lying around in my work
> area. In fact, some of them were in my desk.

This woman bristled with frustration and rage as she retold her
painful story. Notable are the stages of her increasingly aggressive response to overt discrimination. Beginning with verbal
protests, she later filed complaints with the EEOC. When that
was not successful, she sought her day in court. While the decision to fight became part of an ongoing drama of negotiation,
her attempts at redress did not lead to white concessions but
rather to more harassment.

After listening to many such accounts of job discrimination,
the untutored observer might wonder why they are still common, especially given the fact that the 1964 Civil Rights Act and
subsequent legislation make up a tough set of employment discrimination laws. Sadly, the federal agency with the mandate to
enforce these laws has been inadequate to the task. In a 1990
review Herbert Hill concluded that the EEOC "operates as a
claims adjustment bureau, not as a law enforcement agency. The
commission seeks voluntary, negotiated settlements with emphasis upon the quick resolution of issues, usually by extended
compromise. . . . As a result, there is no genuine conciliation,
little threat of litigation, and minimal substantive compliance

with the statute."[34] Businesses and unions know that the government civil rights enforcement agencies, especially as weakened under the Republican administrations from the 1980s to the early 1990s, are often "paper tigers." As a result, there is no real equality of opportunity for African Americans in most U.S. workplaces. Employment discrimination is one type of law violation where the *victims*, not government enforcers, are primarily responsible for dealing with the violators, even to the point of enforcing the law in their own private lawsuits.

Dealing with White Customers and Clients

Discrimination by customers can present serious difficulties for black employees who work in sales. They may be victimized by stereotyped notions of black incompetence held by white customers who may not have encountered a black person in such a role. Or they may be victimized by the concern of whites that a black salesperson knows more than they do. A black manager in an East Coast bank discussed how some of his clients viewed him:

> In the bank, I face discrimination daily. A lot of times when I'm dealing with customers—especially when you're dealing with millions and millions of dollars—nine times out of ten, you're going to be dealing with an older white person, who has just got [it] in his mind that there can't be an educated black person working in a highly respectable position in the bank. . . . In fact, there has never been a black on the board of directors at the bank that I work for. There has never been another black in my department. So, right now, I'm creating history for the bank that I'm working for. . . . And a lot of times, you know we deal with millions and millions of dollars, we have lots of accounts, we have keys out to vaults, and a lot of times I see people like even

hiding things from me, like keys to vaults, and put them in
a certain drawer, like hide them from me, like I might steal
it or something.

A mid-1980s study in banking found that blacks were being
brought into management at a slow rate, and that 80 percent of
black managers felt their chances for promotion were not as
good as those of their white peers.[35] Unaccustomed to seeing
black bank tellers or managers, many white customers may
assume black employees are menial or lower-paid clerical workers and treat them with discourtesy. We also see the power of the
stereotype of black men as thieves. Even the man's coworkers
felt they must protect the vaults against him. Such encounters
with customers and coworkers are reminiscent of the degradation "rituals" forced on blacks under legal segregation.

A college senior working as a salesperson in a southern city
commented on how he was viewed by white customers:

> Sometimes I don't think that I'm taken seriously. For in-
> stance, in my job situation now, since I'm in retail sales, I
> find myself having to prove I sell computers. So I have to
> prove my knowledge of computers and get past what a per-
> son's perceptions are of me. They have to listen to what I
> have to say, and again say, "Well, he *does* know what he's
> talking about. He *does* know what the equipment is. He
> *does* know how to set up a system, how to make it work."
> But I have to get past a person's original perceptions of me
> before I can go on. . . . Well, I deal with a lot of white cus-
> tomers, and they don't seem to like to deal with a black
> employee with knowledge of computers. I think it scares
> them sometimes. You have to be very patient and very dis-
> creet.

Considerable energy was expended by this man in his long-
suffering approach to everyday discrimination. Many beliefs

about blacks are so entrenched in white minds, that white customers may be only half-conscious, even unconscious, of their
racially barbed comments and actions. Yet from the black's perspective it does not matter whether the white perpetrator causing the pain was consciously racist.

A senior psychologist at a large, historically white university
commented on her experiences with white student clients:

> In the nine years that I've been here, there have been a
> couple of times when I've been seated with a client that I'm
> working with, an Anglo, white client, and I've been called a
> "nigger," or "nigger" has been used in the context of some
> discussion that the client is making in my office to my face.
> I've also had clients get up and leave my office. One wom-
> an told me she didn't want to work with me because I was
> black, that she had never worked with, or lived with, or
> gone to school with blacks, and she just had great difficulty
> with it. . . . There have been a few others. The occasional
> being called a "nigger" as I go across campus still happens
> today.

As the hostile epithets show, there is no subtlety in the white
attitudes expressed here; the hostility is often conscious and
flagrant. A forceful person, this professional indicates elsewhere
in the interview that her reaction to such incidents is not deferential but straightforward and, when possible, vocal. The accumulating discrimination she faced at this university eventually
led her to search for a position elsewhere.

Unwilling to place themselves in a role subordinate to a black
person, some white students refuse to acknowledge their traditional position in the student-teacher relationship. A law professor at an eastern university gave an account of experiences
with white students: "At the university, some of the discrimination you find may come from students who are reluctant to
accept your authority, or your expertise. So, it may show up in

the form of anything from refusal to respond to questions or [to] take them seriously to just a kind of ridicule." And a faculty member at a white university in the South spelled out the professorial authority problems in detail:

> Discrimination is an ongoing process in this environment, and you face it at all levels. All up and down the line. It makes your job more difficult, and what is worse about it, you can't always complain about it because the people who you would complain to can't imagine that you would run into the problem. Let's just take it first with the students. They're racist in the extreme. And it's not just me; I've gone to conferences and talked with other black professors, and they have the same problem. . . . You do not have the benefit of positive presumption, so you go into the classroom— white folks think you're dumb. I don't care what your degrees are. If you've got good degrees, they figure you didn't earn them. Figure someone gave it to you. So right away, you got a problem. Now these folks have never had a black person in authority over them. They take out that hostility. . . . What you have with the ethnic minority professor is you find people wanting to test you and giving you a hard time.

Both professors encountered similar challenging of their authority and questioning of their expertise. The last respondent continued with accounts of discrimination at the hands of the secretarial staff and other whites on campus, by which he illustrated the all-pervasive nature of the racism he daily faces.

Racism and Sexism in the Workplace

On occasion, some observers of U.S. racial relations have asked whether black women face more or less discrimination than black men in pursuing their employment goals and careers.

Explicitly addressing a question on this subject, our respondents were often very thoughtful in their replies. A male college graduate in the West saw some important differences:

> There are definitely systemic differences. [Black] women are perceived as being less of a threat, more passive than men. They are seen as feminine, weak. [White males] feel like they can manipulate women by virtue of their sex, manifest many different ways, through sex bias jokes, or gender type things like, that's a man's job. Or, "honey you don't want to get your dress dirty, or something." . . . Black males are perceived to be powerful, a threat.

In his view the black male image that is frightening to many whites on the street has a counterpart in the workplace. Black women are seen as less of a threat because they can be manipulated in sexist ways.

A psychologist at a major university was quite clear as to how she saw the differences:

> Well, it's hard to measure who's being discriminated against the most, and who's hurting the most. Both black men and black women are hurting. But this society shows its racism in a sexist way. Black women may be tolerated, so that then they may be more likely to be let in the door and hired. But *then* they're devalued, because we still devalue women in general, and women still make less money. And women, then, are perceived as less of a threat to male dominated systems. Black males on the other hand can compete with white males, and because they can compete, or are perceived as competing with white males, they evoke the intimidation, and they invoke lots of fear and threats from white men. So, black men get attacked in some very troublesome ways as a result of this. They are perceived as a greater threat and challenge to white male dominance.

. . . Black men in some areas, the door is opening and slamming all at the same time. It means that society is discriminating against us, both racially and by gender. And the purpose of that is certainly to keep the community apart.

Asking whether racism or sexism has been the primary source of oppression for women of color, the Dutch psychologist Philomena Essed conducted a comparative study of small samples of black women in the United States and the Netherlands.[36] In the lives of these women Essed found both racism and sexism, often in the interactive form of the "gendered racism" noted in the last two comments.

That black women are often viewed as sex objects by white men was underscored by one of our female respondents, a successful entrepreneur:

[White men] think they get so familiar with you that they can say certain things, or do certain things. It's just like my husband worked with this guy, Anglo guy. And he called one night, and he was drunk. And my husband was not at home. And I told [him] that he wasn't at home, and I said, "you really need to go home, because you seem like you need to get off the streets." You know, he made a pass at me. Hey, don't put your hands on me, I don't want your white hands on me! Don't touch me!

Black women encounter a variety of sexist attitudes, often mixed together with racist attitudes. An assistant vice president spoke of gender and racial hurdles:

I've had things said to me like, "We didn't give you a certain position because we knew you had a child, and we knew that you would not want to be that far away, or, you cannot do this." It was always something that they assumed. They are trying to govern your life for you. That was one as far as being a woman. As far as being black, [with] the education that I have, I should have been in— probably in corporate headquarters now. I've seen people who were in this same management training program as myself who were white males. They have since almost tripled their salaries. And of course their titles are much more, or better, than mine. And they have, most of them, have less education than I have, have less experience than I have. Their ratings have been less, because that was one of the things that they had to produce when I brought the charges against them. They use, my lawyer said, the common defense of "what was good for the company."

There has been much debate in the stratification literature over whether race, sex, or class is the best framework for interpreting the multiple social hierarchies in the United States. Some analysts reduce one system of discrimination and oppression to another, as when orthodox Marxists insist on interpreting racial discrimination primarily in class terms, or when some feminists ignore the racial dimension in exploring the conditions women face.[37] A comparison of the workplace situations of black men and black women, as a number of respondents demonstrate throughout this chapter, provides illuminating insights. We have seen some of the ways in which patterns of racial discrimination interact with gender discrimination. Black women face a type of double jeopardy, for their hiring or advancement may be blocked by racism or by sexism. Because they are women, they may be more likely to be hired, but once they are in the door, as one respondent put it, "they're devalued, because we still devalue women in general." Black men can compete without facing gender discrimination, but for that very reason many white men may feel more threatened by the presence of black men in the workplace.

Conclusion

The few national studies, such as *A Common Destiny*, that discuss the current employment barriers that African Americans face have not analyzed in detail the situations of those in managerial, professional, and other white-collar positions.[38] Emphasizing the difficulties faced by lower-income black workers, these studies usually attribute their lack of advancement to limited education or conditions linked to poverty or a so-called "minority subculture." These national studies have not documented the discriminatory behavior that targets middle-class black employees.

The men and women whose accounts make up most of this chapter have moved into historically white workplaces in recent decades. They speak from experience about racial discrimination in the hiring process and show how success entering the workplace often does not carry over to egalitarian treatment there. In many cases, entry-level changes have not brought about the necessary internal changes in the white-collar climate. Discrimination can vary from outright exclusion, to discrimination in salary and promotions, to unpleasant and restrictive working conditions. Our interviews underscore how workplace exclusion and restriction, often carried out by white males, remain critical problems.

The psychological costs of racial discrimination are cumulative, painful, and stifling. The economic costs include lost promotions, small or no raises, and disrupted careers. Crossing the threshold of white workplaces has not meant thoroughgoing integration for black Americans, for the dominant white culture has not taken black concerns and perspectives into its core. In the employment accounts we often see normative conflict—the intentionally created anomic condition in which a black person cannot be sure what the actual governing rules are because whites may change them. Conflict between the ideal of equal opportunity and fairness and the real norms shaped by white hostility can create the humiliation, frustration, and anger audible in the accounts of mistreatment.

Each year seminars are given across the nation for black managers to help them deal with racial discrimination and related racial problems in the workplace. Judging from our data, such programs might well be expanded to cover all black employees. For African American employees it is rarely possible to go through a work week without being reminded, a least in a subtle way, of society's negative evaluation of their blackness. There is an enveloping sense of oppression. The detention officer we quoted in regard to initial job restrictions expressed the feelings of many when she spoke with biting humor of the "black cloud" hanging over her head. The adaptive reactions may be creative and successful or destructive and deadly.

In several of these accounts we again sense the influence of a strong belief in human and civil rights on middle-class black Americans. These accounts suggest how much middle-class blacks depend on civil rights legislation and court enforcement of such laws to develop white-collar careers in traditionally white workplaces. Although black employees may be skeptical about seeking court redress, many feel they must use this means to fight back.[39] Recalcitrant white employers often deliver the message: If you want to eliminate racial injustice, "you have to go the whole nine *miles*," to quote a black clerical worker who recently won an employment discrimination case against a southern university. But winning in court also means losing, for there is a fundamental contradiction between legal rights and everyday experience when a black person cannot even take the civil right of equity for granted but must fight an expensive and emotionally draining court battle.

Whites who control and run U.S. workplaces, including the corporations, are often said to be motivated mainly by concerns for business profit and growth. According to the usual business analysis, risks are held to a minimum, and social consciousness, if present, is a minor motivating factor in daily decisions. Because bringing black employees into historically white companies is often considered unnecessary or risky, middle-class blacks have often had to overcome tremendous odds in entering and excelling in them. For more than a century the preferential treatment for whites in corporate and other workplaces has not been defined as "preferential treatment," yet the relatively recent and generally modest affirmative action programs and preferential goals for African Americans are often defined by whites as unfair, if not as "reverse discrimination." A 1990 national opinion survey by the University of Michigan found that about eight in ten white adults opposed preferential hiring of black job applicants.[40] This lack of enthusiasm for affirmative action is found among younger whites as well. A 1991 national survey of young people by Hart Research Associates found that half the black youth thought that to "require companies to hire and promote adequate numbers of minorities" would "help a lot" in dealing with racial problems in U.S. society. In contrast, only 16 percent of the white youth felt such aggressive action would help a lot.[41]

In such assessments most whites focus on the operation of remedial programs and ignore the backdrop of real-world discrimination. Yet the racial discrimination documented in this chapter requires major remedies, including both private-sector and public-sector affirmative action programs.

Chapter Five

Building a Business

A MERICA'S premier real estate entrepreneur in the late 1980s, Donald Trump, commented to an interviewer that "A well-educated black has a tremendous advantage over a well-educated white in terms of the job market." Then he added, "I've said on one occasion, even about myself, if I were starting off today, I would love to be a well-educated black, because I believe they have an actual advantage."[1] Trump, who wrote a best-selling book on the "art of the deal," was until his serious financial difficulties in the early 1990s a leading model of the successful entrepreneur, the type of model often held up to African Americans by advocates of black capitalism. The American dream advocated by Trump and other business leaders is predicated upon the belief that a person can work hard, put aside some money, start a business, and make good. In recent decades many white analysts and some black neoconservatives such as Thomas Sowell and Shelby Steele have argued vigorously that the solution to black economic problems is a hard-work, start-a-business philosophy.[2]

Successful black businesspeople are sometimes celebrated in

scholarly writings and the mass media as proof that there is great opportunity in the United States—that the attainment of the American dream is possible even for the oppressed. Indeed, many whites' conceptions of black opportunities go beyond this optimistic view to a broader mythology of black privilege and white disadvantage. In his comments Trump expresses the belief, apparently common among whites at various income levels, that social and economic conditions have improved so much for well-educated black Americans in recent decades that they are actually better off than affluent white Americans. This white illusion is far from the reality. A black journalist later commented on Trump's statement: "Too bad Trump can't get his wish. Then he'd see that being educated, black and over 21 isn't the key to the Trump Tower. You see there is still the little ugly problem of racism."[3]

Black capitalism is often presented as though it were a recent idea for African Americans, but in fact African Americans have worked hard and struggled against racial barriers to be entrepreneurs since the eighteenth century. Sociologist John Butler has demonstrated that as early as the 1700s there were many black businesspeople in northern and southern cities, serving black and white customers, and that over the next two centuries thriving black business communities developed in cities from New York and Philadelphia to Chicago to Durham and Tulsa.[4] Nineteenth- and twentieth-century black business activity is impressive against the backdrop of both legal and informal discrimination. The exclusion of freed slaves and their immediate descendants from much homesteading land after the Civil War made the accumulation of wealth very difficult.[5] Generally excluded from owning productive land after slavery, most black people worked as tenant farmers or low-wage agricultural and urban workers. Still, some began small businesses on a shoestring, and by the early twentieth century there were thousands of small black businesses. Yet in the 1930s the ravages of the Depression and racial discrimination decimated many of them.

In the decades since World War II there has been a resurgence of entrepreneurial activity. By the late 1980s there were 424,000 black firms, about 3 percent of all firms. Today most black businesses are small; African Americans own nearly 4 percent of the firms with receipts of less than $5,000 annually, but less than 1 percent of those with receipts of $1 million or more annually.[6] The failure rate is higher than that for whites. Only a third as many middle-class black Americans as whites have an equity in a business, and the median equity of blacks in business is only 40 percent of that of whites.[7] Interestingly, opinion surveys of black young people show that they still dream of owning their own businesses. A 1988 survey of eighth graders by the U.S. Department of Education found that 5.8 percent of the black students expected to own a business by age 30, not much less than the 6.3 percent of white students with the same expectation.[8]

Building a Business: The Difficult Rules of the Game

Many Americans put owning their own business at the center of the American dream itself. A 1992 Roper survey found that 17 percent of those in the Northeast thought "owning your own business" was a very important part of the American dream. In other regions of the country the proportion hovered around one quarter.[9] While we do not know of any similar surveys on African Americans specifically, it is clear that for many who have faced racial discrimination in the workplace being one's own boss is seen as a recourse, although a difficult one.

Some of our middle-class respondents have sought the American dream by becoming entrepreneurs and independent professionals. Contrary to the common white stereotype that blacks are "not willing to work hard,"[10] the businesspeople in our sample have worked very hard. Most have obtained a good education, saved their money, started their own businesses, and labored to succeed. Like comparable whites, they want a just distribution of rewards for their efforts. A chef at a large western hotel who tried to start his own small business on the side explained this: "I used the word 'American dream.' From childhood you're taught in order to achieve anything: Hard work. And that is the way, basically, I was raised. I was brought up believing if you're honest, hard working, then good things will happen to you."

Like desegregated schools, the business milieu might be expected to be more protected for middle-class blacks than public accommodations, yet racial discrimination remains a chronic problem in the marketplace. The entrepreneurs and independent professionals we interviewed described a wide range of discriminatory experiences, from being excluded from professional networks, to being denied credit, to having their business locations restricted. Building a new enterprise is difficult under any circumstances, but black businesspeople face an additional set of obstacles and deterrents.

Changing the informal rules of the business game to assure the exclusion of blacks is a common tactic in the white business world. The successful owner of a small consulting firm in a southwestern city described her experiences in the business world:

They say get an education, go out and be entrepreneurs. Pull yourself up by your bootstraps. What bootstraps? Hell, we got to first get the boot in order to have the straps. We try to do all these things. We learn the rules of the game, and by the time we have mastered them to really try to get into the mainstream, the game becomes something else, because now we have learned how to play it. So, it changes constantly, constantly. It always keeps us on edge. I can give you a good example. I have a contract right now with a city government; and I practically gave my services away. I had to become very creative, you know. I wanted the contract because I know I could do the work, and I have the background and the track record to do it. However, in negotiating the contract, they wanted to give it to all these other people who never had any experience . . . simply because they're a big eight accounting firm, or they're some big-time institution. So, I had to compete against those people. But it was good because it proved that I could be competitive, I could give a competitive price, and I could finally win a contract. But it was a struggle.

She continued:

After the evaluation panel had made a decision that I had the highest points, the best management program, and the track record, they recommended me. And they took it back to their department. And the director of their department made a very racial statement, that "they were very sick and tired of these niggers and these other minorities because what they think is that they can come in here and run a business. None of them are qualified to run a business, especially the niggers." (Now, a white person, female, heard this statement, and because they had some confrontational problems—I think the only reason she really told me was because of that.) He was going to use that, not overtly, but in his mind that was going to be his reason for rejection. . . . And, I had to use that racism part to get my contract. Even though they all recommended me (I got all five consensus votes), he was going to throw it out. . . . I had to really, really do some internalizing to keep myself from being very bitter. Because bitterness can make you lose your perspective about what you want to accomplish. Because you know there are so many roadblocks out there—it's just stressful trying to do these kinds of things—but I really had to do that just to keep from going off the deep end. So I had to handle him very professionally. . . . If I had not known [about the racist comment], I could have possibly not had this contract. I used racism to get something that I wanted. But then you have to fight continuously. You have to cross every "t" and dot every "i," you have to be much smarter, much brighter.

Small black companies start with a disadvantage in an economy where the size of a business is directly correlated with economic power. Facing exclusionary discrimination, and possessing limited economic power, these black firms may find that their only chance to secure a contract is to bid low, leaving little profit. This respondent was fortunate in having some proof of the attempt at exclusion; without such evidence many whites hearing about the rejection of a black businessperson for a contract might view the claim as paranoid. Almost apologetically she relates that she had to use this knowledge to insure fair treatment. It is important to note the fairness in the respondent's statement. She gave credit to the presumably white evaluation panel for being fair in rating her and mentioned the help of a white worker who told her about the racist decision-maker.

Racial discrimination can involve the intentional creation of normative uncertainty, similar to what sociologist Emile Durkheim long ago termed "anomie."[11] An unpredictable milieu that keeps a black person on edge produces a modern type of anomie. The rules change because blacks have learned the rules and whites in authority have decided to exclude blacks from the rewards of playing the game well. Note too that racial exclusion violates the equal opportunity canons of public law and represents a corruption of public authority.[12]

Business Networks and 'Ole Boy' Connections

Much has been made of the impersonality and formal regulation of work within corporations and government agencies, but informal networks are at least as important as formal rules and procedures in shaping the way business actually gets done. Exclusive social networks are a problem for black businesses. For example, after the 1992 riot in South-Central Los Angeles black contractors interested in some of the reconstruction business found that they were unable to break into the network of white firms recommended by insurance companies for that work.[13] Reflecting on his experiences, an auto dealer noted that

> We still operate off the 'good ole boy' syndrome, the nepotistic element of business relationships. Because black people in general, in business, have not become part of that system, they will tend to get rejected more so than the majority. We have not been around that long. We don't have those kinds of connections. We don't have that kind of fraternity with the majority. I don't think there is really too much you can do. It's just a matter of time. I think when you really become part of the total system—right now we are basically on one side and the majority is on the other side, when it comes down to the power that's involved. It's not going to happen now. It's not going to happen in the next five years. Maybe after the year 2000 we'll see a different climate.

Like many other African Americans, this man has a developed sensitivity to inequality of power and its consequences. Even partial exclusion from informal interaction with one's counterparts and from other important business contacts can be a for-

193

midable barrier to a successful enterprise. Here one senses a defensive pessimism, yet some hope, in the speculation that blacks are not an integral part of major networks because they are neophytes.

Support and exchange networks operate in complex organizational arrangements that include more than a few "good ole boys." The owner of a baking company in the Southwest described networking problems:

> I guess five years ago I was naive in the sense that I felt like if you had a better product, if you had a good product, and if you worked hard, that you could make it. And what I have found is that . . . everything is set up structurally, all the major companies and all the major forces, everything is set up structurally so that one way or another, you're going to get blocked out. . . . And the only way that you can get around it, on top of being better at everything—which you have to be first of all—on top of that, you have to use . . . political pressure if you can. You know, if they have government contracts . . . then they have an obligation to maybe local vendors, or minority vendors, or maybe both, and that writing letters about that, and maybe talking to your congressman, or people that are pretty high up who have some political power, and letting them know that you're going to do that.

To be sure, lack of access to "good ole boy" connections may hinder some new white businesses as well. Black entrepreneurs, however, face the double handicap of newness and "blackness." As this person learned, black businesses are seldom judged by the same criteria as whites; the rules of the game can shift. Blacks are excluded by subtle run-around tactics and blatant door-slamming tactics. In this case the presence of government minority participation programs did not guarantee fair treatment. This entrepreneur delineated the sabotage techniques used by several corporations that purported to support minority businesses:

[They] made us promises that they were going to give us business and this sort of thing, and that they had a minority program, and that they wanted to help minority companies, and send us samples and send us paper work. And you know, a year and a half went by, we lived up to our obligations, but they didn't give us one bit of business. And it was just all lies and false promises, and they would usually have a black person in the company that's supposedly heading up the minority section of this company, right, but this person is just a front. He's just there, or she's just there, to make it look like they have a minority program and they really don't. And they set it up paper-wise, and they have brochures that say, "yes we have a minority program, and we want to help minorities," but that's all just show. . . . They know that they've got it set up [so that] in order to even get through the system it's going to take such a long time that as a small company you're not going to have the money to wait that long to get the business. So, you're either going to go out of business or you're going to give up in the process. . . . So, you have to go through the system that they have lined up for you, and it's very tedious and it's a very long steady process. And once you've done all those things and fulfilled all those obligations on your side of the table, then at that point, if they don't respond, and you find out that they've just been, excuse the expression, jerking you around for the last year and a half, two years, then at that point, you take other measures. As I said, using the political system, a lot of these companies have state obligations and government obligations and they're supposed to help local vendors and minority vendors. So, you can use that avenue, once you've gone

195

> through the process first. If that doesn't work—it's like
> Martin Luther King, when he did the bus boycott, and that
> was the only thing, the main thing that really
> worked, . . . when you hit them in the pocketbook.

White discriminators in the business world seem to expect their black counterparts either to ignore the discrimination or to accept it quietly as part of a natural order. But this woman, using political pressure, reacted to the mistreatment directly. An imbalance of power is recognized as the heart of the matter, and she called it by its name. One senses in her comment about "lies" more damage to the black psyche. False promises, psychologists John Mirowsky and Catherine Ross note, result in "the belief that others are unsupportive, self-seeking, and devious, which is highly distressing."[14]

In a 1990 study of black businesses in a southeastern city, Joe R. Feagin, using black interviewers, conducted interviews with seventy-six black businesspeople in the construction industry. Numerous specific barriers faced by the black construction contractors were found to be linked, directly or indirectly, to a white ole-boy network in that large metropolitan area. For example, the owner of an electrical construction company that grossed several million dollars in the last year talked about dealing with whites in the bidding process, emphasizing the "buddy-buddy" networks between white general contractors and white subcontractors that undergird long-term working relationships:[15]

> See, it's difficult to know whether or not you're the low
> bidder. The [white] contractor can make it whatever he
> wants because you are not privy to the other bids he gets.
> So you know, all you know is that he's not using it; he's
> using the same people he's been using for twenty and thirty
> years. So you can . . . bid low/high, and you're still not

going to get the job, because there are still a lot, [a] buddy-buddy system.

A college-educated air-conditioning contractor also described how a white "fast shuffle" preserves the white networks:

When you've been at this business as I have, many years, you *know* when a [white] man is giving you a fast shuffle. You know when he's not dealing fairly with you, you know. Because he can't get anybody to do the job any different. But the way in which he manages the work tells you whether he wants you to fail or whether he wants you to succeed. And these people are very sophisticated in the manner in which they discriminate. They're not going to come out and tell you, "Oh, you know, I'm not going to deal with you because you're black." They're not going to do that. You know, it's the same thing with the bidding process, right? They'll call you up for a price, but they'll ask their buddy, "Can you beat this price?" if your price is low, and the buddy will say, "Yes, put me in."

Repeated experience with discrimination has caused many black firms to be wary of white contractors. In this particular metropolitan area the local government has a special "goals" program that requires white general contractors to involve black contractors on many government projects. Yet black contractors have reported few requests for bids on private sector projects, despite having worked for white contractors on government construction projects. Whites generally prefer to work with white firms with whom they have established working relations. Some may also fear the loss of clients if they use black contractors. Like the "social cloning" of white employees noted in the last chapter, white firms are chosen to replace previous white firms in a never-ending succession.

197

These construction industry findings, as well as the data in this chapter, are in line with Carmenza Gallo's unpublished study of white, black, and immigrant contractors in a sector of New York's construction industry. In New York she found that successful contractors depend on social integration, "expressed by membership in industry organizations and by informal connections and the achievement of standing in the community from which the firm's clientele is likely to be drawn."[16] Ties to important industry organizations and existing informal networks in construction were found to be critical to getting good workers, to building a significant clientele, and to establishing a long-term business. The white construction firms, the best integrated in core networks, had the widest access to commercial, governmental, and residential construction projects in New York. Gallo reasoned that the disproportionate reliance of New York's black contractors on government programs for construction projects was not because they were less efficient than others or because they needed special favors, but because of the difficulties they had in finding a color-blind clientele elsewhere.[17]

Problems of Location and Capital

Building a business normally requires a place to do business, which frequently involves working through white-dominated real estate and banking networks. A parole officer in a western city, who tried to start a child care business with a friend, reported on real estate transactions:

If you're a minority, they predominantly want you to go to black, minority areas of town and locate your business there. When in fact, all the money isn't in the black areas of town, it's in the white areas of town. Yes, . . . we wanted to open a day care center in the predominantly white area of town and it was, it was never written down, but we were informed later that we were two young black men, and that wouldn't look good that two young black men would open up a day care center in a predominantly white area of town. . . . When they said that the residence that we bid on was given to someone else, one could look at that and say, "Hey, that was racially motivated." Our bid was the highest. The person with the second highest bid won the bid.

Prejudice such as that described here, Herbert Blumer has argued, is not simply antipathy felt by members of the white group for blacks but rather is "rooted in a sense of group position," which may have a territorial dimension.[18] In this case the whites create and justify a condition of spatial apartheid, probably thinking that other whites would not accept black men in that type of business.

Getting the necessary loans for a business can also be a problem. It is significant that in the late nineteenth and early twentieth centuries, freed black slaves and their descendants established no fewer than 134 banks to support numerous local and regional businesses. However, over the intervening decades blatant racial discrimination, including white violence, and economic depressions took their toll, and by the late 1980s there were only three dozen black-owned banks, all with modest assets.[19] As a result, most black businesspeople today have to turn to white-owned banks for the loans and lines of credit. Substantial collateral is not available to most, for neither they nor their close relatives have had the opportunity to build the economic base many whites have developed. Even for those with collateral, bank loans are hard to acquire, a fact underscored by a number of recent research reports by government and private agencies.

A 1992 report by the U.S. Commission on Minority Business Development found that the lack of access to financing was a major barrier to the development of a black business.[20] Moreover, looking at 10,139 businesses in twenty-eight cities, economist Timothy Bates found that black entrepreneurs had a harder time getting loans than whites did, and the loans blacks did secure were about 40 percent smaller, for the same amount of business equity, as loans to whites.[21] A veteran contractor in a major city in the Midwest explained the current situation for black businesses:

> I like the challenge and independence of being in business for myself. I am in the construction business. I would like to build my business into a thirty to forty million dollar business and be very competitive with everybody and be competitive not just as a black contractor. You need to get a line of credit to be successful. If a minority contractor doesn't have this, he won't get far. This is one of the toughest things to get over. This obstacle keeps minorities down. A white contractor can get a line of credit with less collateral than a black contractor.

A dentist in a southern city, a man of considerable attainment, described the business barriers he has faced as a "glass ceiling." As he noted, discrimination in access to capital not only hinders blacks' entry into the business world but also limits blacks' success in building strong communities:

> A white with the income of mine and the assets that we have would probably have a greater access to greater dollar values, thereby allowing that person the ability to capitalize on the financial basis by which the system is done, either via credit and/or access to information. I feel as though, that at the higher income, the higher echelon you get, the less information the white man wants you to have, because he does not want you to be able to overcome his thing. But he also is conscious that the more control that he can keep

over you through access to money, and I'm talking about
millions and above, my basic kind of example of this is
[a prominent white surgeon]. [This surgeon] showed in
his bankruptcy proceedings that he had $93 million worth
of unsecured loans, $93 million! I don't know one black
man in this state today that can get $1 million worth of
unsecured, or even $93 thousand worth of unsecured
dollars. . . . You see, there's a parallel there between
what is really the cause and effect of us developing our
own direction and developing our neighborhoods. It's
access.

When we asked how many of his friends had faced banking
discrimination, he replied:

All of them. All of our friends. I don't know a black man
in this city that does not have a good economic discrimination suit . . . that's borrowed $20,000 compared to $50,000
to the same [white] man with the same income with the
same situation. It's just rampant, it's throughout the whole
system. You almost have to pawn your grandmother to get
a loan.

In the previously mentioned study of black construction contractors in a southeastern city by the first author, many respondents spoke of having experienced some type of discrimination
from white-controlled banking institutions. A college-educated
flooring contractor with a good credit record described what
happened when he tried to get a loan:

Last year the school board had a bunch of bankers that
said that they wanted to help minority people get money.
We applied to a bank, which is called [Bank B]. We put [in]
our paper; we did the income tax and everything, plus the
fact that the job was bonded. So therefore, payments are
guaranteed by my bonding company. From November 1989

201

through January 1990 we couldn't even get an answer from
them. The school board couldn't even get their calls answered. Finally, we sent in even more information. They
said they didn't want information. We sent them information, and to this day we never heard from them. . . . [What
evidence can you give that race, and not some other factor,
was the reason for that poor treatment?] Well, how do you
explain that you go to a bank and, first of all, when you
approach anybody in a bank, okay, even the secretaries
look at you like, "Is this guy come to talk to me or to stick
up the bank?" That's number one. No matter how you
look or how much you dress [up] you receive a lot of questions. You are investigated very thoroughly and end up getting nothing, irregardless of your record. We had rates with
[a major rating firm], we have an A rating with that company. We are cleared for a million dollars in [business]. We
have a record of finishing all our work. We are bonded,
and yet we can't get a bank to give us a penny.[22]

This black contractor's problems at white banks start when he
walks in the door and is met with suspicion. Even after intensive
investigation by the bank he still does not get the loans that his
accomplishments suggest he deserves. There seems to be a widespread perception among whites that blacks cannot succeed in
business. Some businesspeople have devised sophisticated ways
to circumvent the problem. For example, a *Money* magazine
article profiled a black entrepreneur in St. Louis who sought a
loan to start an independent oil change operation.[23] Although
he had a good business record, he was rejected by three banks
for different reasons, all lacking substance. As a result, he
turned to a white friend, a developer, who obtained a loan on
the land and leased it back to the black entrepreneur.

Most small businesses, black and white, secure a substantial
portion of their startup funds and initial operating expenses

from informal financing, such as personal or family savings, salaries foregone, or supplier credit. A study of newly created firms in Minnesota found that those started by whites secured much more formal capital than the minority firms, with real estate loans, on the average, being the most important source.[24] Commissioned by the *Wall Street Journal*, a 1992–1993 survey of 500 black entrepreneurs with an annual revenue of $100,000 or more found that more than 90 percent had been turned down by banks when seeking loans for a business. Three quarters felt that it was much more difficult for a black firm to get loans than white firms. As a result, 70 percent reported that they had used their own personal savings to finance their business. On the average, financial institutions provided only 6 percent of their total capital. And nearly two thirds felt that black-owned businesses were charged higher interest rates for capital than white-owned businesses.[25]

Perhaps the most visible impact of past discrimination can be seen in the severe racial inequality in the economic base necessary for successful entrepreneurship. In the most recent federal survey of wealth the net worth of the average white household ($39,000) was twelve times that of the average black household ($3,400); only 13 percent of black Americans had assets of $50,000 or more, compared with 44 percent of whites.[26] Punctuating his comments with some laughter, one independent professional commented on what he would like changed in the larger society:

> Distribution of wealth. It would be good if we were able to get our portion of the American dream, so that money could come, jobs, opportunities. I think that would, you know—hey, they can think what they want about black people. But hey, if we were getting the same amount of money it would help, it would help a lot. You know what I mean? The same jobs, opportunities.

Denied loans by banking institutions, black businesspeople may fall back on local organizations. The president of a community credit fund in an eastern city discussed exclusionary discrimination by lending institutions:

> I've seen some attitudes . . . within the financial community toward minority entrepreneurs . . . saying that they have no skills, they have no ability to manage, or to borrow and successfully use those borrowed funds. I've seen people who've been turned away from financial institutions, who've come to us, and we've helped them. And I cannot understand why those commercial banks, or savings and loans haven't helped them.

That this community credit fund has fostered successful black businesses argues strongly for an end to discrimination in white-controlled commercial banks. Such success may argue for the expansion of community banks as an antidote to discrimination in mainstream institutions, although the limited amount of capital they usually have does not make this approach a panacea. Federal government intervention would seem to be the way to provide adequate funds for business expansion.

Professionals in Business

In recent years some commentators have complained about the scarcity of African American health-care professionals. Lack of motivation, low educational attainment, and insufficient role models are sometimes cited as reasons, explanations similar to those given for black student attrition (discussed in Chapter 3). Too often ignored is the fact that black professionals face discrimination at every step in a medical career, from early education, to medical school, to actual practice. Until the 1950s doctors in the American Medical Association kept the organization all white and discriminated against black Americans in their organizational activities. As a result, black professionals organized separate societies, such as the National Medical Association.[27] These societies were, and often still are, the only groups that permit the kind of open professional exchange and extensive networking black professionals need for support and advancement.

Some progress has been made, but American medicine is still substantially segregated, with many black physicians having mostly black clienteles and few white doctors locating in black communities. Although many black people are patients of white doctors, others prefer black doctors because they do not have to fear unfair racial treatment.[28] The roots of the distrust of white professionals run deep in living memories, especially of older African Americans. Some remember the chilling news reports since 1972 of the Tuskegee, Alabama experiments by the U.S. Public Health Service's white doctors on black men with syphilis. About 430 black men with late-stage syphilis were regularly examined and studied for several decades from the 1930s forward to study the effects of the disease. Even after penicillin was found to be a cure in the 1940s, the study participants received no treatment from the white physicians; most were allowed to think that they were being treated for rheumatism, bad stomachs, or "bad blood." Lacking treatment, some died horrible deaths.[29] In 1973 the attorney for the surviving men sued the government, calling the study a "program of controlled genocide." The revelation of the Tuskegee experiments deepened many blacks' distrust of white doctors and undermined others' faith in white-controlled medicine. Journalist Tom Junod recently quoted the comments of a black medical outreach worker in Atlanta about the advice given by her grandparents: "Don't ever let a doctor do an experiment on you."[30]

There are also many stories of white physicians carried in the collective memories of black families. One retired black educator described an incident in his boyhood long ago in the Midwest that still infuriates him. He and his six-year-old sister were in an auto accident in which his sister sustained a broken nose and gash on her forehead: "We were taken to a white doctor, who put one stitch in a wound that later required three stitches, used nothing to deaden her pain, and did not treat the broken nose. After a three-hour drive home, our family physician, who was black, was furious at the poor treatment."

For any doctor, professional connections are crucial to developing a viable medical or dental practice. Indeed, these professions *are* networks, for without referrals and the dissemination of knowledge along networks they would not exist. Exclusion from a professional network is a major disadvantage, yet even inclusion in a network does not necessarily confer equal status on a black doctor. Some black physicians find that their white peers sometimes see them as receptacles for poor and other unwanted clients. A doctor in the Northeast commented on the selective nature of referrals he received: "I find that referrals from agencies, white agencies, to me are apt to be patients that other physicians, white physicians, would not accept. For example, patients who don't have the money to pay. Patients who may have certain forms to fill out and the white physicians won't want to bother with it. They'll send them to me."

White administrators and doctors control admission to most hospital facilities. A physician in another East Coast city described problems that her husband, who is also a doctor, has faced:

My husband has faced discrimination. And he's a neurologist. And his problem has been because he's black, and because the hospitals that we practice in, it's very cliquish, WASP-ish. They are very threatened by him, because of course they feel that he will take their black clientele. And so they have put barriers in his way to try to hold him back—as far as monitoring his charts, holding him up for the operating room so that he's late for his case. I mean, he's faced obvious discrimination, much more than I have.

A physician in a southwestern city explained in some detail how this exclusion works:

A lot of the physicians have formed contractual arrangements with different companies and different insurance companies, okay? And if you don't have a job, you don't work, and you don't have insurance, then it's difficult to be seen by one of these physicians. . . . I signed up to join a local hospital's health care organization, which provides health care to the employees of that hospital. And I was told that the reason that they weren't going to accept me into their organization was that they had too many doctors in the downtown area in the plan already. . . . I said, "Well, I'm not downtown, I practice on the south side of this city, in the black community. And all I want to do is—I just want to be able to take care of the people who live on the south side who are in the plan, okay?"

For medical professionals like this man aggressive action against discrimination can be risky, because it may endanger the often tenuous professional networks one has already established. Yet his anger at his impotence is unmistakable. This independent professional continued with a description of how black physicians are not included in joint ventures undertaken by white administrators and doctors, then discussed other impediments, such as special scrutiny:

If you're a doctor, say, in this community . . . and they don't allow you to have hospital privileges, for instance, then that cuts you off from hospital access. And if you don't have hospital access then patients aren't going to come see you, because they say, "Well, if I get sick, he can't put me in a hospital, or come see me when I'm in a hospital." So that, in turn, can make a doctor leave a community and move to another one. . . . It used to be, like back in the '50s and before that, they just told you that because of your color you couldn't belong and then throw your application in the trash can. Now they do it a little more shrewdly, because of the civil rights law and that kind of thing. In other words, it's the same old game, it's just that the rules are different. . . . They may let you in the hospital, and then limit what you can do while you're there. Or they may let you in, but then they have you under such scrutiny that they try to find anything that they can to put you off the staff. In other words, it's a double standard. What they'll do is, like, a black physician, if he doesn't cross every "t" and dot every "i" then he's kicked off the staff. Whereas, a white physician may have had a lot of serious infractions on his record but not have been punished or reprimanded or anything like that.

A theme in our interviews is this white questioning, sometimes explicit, sometimes subtle, of black competence, whatever the setting. In a northern metropolis a doctor with a busy practice and her own nursing home explained how she was subjected to surveillance by white members of her profession:

I've had [white] people who've tried to come in and investigate my practice, who've tried to form peer reviews of my practice to see if the quality of care was up to standards, because there was no way that someone could provide a quality of care and do it as a solo practitioner and be black. Of course, nothing was found, but I did face that problem. About four or five years ago I came through it with no problems. . . . When I went through that period, it was strictly racially motivated. And I filed a countersuit against the board.

208

In her interview she also said that she shudders at judgments of her work based on white perspectives and values she felt to be inappropriate to her situation. Black professionals undergoing such scrutiny fear they will be held to excessively stringent standards, to higher standards than are their white counterparts.

Refusal of the mostly white dental establishment to accept a black person can lock a new professional out of a successful practice. A black dentist noted that when she started she was

> one of the only females practicing dentistry in my city, and because of that I was definitely not accepted by the white males. So I had no choice as far as my business was concerned, than to open up another, open up my own business, because I was not going to be insulted by whites in going to apply to be an associate in their office. That was just not going to happen. I also attempted to be part of various study clubs, and I was always told that they were filled, or no one ever got back with me.

In this case, she was undoubtedly excluded both as an African American and as a woman. In later comments in the interview she explained that her practice has been limited primarily to black patients, many of modest means, and for that reason she has begun a small cosmetics business on the side. Sometimes middle-class African American professionals must start a second business to supplement their below-average incomes.

Attorneys also face racial discrimination. A self-employed attorney in a southern city explained that whites sometimes have considerable control over the work that black lawyers get. Some white firms only appear willing to give black attorneys less desirable work, a situation similar to the selective referrals black medical professionals get. White firms may exclude black attorneys from important joint ventures. One lawyer observed that exclusion from the field of law in the past continues to work against black attorneys in the present, since access to some legal work in the present requires experience that past discrimination kept them from obtaining:

> We've met some resistance from some firms who think that if, let's say, the city or the county or the mass transit system here, any one of those entities, do more business with minority firms, law firms, that it will take away from what they're doing. And consequently they're resisting that. . . . So they try to minimize what work is given out, or they try to give out work that they themselves may not want to do or [that] may not generate that much revenue. . . . Or if you're talking about funding municipal bonds and things of that notion, in order to do that work you have to get in what we call "the red book." And there're so few minority attorneys, and even fewer black attorneys, in the red book that are qualified to do the work, but in order to get in the red book, you must do some of the work. So they don't want to bring in, or do joint ventures with other black law firms or black lawyers that would qualify them to be placed in the red book.

Excluding black professionals does not seem to be enough for some white firms, which also covet the small amount of business sometimes set aside for minorities by local and federal governments. In the study of the construction industry in a southeastern metropolis discussed previously, several black contractors reported that white general contractors had offered black firms money just to sign a "letter of intent" so the white firms could appear to meet minority hiring goals in bidding on local government construction projects. Yet many white contractors had no intention of actually using the black businesses.[31] The attorney quoted above described his encounter with a similar problem:

> In terms of work that's being done in this city and this county, whether it be city, county, school district, we have negotiated with certain firms, other firms, for joint venture arrangements. We have not gotten the work. Not so much because the expertise was not vast, but because in our negotiations we wanted a meaningful arrangement. Well, why should you, a predominantly white firm, engage in business with me, when you can engage in a venture with some other minority who's saying, "Give me my check and you can use my name." When you're going to probably be paying less to that person than you'd be paying to me. So why do business with me? You won't do business with me. Unless there's some moral rationale, reason. And I gave up on that a while ago, but that's what you have. And that's the reality. I don't get upset with anybody for doing that. The only thing that I'm saying is that in the long run, minorities (or people who are in business for themselves who are minorities) do themselves and all of us a disservice by engaging in—what's the word?—in joint ventures that are intended merely to circumvent the program just for a few dollars. And as long as that happens, there is not going to be any real incentive on behalf of the white companies or corporations or firms to engage in serious conversation.

When people of different backgrounds compete fairly in business, most Americans consider it fair for the more skilled person to have an advantage over the other. Yet most black businesses are not allowed to compete meritocratically on the same level with whites. Another respondent noted that when small black firms cannot get business because of discrimination, they may be "hungry enough" to cooperate with white firms illegally in such a "set-aside racket" just to survive.

White Customers and Associates

Black people in business for themselves encounter a range of problems at the hands of prejudiced whites, similar to those that black white-collar workers do, including the refusal of some whites to buy from blacks, the doubting of black capabilities, and even the hurling of racist epithets. It is difficult for black merchants to develop their businesses, serving either the public or the private sector of the economy, if whites refuse to do business with them. An auto dealer who owned a business in the Midwest from 1979 to 1985 occasionally observed customers who "would come in the showroom floor, and they would find out that a black person owned the dealership, and they'd leave."

Knowing that white prejudice exists, blacks whose business places them in direct contact with whites must be alert. Grier and Cobbs argue that black Americans must condition themselves "against cheating, slander, humiliation, physical harm and outright mistreatment by representatives of our society. If not, life will be so full of shock and pain as to be unbearable."[32] The hotel chef quoted earlier also reported his difficulty getting white customers for his new cake catering business:

> You know how employees . . . have a birthday party for
> another employee or a retirement party, something of that
> nature. And a few of the black people here were buying
> cakes from me. One of the supervisors here—a pretty big
> wheel—well anyway, the girls that work under
> her . . . were up in the break room talking about where are
> they going to get a cake. So, one of the black girls said—
> she was the only black one up there and there must have
> been about eight white girls—and she said, "Why don't we

get Sam to do it? He works down in the kitchen." So, I
stuck my head in the door and smiled. And a couple of the
white girls looked up, and looked at each other. And you
can tell with their eyes [they were saying] "Oh my good-
ness. No, no, not him." So, hey, I can take a hint. I just
gave it one of these little Charlie waves and kept going.
Well, they didn't order the cake from me. But you know,
cool. And so that went on for about six or seven months.
The only cakes that I could sell here were to other blacks.
Now, one of the owners of the place here asked me to do a
cake for her son. So, I said, "Sure, no problem." I did the
cake for her son. I did a pretty good job. She liked it and
she was telling all the other people that work here, [in]
management and everywhere else. Now from that day on,
it was just, I was just bombarded. It was like, "If this big,
powerful, rich lady would buy a cake from him, he's what's
happening. I want to buy a cake from him, too." You see?
That type of prejudice I have run into quite often.

The chef's "little Charlie waves" and "cool" reaction probably
masked anger and hurt at the white workers' assumption that a
black person would not do as good a job as a white person. In
the waves we glimpse a kind of protective device, a feigned,
nonverbal expression of amiability and nonchalance. Thomas
and Sillen have suggested that "a traditional feature of the racist
syndrome is the interpretation of strength of feeling in the black
man as primitive emotionalism,"[33] a white attitude that causes
many black men and women to repress their justified anger in
order not to be stereotyped by whites as out of control.

This account also illustrates the leadership role unprejudiced
whites can play in discriminatory situations, setting a precedent
for others. The relative ease with which whites sometimes
change certain prejudiced notions and discriminatory behavior
underscores Thomas Pettigrew's point that prejudice and dis-

crimination can be changed if the benefits of change outweigh the advantages of holding firm.[34]

Dealing with prejudiced clients creates a dilemma for black businesspeople. Some brazenly prejudiced white customers are simply not worth the effort, yet not putting forth that effort leaves the black person vulnerable to the accusation of being lazy. The owner of a chemical distributing company in the Southwest reported that

> You're going to find some racist buyers out there. You have to recognize when that situation occurs and move on to something else. . . . There've been times when I've told our salespeople to move on to some other account. For various reasons, this person's not being fair with you. I don't know if it's because it's just that he's not a fair person or because of skin color. One or two, [maybe a] combination. Then you just move on to something else.

Black businesspeople can realistically expect to be insulted, and most prepare themselves to cope with the insults and, if possible, to negotiate with the white antagonist. In a business context, restraint may stem from fear of losing a client or of being the target of white retaliation for being aggressive. Here, as in other black dealings with whites, a restrained response can bring distress from the feeling of impotence, which in turn may contribute to stress-related physical disorders such as the hypertension that plagues African Americans.[35]

No matter how experienced and able they may be, black businesspeople may be subject to the automatic assumption from whites that their products or services are inferior. A successful contractor in the Midwest explained: "It's not as easy for a black contractor to negotiate design changes as it is for a white contractor. The stereotype is that your qualifications are not up to par." A lawyer in a southern metropolis explained that he was treated as competent by officials who knew him but not by strangers:

214

When I pick a jury of strangers who don't know me, I have to constantly be on guard of the potential racial ideas that those jurors might have. When I interact with court personnel who may not know who I am, I run into an assumption sometimes that because he's a black lawyer, he must not be as sharp as his white counterparts, or his pleadings might not be as good, or basically he's just not as good a lawyer. And when I interact with my black clients, who have been victims of racism, some of them have apprehensions sometimes with having a black lawyer represent them, because they feel for whatever reasons that maybe he's not going to be as good as a white lawyer. Or, conversely sometimes, I have white clients who come and I represent, and I feel that I have to prove to them that even though I am black, I'm a hell of a lawyer. Those are all examples of the way racism is still alive and well in the American judicial system.

Doubtless most black clients know there are competent black lawyers, but many choose white representation because they fear the prejudices of a white jury or judge or because they too feel white is better.[36]

Another distressing attitude black businesspeople encounter is a lack of respect from white customers. A respondent in an eastern city related her husband's experiences: "I know that the [white] attitudes may not change, but I'd like to see the behaviors change. An example of that: My husband had his own business in the south part of the city. There are white people there who are on welfare who consider themselves better than he. They still consider all black people, even though they're destitute, to be lower than they are." Poor whites' condescension and emphasis on blacks' racial status over the class status they have achieved have a long history in this society.[37]

Reflecting on years of consulting experience, a retired professor commented on how he had been treated by white clients and on the marked discrepancy between the respect and compensation he received compared with his white peers.

> In my consulting, I have great difficulty getting half of what a white man would get for doing the same job. There was an instance where I did some consulting at the state Department of Corrections. I worked teaching their counselors for months. I became ill, had a heart attack, and sent another [white] young man to complete the two or three days of work. He went in and did an excellent job, completed the job. Months later when I came back on the job, I looked on his wall and saw a certificate of appreciation for all he had done for the Department of Corrections counselors and what he had meant to them. And not one even sent me a card while I was ill. . . . And right now, blacks are limited in consulting because whites really don't want to pay them the same fee they pay a white person for doing less.

The devaluation of professional activity reported here reminds us of the defective white vision about which Ellison wrote in *The Invisible Man*. What might seem to some white readers as hypersensitivity in the professor's interpretation of these events as discriminatory is the result of decades of experience with racial insensitivity and animosity consulting in this and similar government agencies.

Doing business with whites who devalue one's abilities is bad enough, but there is always the additional possibility of the racist epithet, the crude racial remark in the business setting. Racist comments sometimes come from white workers who supposedly have lower social status in the workplace than black businesspeople, or racial slurs come from business associates at the same status level. In the 1990 study of the construction industry the first author found a number of black contractors who had been taunted by comments on the job. A well-educated steel contractor from the Caribbean described his experience with whites while working for a white-run firm:

> Oh, with [XYZ company], ho. They come along, and
> they'll yell on the job. And they'll be asking you,"Why you
> all leave where you are from and come here to work?"
> "Which boat you land on?" It's a common thing, alright?
> They come around, and you're doing the work. And they
> say, "You know, the place where your forefathers come
> from, they don't do this kind of work, they use only sticks
> and leaves to make buildings!" And you know, it's kind of
> degrading, like, "Hey, you see that we can do the work,
> you see we are doing the work." And I always say I'm
> from the islands . . . and as far as I'm concerned you don't
> have any building here that we don't put up there. Alright?
> And it's always, it's aggravating. . . . So we're tired of
> it. . . . As soon as it became a black crew on the job, you
> go into the restroom: "Niggers, we don't want you here."
> "Niggers, go use the bush."

In settings like these the black businessperson senses viscerally the whites' view that blacks are less than human, a perspective with an ideological lineage running back through legal segregation to slavery.

Another example from a quite different work setting was given by a black attorney who recounted an incident with a white associate at the end of a work day:

> I was sitting in the offices one day after 5:00 P.M. You
> know, people come together in the office, and everybody's
> talking and shooting the b.s. . . . they were talking about
> the attorneys or the people or the clients and everybody's
> laughing, and everybody's getting loose. And then one
> [white] attorney said, "Yeah, that nigger." And you're sit-

ting there. . . . Well, they say what you do in private comes
out in the light of day, so he must have been saying it other
places. And it just came out. When he said it, everybody
else heard it. He recognized it when he said it. I'm sitting
there and I said nothing. I wasn't going to say anything. I
did not laugh at it, but I wasn't going to say anything. And
my point was, he knew he said it, they knew he said it and
they heard it, and they knew that I heard it. Now let their
own consciences deal with it. Now, maybe in another setting, I may have commented or I may have said something,
but there was no need to say anything, you know? So my
attitude was: I won't say anything, you know I heard it,
now I'll let you think what I'm thinking.

Laughing periodically, he discussed subsequent events:

So for the next two or three days, he'd come to my office,
see how I'm doing, you know. [I'd say] "I'm doing fine. Because I knew you were racist way before you said it; all
you did was confirm what I had already thought." . . . Like
I told him, I said, "Y'all are sick. My attitude is that you
white Americans are in general sick. Y'all need help. And
my training and where I was brought up, you help the sick,
feed the hungry, clothe the naked. I can't get mad at you
for your racism; you're sick." And I think that's the attitude
that black America must have towards white America, especially those who pronounce racist views or hold racist
views or practice discrimination, and that is that those individuals are sick. And instead of us getting so bent out of
shape and angry and frustrating ourselves, we treat them as
patients. And for some, you can nurse back to health; for
others, you must diagnose as being terminally ill.

Again we observe what being black in a white world means on a
daily basis, for one must be prepared to assess a situation rap-

218

idly and then exert energy to decide on the appropriate response. We see here a reluctance to confront his colleague aggressively at the time of the remark; he decided instead not to
display any response and in a measured reaction forced the
white man to reflect on his ill-considered action.

Conclusion

Some white scholars view African Americans as just another
immigrant group that can work its way up if it adheres to the
American work ethic. Sociologist Nathan Glazer has argued
that although differences exist between the experiences of black
Americans and of white-ethnic immigrants, there are more similarities than differences: "The gap between the experience of
the worst off of the ethnic groups and the Negroes is one of
degree rather than kind. Indeed, in some respects the Negro is
better off than some other groups."[38] Thus relatively recent
nonblack immigrants to the United States, such as the mostly
white Cubans who migrated to Florida beginning in the late
1950s, have been viewed by many white analysts as more or less
comparable to black Americans in the difficulties they have
faced getting into business. They are celebrated among those
advocating "free enterprise" solutions for black Americans.[39] If
these Cuban immigrants "have made it," this reasoning goes, so
can African Americans if they will only come to terms with their
weaknesses and work much harder. Yet this common white
view ignores the major dissimilarities in the situations of African Americans and immigrants such as the Cubans. There are,
for example, differing times of entry into major cities and significantly different amounts of wealth and other resources to consider. And there is the virulence of antiblack discrimination
among whites. Discussing the Cuban American community in
Florida, Alejandro Portes and Robert Bach have argued that a
chief reason that the mostly white Cubans have done well eco-

nomically is that they migrated not as poor individuals but rather as an officially recognized group with substantial economic, educational, and political resources. Many came with the education and credentials that enabled them to become professionals or businesspeople. The Cuban immigrants were also covered by federal legislation providing a substantial social welfare program that helped many get a new start, including a start in business. They did not "make it" only on their own.[40]

Unlike Cuban Americans, African Americans have faced major racial barriers in getting into business for several centuries and have not benefitted from a concerted, large-scale governmental effort to break down business barriers. Our respondents speak eloquently of obstacles to building a business, either as a merchant, contractor, or independent professional, and of the deliberate and unconscious discriminatory actions of whites, which can be impediments to success in business. More than one respondent told of being the victim of behind-the-scenes maneuvering by white officials working against their bids for contracts. Examining racial barriers in her study of discrimination in the New York construction industry, Gallo concluded that a businessperson's reputation depends more on subjective factors such as social acceptability than on objective criteria such as cost and efficiency.[41]

One of our respondents commented simply that many whites do not want blacks to have a "piece of the pie." Because of barriers to black opportunity, whites can command larger segments of business markets than they would under free competition. A self-employed lawyer put his desire for changes in the business world and other areas of daily life this way:

> If I had the magic wand and could wave and get an instant result, I would create in white folk an attitude that would allow them to disregard considerations of race when it came to making judgments about us. I think Martin Luther

King's dream is very, very apropos. I'd like to see this society in which the worth of an individual is measured in terms of the content of the mind and the character, as opposed to the color of the skin.

Our respondents show how discrimination in business and experiences with white racism shape their approach not only to business but also to life itself. For example, we see a certain resignation to the inevitability of discrimination in such comments as, "It's not going to happen now" and "Maybe after the year 2000 we'll see a different climate." One glimpses in the interviews humiliation, frustration, and anger. A black businessperson pays a heavy psychological price in order to gain access to the white world. One entrepreneur spoke of the emotional strain:

You always have to watch and really think and really concentrate about what you're saying, so that you're not emotional, because you know black people are "so emotional" and "so defensive," and so you have to always be cognizant of that. And that's a mental strain and a mental drain on you.

Asked what she does to keep a balance, she replied with some laughter:

I come in here and scream! I talk to my friends. I come in here and talk to my assistant. She's even seen me cry because I'm so angry 'til I am to the point of violence. But I know that I have to really, really be cognizant of what I'm doing, because why go to jail for nothing? . . . So I just call my friends and get it off my chest with them, because they understand.

Particular incidents of discrimination not only have a devastating impact on African Americans but also perpetuate institutionalized racism. The recounted incidents and others alluded to give us a picture of the web of discrimination faced by black businesspeople in traditionally white business sites. The market does not work fairly or freely with ole-boy or buddy-buddy networks at its heart. Frequently the white discriminators in these accounts are not the stereotyped blue-collar bigots but rather middle-class whites. Significantly, Walter Rodney considers the notion that "free enterprise," individualism, and great effort will pay off handsomely for African Americans to be destructive: "It is a common myth within capitalist thought that the individual through drive and hard work can become a capitalist. The acquisition of wealth is not through hard work alone, or the Africans working as slaves in America and the West Indies would have been the wealthiest group in the world."[42]

Over a lifetime of facing racial discrimination in America, an African American comes to see that the promise of truly equal opportunity is a "white lie," a betrayal that the professor with his own consulting business feels keenly:

I feel angry. I feel betrayed. Sometimes I feel very cynical. Most of the time I feel that I live in a country where I'm still not respected as a person. I lived at a time when I was told that if I got a good education, did all the right things, that I could be anything I wanted to be. I got a good education. I did all the right things, but even today I run into situations where my opportunity structure is limited because I am black. So, I found that all along that no matter what I did, no matter how hard I tried, limitations were placed on me strictly because of the color of my skin.

Chapter Six

Seeking a Good Home and Neighborhood

A T the top of the list of material goods promised by the American dream to those who get a good education and work hard is a decent apartment or house in a pleasant neighborhood. Like middle-class whites, middle-class African Americans greatly value this promise. Speaking of conversations with her husband, a teacher articulated this dream: "I would like to have my dream home in the next year, and I'm serious. Because no matter what you do, no matter how much money you make, you're always going to owe somebody. So I said, why not go ahead and get our dream home now?" A house is a visible manifestation of accomplishments, one's standing in society, even one's character. For homeowners the house is also a sign of equity, of wealth that can be passed to subsequent generations. Yet racial discrimination has historically played a major role in keeping most African Americans from building up much housing wealth. Today they are still less likely to be homeowners than whites; according to the U.S. Census Bureau just 43 percent of black Americans own their homes, compared with 67 percent of whites.[1]

Home as a Place of Refuge

To black families, home represents one of the few anchors available to them in an often hostile white-dominated world. Home is for African Americans the one place that is theirs to control and that can give them refuge from racial maltreatment in the outside world. Putting the point succinctly, a corporate executive said: "The only place it probably doesn't affect me, I guess, is in my home; specifically, actually, in the interior portions of my home. But outside one's home, it always affects me." A manager at a major electronics firm commented, "Well, I think you really kind of lead dual lives," one at home among black people and one at work among white people. And a substance abuse counsellor explained that home means support: "Because I can come home and talk about the situations. That's one thing that I have in my favor, because my family, they are understanding, and if anything like this should happen, I can come home and talk about it and get it resolved." Numerous respondents criticized the air of unreality in the portrayal of the lives of black middle-class families on television. The nearly perfect family on the Bill Cosby Show, for example, does not face racism from its white neighbors or coworkers. In this regard the Cosby show is mythological, because it shows neither the racism that middle-class blacks ordinarily experience nor the role of the family in helping individual family members cope.

Even white friends are rarely able to relate to blacks in the intimate way that family and black friends can, as an airline manager suggested:

So I can't discuss it with white friends, and I do have white friends, but they're just, I mean, like I said, in the industry, the neighborhood, the situations that I'm in, there just aren't that many black people. So my husband and my family become the stabilizing force for bouncing off situations.

A student at a mostly white university described retreating to home regularly during his freshman year because of his difficulty dealing with the culture of his university:

Everything in the environment here [causes stress]. Everything. Every single thing—the parties, the music, the teachers, the classroom discussions, the meals, the new prejudices, the new stereotypes. . . . I think part of the reason I went home every weekend in [my] freshman year is so I wouldn't have to listen to [white students'] music that I didn't necessarily want to listen to, blasting all Saturday night, all Sunday night.

Home is the place where one can get support in an intimate way to deal with problems beyond the home. While we will return to this matter in detail in the next chapter, two brief comments will underscore the valuable functions performed by the black home. A professor in an eastern city pointed out how home serves him as a place to laugh at insults:

For my own self, I think one copes, I cope with the experience of the work world by having a very secure, good family life and things that, you know, when you can come home and laugh at many of the things that are very outrageous and insulting [laughs], but you can come home and laugh about it, in a sense, because you know very well that it's not true.

The black home can be the one place where one does not have to be on guard, as a business manager at a mostly white university described: "The [white] smiles and so forth, understanding what those mean, and so therefore my intent is I've got to be suspicious and that's just survival. So I live in a world of survival in that sense, in terms of what it is to be black. The place where I don't have to justify, in a sense, and can let down that guard is, yes, it's at home and with my family."

Segregated Housing: U.S. Laws and White Attitudes

Without the foundation of home and family there would be no black middle class. In the search for a decent house and a safe, well-equipped middle-class neighborhood in which to build home-castles, the black middle class faces the major dilemma of whether or not to venture into white residential areas. From the late-nineteenth century to the last third of the twentieth century, municipal ordinances, state laws, private deed restrictions, and brute force were used to keep African Americans out of most white communities, North and South. From the 1930s to the 1960s Federal Housing Administration (FHA) policies reinforced or increased racial segregation by effectively restricting FHA housing loans to segregated areas and by locating public housing for African Americans in historically black communities. Only in the late 1960s was federal protection from blatant housing discrimination officially extended to most black Americans. Although government-backed housing segregation has not been the rule for more than two decades, the United States still remains a very segregated society. One 1989 report on the twenty-five largest cities noted very high levels of residential segregation in 1980, with only a modest 7 percent decline in the continuing high levels of segregation over the civil rights era between 1950 and 1980.[2] And a recent study by Douglas S. Massey and Nancy A. Denton of housing segregation in the thirty northern and southern metropolitan areas with the largest black communities found little change in the massive patterns of residential segregation since 1980. The very small declines in their indices of housing segregation for 1980 to 1990

226

were even less than for 1970 to 1980. As of 1990 the indices indicated that, on the average, 67 percent of the black residents of southern cities and 78 percent of the black residents of northern cities would have to move from their present neighborhoods (census tracts) in order for there to be a completely desegregated housing pattern.[3]

This continuing segregation is by no means voluntary on the part of African Americans, for their housing choices are constrained immediately or indirectly by white attitudes and actions. Opinion surveys show that today many white Americans believe housing discrimination by white homeowners should be government-sanctioned. In a 1990 NORC opinion survey nearly four whites in ten said they favored a law giving a white homeowner the right *not* to sell a house to a black person over a law prohibiting such discrimination.[4] And a substantial majority of whites have a negative reaction to the presence of blacks as neighbors when the numbers increase beyond token levels to a significant proportion. In a 1976 Detroit study only one in six whites said they had a favorable reaction to the idea of moving to a neighborhood that was half white and half black. Most black Americans, in contrast, prefer this type of blended neighborhood. The Detroit study found blacks' ideal choice was an area 55 percent white and 45 percent black.[5] This desire for a mixed neighborhood still seems to be the ideal for many black Americans. With this desire for integrated housing, and with the proportion of whites with negative views of black neighbors so high, there is a likelihood that many black families will encounter discrimination when seeking to buy or rent a home.

Several housing audit studies show that racial discrimination by white landlords, homeowners, and real estate agents is a primary cause of residential segregation. Over the last two decades studies in dozens of metropolitan areas have sent a black and a white auditor of similar socioeconomic backgrounds to white real estate agents selling homes and to white agents renting apartments. Whites were more likely to be shown or told about more housing units than blacks. In a recent federal survey involving 3,800 test audits in twenty-five metropolitan areas, black renters faced some type of discriminatory treatment about half the time, while black homeseekers faced discriminatory treatment 59 percent of the time. Discrimination was found in discrepancies in information about housing availability and during the transaction with the seller or agent.[6]

A 1989 ABC/*Washington Post* opinion poll found that half the black respondents felt there was serious discrimination against blacks in getting decent housing; the proportion had increased a little since a similar 1986 survey. Also, in that earlier survey 26 percent of the black respondents reported personally having experienced racial discrimination in getting decent housing.[7] This latter percentage seems low; the proportion reporting discrimination might have been higher if more specific questions about the finding and financing of housing had been asked. In addition, survey data for middle-class black homeseekers have not been reported separately. Because middle-class black families often seek housing outside of traditionally black communities, they may be the most likely to face housing discrimination. In a 1990 NORC national opinion survey 46 percent of all black respondents felt there was housing discrimination, while among the most educated respondents the proportion climbed to nearly three quarters.[8]

Renters: Seeking and Securing Housing

In cities or suburbs blacks are less likely to own their homes than whites are, because of historical and contemporary patterns of discrimination in employment, income, wealth, and housing.[9] Many black Americans in their search for houses or apartments to rent report having been mistaken for whites over the phone, then rejected in person, such as this minister in an eastern city: "Now, at the present location that we're living at, we've had to deal with whites, and we've faced discrimination. At first, they didn't realize that we were black in applying for the housing. And when my wife was persistent, she found out on the phone that they had vacancies. And then when we got there, we found out there were no vacancies. But in our persistence, we found out that there was an opening for us that wasn't there before." Good housing opportunities may appear in the search and be promised over the phone but then evaporate suddenly. Aware of the problem of accepting black renters over the phone, some savvy whites may listen carefully to the accent of the potential renter, as in this example given by a high school teacher in a northern city:

> I had a friend who was an LPN. And she wanted an apartment, and she saw one in the paper. She called, and they told her that the apartment was rented. And she called me on the phone and said, "I'd like for you to call them." I said, "Why?" And she said, "Because you sound like a white person." And I called, and the apartment was still unrented. So . . . this hasn't been a hundred years ago. This is like in the last two or three years that this happened.

The intentional use of a "white-sounding" voice, either one's own or a friend's, is one painful strategy middle-class black homeseekers have developed to get around some discrimination.

A HUD researcher commented recently on the great variety of strategies white landlords use to exclude blacks: "HUD gets plenty of instances in which the person shows up after a phone call and the agent suddenly has to leave; doesn't open the door; says the apartment was just taken; slams the door in their face; tells them they'd be unhappy there; unleashes the dog."[10] White homeowners who are landlords play a role in this exclusionary behavior, as in this case reported by university administrator in

229

a northern city: "But I think one incident that made an impression on me was a woman [who] answered the door when I came to look at a house. This was to rent. And she just laughed, just started laughing when she saw my black face, and closed the door in my face. And didn't even respond."

Since the 1950s, housing discrimination laws have had an effect on many white landlords; the laws have made the old forms of outright exclusion on racial grounds less likely. Yet there are many ways to reject a black renter other than by slamming the door. One runaround strategy was described by a public administrator in an eastern city: "I remember specifically, I would go by this apartment building a lot of times. There was one apartment in particular that I really wanted to live in [in] this apartment building, and I applied. They said there were no vacancies. And I asked them, please, put me on the waiting list." Continuing with the account, she laughed and said, "And it's been over five years, and they've not called me yet, and I know people have moved out of that building!"

A drug abuse counselor discussed a creative excuse for exclusion:

> Recently we went to rent a house, and probably they
> weren't expecting us [to be black] after they spoke to us on
> the phone. . . . when we got there and we saw the place,
> they had no recourse or anything like that to say that they
> couldn't rent us a place. She made a promise that she was
> going to rent us a place and everything. And then when she
> did the financial check, she came back with an excuse, like
> "Well, you know, people [like you] normally move, and we
> want someone who is going to be staying there for a period
> of time."

When racial characteristics cannot be used overtly as grounds for exclusion, contemporary discriminators may attempt to use income and other class characteristics thought to be associated

230

with racial group, a point illustrated by the experience of an engineer in a southwestern metropolis:

> When I talked to the lady, she said, "Oh yes, come on in and we can approve your application while you're here," and all that. And then when I got there, it was going to take two days to approve. And they checked everything out thoroughly and the guy who referenced me to the apartment was a white guy. And he got his approved in one day. And he's saying, "Oh, why don't you go there, and it doesn't take any time to get it approved." They went so far as to call my job. And one of the people who works for me answered the phone, and the lady from the apartment complex said, "Is it conceivable that he makes X amount of dollars a month?" I mean, that's not something—first of all, if you want to know, call personnel or ask me, but you don't ask somebody who works for me. Well I know they have to have verification of the stuff that you put on your application, but . . . I think that if they want to know bad enough they'd say, by the way, bring in a copy of one of your pay statements.

Intensive background checks can be used to discourage or stall black applicants. Not only was the respondent forced to endure a runaround once color became salient, but he had to go through the degradation of a check with one of his workplace subordinates. Such instances of housing discrimination provide clear indications not only of the energy cost to the victims but also of the processual character of some present-day discrimination.

Another barrier for black renters is quotas that allow only a certain number of minority renters to move into a complex. An accountant described what it was like when she lived in New York City:

> There're certain apartment buildings that you are denied

living there strictly because of your color. . . . There was one particular incident, and it ended up being in the paper. And it wasn't because of me, but I had applied during that same time. There was a huge apartment complex; it's like a city within a complex. They had their own stores, their own schools, everything is right there within walking distance. And they had a quota. The quota was 25 percent minorities, period, which included blacks, Hispanics, whatever. There was a big issue because there were qualified black people that applied and they were denied housing strictly because the management said that they had their quota. . . . And a lot of people got a little angry because they did apply and they couldn't get in and they met all the requirements. And it came out that the housing, the people, management said that they were not going to put any more blacks in there or other minorities because they had met their quota as far as—I assume there was a minority requirement—that they had to have in order to continue to get whatever [government] money they were getting.

This privately owned complex had received federal housing subsidies and had set up a quota (actually closer to 40 percent) in order to limit the proportion of minorities. Such "integration maintenance" programs use race-conscious quotas to maintain "balance," because the white demand for integrated housing is usually weak, and small changes in the proportion of minority residents can trigger white flight or keep whites from moving in. Yet much of the human cost of this type of managed housing integration is paid for by potential minority renters, who must again adapt to the racial prejudices of whites. In most cases the effect is to keep black residents as the statistical minority in the complex and to create very long waiting lists for black families seeking such housing. Meanwhile, white waiting lists tend to be short. Some white developers and landlords have learned to use federal housing loan and development programs to their advantage, knowing such programs can provide essential capital, and perhaps expecting little surveillance by federal authorities to enforce housing justice.[11] In this case they miscalculated, for the Department of Justice did sue the management for racial discrimination.

Having overcome barriers in the search for rental housing, a black person who moves into a substantially white complex may find that the facilities provided are inferior, as a flight attendant in a western metropolis discovered:

I guess one funny thing happened when I took an apartment in a well known area of California, and I did the application for the apartment over the telephone. And when I went in to sign the lease, the owner in fact emphasized the fact that I did the application over the telephone. And I distinctly felt as though they didn't know I was black. And then when I showed up and I was black, he just came right out and said, "Oh, you did the interview over the phone." I think he said it without really thinking about what he was even implying when he said it. . . . At that point, there was really nothing he could do, because it had been approved. [So, was it your feeling that if he had known you were black there might have been a problem?] Oh, for sure, because of the way he said it. . . . After I got moved into this particular apartment, I wanted to get a parking space there. And they told me that my apartment didn't come with a parking space. But next door to me, a white guy lived there, and we had the same exact apartment. In fact, he was paying a few dollars more than I was only because he moved into the building after I did, and his apartment came with a parking space. And when I asked the owners about it, they tried to tell me that his did and mine didn't. But my question was, but we have the same exact apartment, why

233

does his, and why doesn't mine? And after some discussion, after about twenty minutes, I actually had to accuse the owners of discriminating, because I couldn't find any other reason why I couldn't have a parking space. The owner re-lented and did give me a parking space. So, I had to assume that there was no real reason why I didn't have one.

Not only did the respondent encounter a landlord who had apparently taken her to be white over the phone, but she had to struggle to get the same facilities as a white renter. Middle-class black renters can demand fair treatment, but the personal ener-gy costs can be high. Some we interviewed suggested that they found discriminatory treatment to be so unbearable that they had moved out, or considered moving out, perhaps permitting a white landlord to say "Well, I rented it to them. I can't be responsible for whether they stayed or not."

Homeowners: Seeking and Securing Housing

The 1980s were the first decade since the Great Depression in which there was a decline in the proportion of U.S. home-owners. The reason: the increasing cost of houses relative to incomes. While home ownership is still central to the American dream, buying a house has often become more difficult. This situation has become especially serious for African Americans. Nonetheless, since the 1970s significant numbers of middle-class black families have sought the American dream of owning their own homes, often in predominantly or entirely white areas.

Denial of access is the most basic constraint facing black families seeking housing in formerly all-white areas. We cited earlier the federal study of U.S. metropolitan areas that found black homeseekers faced a better than 50–50 chance of encoun-

tering racial discrimination. Attempts to secure suburban housing can involve great expenditures of energy. In particular cases
the attempts to exclude blacks can be complex and involve
extended racial bargaining, as in this one described by a dentist
in a southern city:

My first encounter with discrimination in my present location ironically had to do with a very basic thing that most
people look forward to, and that's their home. . . . That
evening she [the white real estate agent] called me at home
and said she thought she'd accidentally stumbled onto
something that might interest me and would I be interested
in looking? I said yes. She arranged to show me the home,
which turned out to be the first one that I bought here. It
was a home owned by a major insurance company executive who had been transferred to another city 100 miles
away. . . . We contacted the owner by phone. She conveyed
an offer; he countered. I countered; he accepted it. I signed
the papers; we sent them to him. We never got them back.
The real estate owner that she [our salesperson] worked for
was totally uncooperative with assisting her. Days went by;
weeks went by; over a month went by. At this particular
time, every brokerage house in town was anxious to show
this house. The young lady, who happened to be white,
who showed me that home went out of town; she took the
keys to the home. She told her children not to give word
that she was home. She did everything humanly possible to
keep from letting that house be shown again. She confronted the owner of the real estate company; he refused to
help her. He refused to look to find out why we had not
gotten the papers back. He simply stated [that] without two
signatures, the home was up for grabs. Well, she knew at
that interest rate, and having known what the owner [now

in another city] accepted, that house would be sold to someone else out from under me in a matter of seconds. And she wanted to keep her word.

It was only after about five, six weeks I said to her: "Don't bother to hide the key any more. Put it back in the office. I'll handle it." And it was at that time that I formulated a letter, and I sent a copy of it to the president of that insurance company, explaining what had happened and stating that we could not understand why there was a delay. I also made note that I sent a copy of that letter to the general secretary of the NAACP. My point in sending a copy of the letter and making note on the president's letter of this fact was not anything that was very casual or accidental. I did it deliberately. Within 24 hours I got a call from the general counsel of that insurance company. He made one statement and he was very emphatic. He said, "Doctor, if any of our executives gave you their word that they accepted the offer on your house, whether it was written or whether it was his word, he has no job if he goes back on it. So don't worry; the house is yours."

Several white actors, including a homeowner and the owner of a real estate firm, play a major role in this mini-drama. We see a white real estate agent denying herself a quick commission for the sake of principle, a sign of some change from the recent past. Yet she was blocked by other whites, including her own boss. The dentist reacted forthrightly to the runaround and attempted exclusion by writing a measured letter to the president of the insurance company, with a copy to a civil rights organization known for litigation victories. Significantly, this man did not make direct use of fair housing laws or government enforcement agencies. Judging from our interviews, black homebuyers rarely consider the possibility of using government enforcement agencies to fight housing discrimination, perhaps because of a distrust of the generally weak fair housing agencies at all government levels and a sense of futility because racial discrimination in housing is so widespread.

Sometimes a group of whites may work together to exclude black residents, as the president of a community credit fund in an eastern city recounted: "When we first came to the neighborhood, the people were very upset, because the neighborhood association wanted to sell all of the homes and therefore control who came in. We happened to make friends with a black family who was already there, and that's when we came in. The gentleman who ran for governor, his wife led the neighborhood association that really did not want blacks in." Here it was members of the local elite rather than working-class whites who led the effort to exclude blacks. The black family's assertive action, facilitated by a family already there, was successful, which signals some changes from the recent past of rigid housing segregation.

In the United States the real estate industry is about as segregated as residential housing.[12] White real estate brokers are often linked together in informal networks through which they circulate information about houses for sale and make home-buyer referrals. Homes-for-sale information is usually printed in multiple listing services' books, listings that may only encompass mostly white suburban areas and certain city areas. Distribution of these lists tends to be limited to the white real estate brokers who have listed houses in such areas. This type of marketing of housing restricts the information that is available to black homeseekers currently living in segregated areas, since real estate brokers serving black areas are often not well integrated into the white real estate networks.[13] As a result, the searches of black homebuyers for housing are usually less efficient than for comparable whites.

A university administrator in a northern city reported that her experiences trying to rent a place were so unpleasant that she turned to buying. Here she discussed the reaction of a white woman who was apparently a real estate agent:

> So I worked two jobs so that I'd be able to buy a house, and saved the money from the second job to be able to buy the house with, because it took all the money from the first job just to live, because I have a large family. And I had a woman tell me on the phone that I would like the neighborhood because there were no blacks in it. And I said, "Well, my dear, you're in for a big surprise, because if I buy it, there will be a black there then, because I am now, I am a black." And she gasped, you know, and just hung the phone up.

White realtors and their agents use several mechanisms to perpetuate racial mapping. The procedure whereby black and other minority homebuyers are systematically shown neighborhoods different from those of their white counterparts is often called *steering*. A 1991 federal study of housing discrimination found the steering of minority homebuyers in a fifth of the cases where white and minority auditors were shown housing or where addresses were recommended.[14] With an angry tone to his reply, the director of a drug abuse program in a midwestern city commented on several recent instances of poor treatment:

> Have I ever been discriminated [against] in housing? Oh, yes! . . . We saw [a house] in the newspaper, called the girl up and told her we wanted to look at this house. We got out of the car and we could see the lady sitting at the table, the owner of the home, as we got out of the driveway. And I actually saw the expression on her face change as she saw this young black couple walking up the driveway. I guess she figured we couldn't afford a house, or else she didn't want to give us one in this neighborhood.
>
> The area I live in is called Stonebridge, which is predom-

inantly white. Right across the street is Stonebridge
Heights, which is 85 percent black, and across the street
from there is Stonewoods, which is 99 percent black. So after [the agent] got through showing us this one house, she
drove all the way to the other side into Stonebridge Heights
to show us another house. The house that I bought eventually was right around the corner from the original house we
saw, which is a 99 percent white neighborhood. We're the
only blacks in the neighborhood, on the corner. And the
other thing that made me realize that it was discrimination
—how many of you have ever seen a real estate agent who
has never called back a prospective buyer? This woman
never called us back, never wanted to know if we were still
looking or interested. And so, yeah, I have experienced it.
It pissed me off.

The housing of this particular city is substantially segregated
along racial lines, much like the rigidly segregated housing of an
earlier era. Unlike earlier black homebuyers, however, this man
had the ability to thwart the attempted steering by a white
salesperson. Reviewing his experience, he added this comment:

As far as being discriminated [against], I mean, they're
going to discriminate against us till we leave here! And I
don't let other folks' problems become mine, as far as discrimination is concerned. That's their problem, you know;
they got more of a problem with me being black than I got
with being black!

Our respondents use their middle-class resources to fight mistreatment by homeowners and real estate agents. A financial
analyst at a Fortune 500 company reported:

I hired a realtor to show me around. And I gave her the requirements I was looking for—the price range, the type of
house, and so forth. And at one point in time she steered

me toward a certain section of town which made me feel a little uneasy. And henceforth I had a new realtor within a day or two.

This professional's ability to find a cooperative white agent again marks a significant change from the 1950s and 1960s when few such agents could be found in any city in the nation.[15] Our respondents mentioned a variety of innovative coping tactics. Replying to a question about discrimination in real estate, a teacher replied in an exasperated tone:

Oh! Geez! Yes! I think that's been our problem here in this city. And we've been tempted to get a white friend to—the house that we love—to be the face for us. You know, bargains we've heard of . . . that work for other people, they don't work for us. And I think it's simply because of the neighborhoods that we're looking in. . . . And I think a lot of discrimination goes on as far as housing here in this city.

Even when a sale is well underway, racial barriers may be erected. A manager at a large corporation explained how he foiled an attempt to discriminate against him during the closing process:

We found a house that we wanted. The [white] people, for whatever reason, assumed that upon the closing of the house, they were going to make us aware of some things that they hadn't before, [that] we would not be able to financially follow suit with the house that we wanted. But I think that it was probably because some of the neighbors had indicated that they had not had any blacks in the neighborhood, and they figured out some way of not allowing this particular family into the neighborhood. So when the person presented this [money] figure to us, they kind of indicated, "Well, we know you put down your earnest money and you put down too much earnest money. This

240

will probably be a lesson to you that, don't put down a bunch of earnest money. . . . So we listened, and [I said] "Well, you haven't asked us if we could meet that financial obligation." And I wrote a check for the amount, and the person was just kind of flabbergasted. I found out later from some neighbors that a certain influential neighbor had put up this particular company to figure out some way of not allowing us to buy the house.

The employment of black agents in formerly all-white real estate firms marks a significant change from the era of legal segregation. While black agents in white firms may feel great pressure to cooperate in steering and otherwise discriminate against black homeseekers—indeed, their jobs may be on the line—they may still be a welcome source of additional information. A newspaper publisher recounted her experience with a white realtor and a black realtor in the same firm:

> From a white realtor, one time when I was looking for a house I had asked about certain properties that I was interested in seeing, and he told me that all of them were sold. And he showed me another section in a black area where he thought I should be, I assume. And I proceeded to call back to his same agency and ask if there was a black salesperson. And a black salesperson came on, and I asked about the other houses. And the other houses were not gone.

Clearly, black real estate agents selling in a white housing world face difficult problems, as an administrator at an eastern law school who had previously sold real estate described:

> There have been times when I used to sell real estate that I know that the other realtor will not want to give me a key to show the house because he thinks that the client that I'm showing the house to is black. And that happened about

241

four years ago, where the house was in an exclusive white area. The other broker thought that my clients were black, but as it turned out, both of my clients were white, and more than that, my client's father knew the broker. And when they discovered what was happening, that I wasn't getting the key so they could see the house, they wanted to buy this house, she just stopped. She said, "Stop right here at this phone booth in the middle of the street." And called her father. Her father called him. And immediately when I went back to the office, the key was available. That's the way it works. . . . Yeah, it was all based on their belief that I had a black client.

From the tone of the respondent's comments one can conclude that it was galling for him to see white clients use their own social networks to secure easy access to a house—a result underscoring the blatancy and the cumulative character of some housing discrimination.

Interestingly, a few respondents suggested that housing discrimination often took the form of "green discrimination" and that income, not skin color, was what mattered. A university administrator when asked whether he had recently faced housing discrimination answered, "Not really. And you know why? It's that thing I talked about before. If I were making 30 or 40 or 50,000 dollars a year less, then my answer would inevitably be 'yes.' But this is a capitalist society. And I make lot of money and so, therefore, my color does not mean near as much as the color of my money!" Whites with prejudices may be swayed by money. An administrator at a western university made a similar comment.

I know my way around. I don't rent, I don't have a landlord. I pay a mortgage company. The dollar bill counts for a lot. They don't care. If you've got the bucks, you can live almost anywhere. And so, I live in a predominantly white neighborhood, I don't live in the ghetto by choice. So, finding my house was easy. The realtor that helped us get it—I lucked upon somebody that was real nice.

The final comment does suggest that luck as well as money enabled him to avoid discrimination in this particular case.

It was a corporate manager in an eastern city who suggested the term "green discrimination" for the limitations imposed by income:

I purchased a home some ten years ago. And it was in a re-developing area. In fact, I moved from a predominantly white area to the inner city where the home had been reno-vated. It's like a carriage home. So, basically, it's a mixed neighborhood, more blacks, but we do have whites in the neighborhood. I haven't faced any discrimination. If any kind of discrimination, it's economically. If you don't have the money, you can't go or move certain places. You can't do certain things. That's what I find the biggest discrimina-tory factor nowadays. Not so much race, or color, but green discrimination.

Although he did not explain why, it is interesting that he moved from a white area to a racially mixed, gentrified area where he is now more comfortable. Here too we note an illustration of the effects of government subsidized redevelopment and gentrifica-tion on the housing opportunities of middle-class African Amer-icans. Some areas like this have become scattered exceptions to the usual segregated urban housing patterns. Still, gentrifying areas with reasonable income and racial mixes account for only small portions of the housing market in U.S. cities.[16]

Racial Transition and Resegregation

Often linked to the practice of steering is the illegal practice of "blockbusting," the practice of actively working to shift an

area from white to black. This is often done so that white real
estate agencies can reap profits from panicky whites willing to
sell for less to get out of an area. As a result, many middle-class
black families find themselves living in residential areas, including suburbs, once substantially or entirely white, that have become mostly black. Responding to a question about his neighbors, a school principal explained: "Most of them are black.
When I moved out here in '67, you couldn't see a black here
until you saw my family or the next door people. . . . My son
was the only black in the second grade. Now this place is predominantly black. That church was white; once the Methodist
church was white. Now it is one of the biggest Methodist
churches in the South and it's predominantly black." With a
tone of resignation in his voice an engineer at a computer firm in
the Southwest described how areas become reserved by realtors
for blacks:

> [In] the suburb I moved into, I have seen a tendency of
> them gearing, seems like, only blacks to where we live.
> There are few whites. When I first moved in that neighbor-
> hood, there were only about twenty families living there;
> now it's about over a hundred families live in that neigh-
> borhood. It was about fifteen white families and five black
> families. As the neighborhood grew and the homes began
> to close out throughout that building [area], I saw a ten-
> dency of—it seemed that the realtors were only selling to
> black people. Seemed like they were trying to set us in one
> location. I mean, you saw it go from 80 percent white and
> 20 percent black, to now almost 80 percent black and 20
> percent white now. And I often wondered, what happened?
> I began to see homes go up for sale of the few white fami-
> lies, and the neighborhood is excellent. Beautiful homes,
> lawns, things are kept up nice. And the neighborhood's
> only been there two and half years. But every white I

244

would see, 95 percent of them, that "For Sale" sign put up from their home. Because it seemed like the realtors were only gearing black people toward that neighborhood, so the whites started moving out when the blacks started moving in.

The short time that it took this suburban area to go from predominantly white to mainly black probably signals cooperation among real estate agents to blockbust the area. The engineer observed that agents were selling there only to black households. This deliberate concentration of middle-class blacks in certain suburban areas, resulting in a hopscotch pattern of black-white segregation, contradicts the arguments of some scholars, such as William J. Wilson, about the black middle class moving out of black inner city communities and successfully integrating themselves into formerly all-white areas.[17] Middle class families sometimes bypass older central city areas, yet find themselves facing resegregation in a variety of suburban areas.

A manager at a computer firm in a large southern city noted the role of whites in shaping the population map in his city:

I came here as a result of a move with a major computer firm. And this neighborhood—I was open to move into any neighborhood, and what ended up happening is that we were somewhat directed, or steered, out to this neighborhood. And when we moved out into this neighborhood, it was one third black and 60 percent white, with the remaining percentage being Hispanics. So at this point the neighborhood has become now probably 80 percent black and probably 15 percent white, and the remaining percentage Hispanics and Orientals. So the neighborhood has changed, and from what I understand—after we've moved here and several years later—this whole southwest quadrant was in fact designated to become black. But that was after the fact, and realtors being very sophisticated in how they han-

dle these things. . . . I was totally at the mercy of the realtors when I came here. We came here in '71; I did not
know anybody. And so we just went to realtors, and the realtors in turn just showed us homes and, ironically, most of
the homes we were ever allowed to see were in the minority
quadrant.

Typical of many blacks looking for a better home, this man is
not fussy about the racial population mix. Yet he has little
control over it. Housing patterns involve more than the preferences of individual homeowners, black or white. The reported
shift in mapping from majority white to mostly minority in the
respondent's immediate area, as well as in that quadrant of this
major city, again shows that much discrimination is not sponta-
neous but rather represents the policy of many in the real estate
establishment to concentrate black families in certain residential
sectors.

A law professor at a southern university commented on local
segregation:

Right around this campus, there's one community that's
predominantly white, has been for years. And the major realtors in the area take great pride in discriminating against
black folks. It's breaking down just a little bit just now.
Again, I've been here ten years. I remember one of my colleagues was looking for a house, and he came to relay this
story because this realtor was showing him houses. And
this realtor proudly told him how he had kept blacks out of
there for a number of years. Proudly. Told him because he
was white, and he didn't think he'd be offended. . . . I live
in a nice neighborhood. It's near here, predominantly black.
And I've had colleagues come who wouldn't even look in
my area. I've had other people look for places. And then I
would say, "Well, look, we've got some houses for sale over
there near me." And I had one say to me, "Any white peo-

ple live over there?" Now look, that's a quote. He didn't say, "Any other professors?" He didn't say, "Any middle class folk?" He didn't say anything like that. He said, "Any white people?" And not, not, not "educated people?" No! Just "any white people" is what he said. It's not a joke. It was a serious question. But it spoke volumes, you know. . . . I didn't make a big deal out of it at the time; I haven't since.

Here one of the respondent's white colleagues informed him of intentional steering, while another asked crudely about the racial composition of a neighborhood. Revealing here is the way in which some whites, in this case the real estate agent, are willing to talk about discrimination with other whites in what they believe to be complicity and mutual understanding. It is significant too that this black lawyer has not taken legal action against the realtors' discrimination.

Over the course of U.S. history new groups moving into cities or suburban areas in significant numbers have seen the racial or ethnic groups already there move out, either gradually or suddenly. However, some city neighborhoods undergoing residential succession can remain significantly diverse for some period of time. Some of our interviews suggest that the whites likely to remain in such areas often may not be a representative sample of the white population. A vice president at an East Coast bank commented on the mix in her neighborhood:

Well, now it's about half and half. When I first lived there ten years ago, it was predominantly white. It's older Jewish type of families that live there, but now it's about half and half. [And during that time, how were you treated by your white neighbors?] Really very friendly. I didn't really have a lot of problems. They really stay to themselves. They would speak, "Hi, how you doing?" And that was it. They didn't make me feel they didn't want me in the neighborhood.

247

A few respondents mentioned that their mixed neighborhoods included Jewish neighbors. A self-employed attorney in a southern city described his neighborhood as "a little U.N.": "We've got Asians and Indians and whites and blacks. But how is my relationship with my neighbors? It's been good." Some racially integrated communities develop a certain stability, at least for a time, as a black professor observed of the neighborhood in a western city: "This neighborhood that I'm in is somewhat mixed. And it's not, I guess, totally typical, because in many, many cases neighborhoods tend to, once they start to being mixed, they tend to resegregate. And once one group moves in, other groups start to moving out; and then so different sections tend to . . . resegregate it sometimes. But in this particular case, I think there's not much of a problem because the balance is reasonable." It is clear in the interview that the respondent's preference is for a racially mixed neighborhood. Not much research has been done in recent years on what keeps neighborhoods like this from resegregating; the commitment of black and white residents to maintaining a balance seems crucial. A few historically white residential areas have tried a type of "managed integration" similar to that we noted for a rental housing complex earlier in the chapter. Suburban areas like Shaker Heights, Ohio and Oak Park, Illinois have made aggressive attempts to keep white homeowners from fleeing; white community leaders help white buyers get special loans, provide insurance to protect the value of white property, prohibit "For Sale" signs in front yards, and encourage realtors to steer potential white buyers into the area. While such solutions can maintain desegregation, they are in effect bribing whites to live in integrated neighborhoods and, as Massey and Denton have argued, "ultimately they operate by restricting black residential choice and violating the letter of the Fair Housing Act."[18] Again we see that much of the burden of desegregating U.S. residential communities has been placed on the backs of African American families.

Discrimination by Lenders

White-controlled banks have a long history of discriminating against African Americans. For decades the federal government intentionally fostered racial discrimination in lending. The Federal Housing Administration's manual discouraged desegregation of housing in its stipulation that loans would not be approved if made in racially mixed areas. Title VIII of the 1968 Civil Rights Act and the Equal Credit Opportunity Act prohibited discrimination in lending. By the 1970s federal housing regulations had eliminated the most blatant exclusionary discrimination in lending.[19] In Senate hearings in the early 1990s lending regulators reported that there was little evidence of widespread overt discrimination in lending and that there were few discrimination complaints filed against lenders.[20] Yet serious questions about differential treatment in lending remain. A 1989 report of the federal Office of Thrift Supervision found that, nationwide, black mortgage loan applicants were rejected by savings and loan associations at twice the rate of white applicants.[21] A Federal Reserve Board study of more than six million mortgages made by 9,300 financial institutions in 1990 found that 34 percent of black applications were rejected, compared to only 14 of white applications.[22] And a report sponsored by the Federal Home Loan Mortgage Corporation found that lenders rely heavily on white realtors for referrals and are biased in favor of white areas in their loan-related assessments of residential stability.[23]

Today African Americans face not only exclusion from loans for homes and businesses, but also more subtle and covert discrimination in the form of poor information, getting the runaround, and added restrictions for loans. Providing a sense of the struggle, a professor of nursing in a southwestern city discussed her experience:

> One of the major sources of discrimination is in the housing market and in the mortgage financing aspect in trying to buy houses. Now, we're skilled home buyers, we're skilled lookers. And we recognize as African American people that any time we approach a mortgage company to buy anything that exceeds $60,000 in cost we're going to have a problem. And we're going to have a problem in the arena of a black moving into a white neighborhood, so to speak. Redlining is not uncommon in this city, just like it is in Atlanta and a lot of other cities that have upwardly mobile African American families. And that's one of the things that we have to deal with, and on a number of occasions in the process of purchasing six homes we've had to challenge that issue. . . . We were denied information about housing, the threat of denial of the mortgage, of [not] being able to purchase a particular home for various and sundry reasons, none of which had to do with our ability to pay the mortgage or our credit rating.

Commenting on her persistence with one bank, a manager in a social services agency in an eastern city highlighted some mortgage problems:

> My husband and I have owned our present home for the last thirteen years. . . . we live in a nontraditional area for blacks within the city. And we were discriminated against in getting a mortgage for our house. We were very much aware of that. That whole—well—the lending institution to which we went, where we have always dealt with our banking needs, was reluctant to give us a mortgage. And it was only through applying pressure, that it was given to us.

In practice, white bankers can decide on the basis of their subjective judgments where it is appropriate for a middle-class black family to live. A probation officer in a southern city described one of his encounters with a bank:

> I owned some property, an acre of land. It's in a predominantly, as a matter of fact, an all-black subdivision area of the city. And I wanted to build a $100,000–$150,000 house. In my opinion, it'd probably [be] valued at more. I went to three different banks—had to post $2500 in their loan processing—and each time they found some reason to deny me the loan. Basically what they were saying in essence is the type of house that I wanted to build couldn't be built in that area for that particular price. And I know— because I've done contracting before and I have been a contractor—so I know what the costs were going to be. I had figured out all the costs, plus added their 20 percent into it. And I know that for $120,000 I could have built that house. I only wanted $90,000 to borrow. Also I'm going to put $30,000 invested money into it. Plus I've got land there, so it was very well secured. So that pissed me off, and it upset me so much that I just went out and bought a house where the "establishment" says that you can apply. And they made the loan real easily. Of course, the house wasn't valued at quite as much. For the money I got a comparable house. But it's not what I want, because my lifetime ambition is to build this dream home. [Do you feel that if you'd been white it would've been different?] Certainly!

Because the house was to be built in an all-black subdivision, the white bankers denied the respondent a loan that probably would have been only 60 to 70 percent of the value of house and lot and thereby killed his housing dream. In making loans white-controlled banks and thrifts have considerable power to

251

shape how, and whether, urban communities grow. Thus when they have decided to finance office towers in central cities, they have contributed to the growth of new administrative centers. When the white real estate elites decide to deny loans to black homeowners in certain areas, they reduce black housing options and help to configure city residential patterns according to their conceptions and interests.

After the Move: White Neighbors

Whether a black family owns or rents, the move into a traditionally white neighborhood typically begins a new phase in the struggle to create a safe and supportive family milieu. In such neighborhoods the white repertoire of negative responses can range from violence, to surveillance, to grudging accommodation. Whatever the white response, including acceptance, the dimension of race usually hovers in the background. One report by the Southern Poverty Law Center covering just two years (1985–1986) counted forty-five cases of move-in violence targeting minority Americans, the majority of these being African Americans.[24] In the 1990s cross burnings aimed at black families moving into white areas continue to occur in all regions of the country.[25] These areas have included DuPage County, Illinois; Pasco County, Florida; Marshall County, Ohio; Suffolk County, New York; Orange County, California; Vidor, Texas; Winter Garden and Orlando, Florida; St. Paul, Minnesota; Phoenix, Arizona; and Bellevelle, Illinois, to name just a few. In the early 1990s a dozen black families had crosses burned outside their homes in Dubuque, Iowa; the cross burnings were part of a broader protest by local whites against a small-scale minority-recruitment plan proposed by a local task force to increase the racial diversity of the city.[26] That such action could take place in a midwestern city with a black population of less than 1 percent suggests that racism is not necessarily generated by whites' contact with black Americans and that such white racism is probably omnipresent in the United States. Black families moving into white areas have been shot at, have had their windows broken, and have fled when their houses were fire-bombed. In our interviews a former secretary, now a hair stylist, recounted the experiences of a friend in a large midwestern city in the 1970s: "I had a girlfriend. When [she and her husband] bought in the same area that we were buying in, their house got fired on three times, you know, before they even got a chance to move in. Her husband had to sit there and sleep with a shotgun. And we are still talking about the 1970s in that city. So you knew, you knew your place." Since the 1970s this city has experienced a series of similar incidents. In such situations some black homeowners have fled, while others have responded by arming themselves and standing their ground.[27]

Several in our sample reported vandalism with overtones of personal violence. A newspaper publisher discussed her sister's experience in an industrial city in the South: "She had a new car, one of those little sports cars. I can't think of what it's called. They kept 'keying' her car, taking a key and running down, scraping the side of it. And she was the only—there are only about four or five blacks who live in this little exclusive complex in the city. Her car got keyed three times, and the insurance company canceled her. And she moved. Nobody else's car was getting keyed." Similarly, one of the black interviewers for our project, a graduate student who was living in a large city in New England in the early 1990s, reported that her car was vandalized in a residential area where there were no other black renters. Nearby cars belonging to whites were not damaged, but hers was dented and defaced several times by unknown vandals. In both cases the destruction of property and implied personal threat pressured the women to move out of the white areas.

Sometimes the opposition of whites, while not violent, is

253

openly hostile. After describing the hate stares he had encountered at a local restaurant, a manager at an electronics firm in the Southwest discussed his reaction to finding racist graffiti in his nearly all white neighborhood:

> [In] the same neighborhood, a half-block down the street, is a junior high school. And my wife and I, you know, we're middle-aged, forties, and we're getting a gut so we wanted to start walking. So they built a brand-new asphalt track at this high school. So we went over there one afternoon to walk. And as we walked around the track, we came on the far end of the track and there was this big brick wall and all across this wall were negative slurs: "Go home, nigger," "Jews die," the German swastika all over the place, "White power," "White supremacy." Now again, in a totally white neighborhood—and when I say totally I'm talking about the year I was there I saw *two* black families—totally white neighborhood and a few Asian, Indian, Arabic-descent families around, but again, white. Now why would we see that type of graffiti on a wall at a white school? Unless the parents had instilled that in those kids. Because those kids don't know negative [things about] blacks, because they don't even live with them, they don't go to school with them, they don't go to church with them. So that had to come from the parents, and that made me want to move. Not because I was running from it, it was that I didn't *have* to be in it, and I was putting myself in it for nothing.

In this case, the hate stares in restaurants and the threat suggested in the graffiti were so disturbing that the respondent and his family moved from the subdivision. Such racially motivated hate crimes, which include racist graffiti and similar vandalism targeting African Americans, have increased in the United States since the early 1980s. This incident did not occur in an inner-city neighborhood, where such graffiti might be more likely, but

254

rather in an exclusive white suburb with manicured lawns and high family incomes.

Most black middle-class families are not the objects of serious acts of violence, but do encounter racist reactions from some of their neighbors, ranging from excessive surveillance, to spreading misconceptions and rumors, to harassment, to white flight. A physician in an eastern city noted two different reactions of her current neighbors in a white suburb: "A lot of people became very threatened and moved. Then it was this, 'How can they afford this, or how can they do this.' Not realizing that I work sixteen hours a day, and so does my husband."

Many white homeowners, fearful about the crime and "status contamination" that they expect to come with their black neighbors, engage in some extra surveillance of the newcomers. A student counselor at a western university related her experience with unneighborly scrutiny:

When we moved in there was a lot of glaring, and I guess when they see you do normal things, things that other people do, then it's almost like you see them breathe a sigh of relief. . . . I, one afternoon, had come in from work early. And this house [we were renting] had trees in front of it, and it was just annoying me that these leaves were always—the lawn was always covered with leaves. So, this particular day, I come in early from work, so I decide to take off my street shoes. And I put on some garden shoes and just grabbed a broom and decided I'm getting rid of these leaves right now. Only to have my neighbor come along, who is white, and say, "Gee you push that broom real swell!" [And you felt that he was making a comment?] He was making a racist comment, he was always making racist comments. He would say things like, "By god, where do you think all those colored folks get all those fine cars that they drive?"

Here the surveillance was reduced when the white neighbors were satisfied that the black renters did not fit the feared stereotypes. This woman noted that she had also felt under surveillance in an elite white suburb where she had rented previously: "But typically I find that the more affluent the neighborhood, the more suspiciously they look at you if you're a black person —trying to, in my mind, trying to figure out how you got there, where you get your money from, how can you afford to live there? In that elite suburb I was a student at the time, and not really working a full-time job, and I really felt that there was a lot of animosity towards me." An experience with white scrutiny contributes to the accumulating fund of knowledge blacks use to judge new encounters with whites.

As we have noted previously, the image of blacks, especially black men, as criminals is deeply imbedded in many white minds. One professor in a southwestern city was informative about her white neighbors' reactions:

I think when we first moved in it was pretty clear that they were a little bit nervous. And once they saw that people weren't driving up to our house at midnight, you know, purchasing small packages of white powders, then they relaxed. And you could see them relax after a couple of months, and then they would wave, and occasionally they would come over and ask if they could take the persimmons off our tree, because I wasn't interested in doing anything with persimmons. And they loosened up quite a bit, but the first couple of months, you could sort of watch the way they behaved, the way they peered out of their curtains, the way they were careful to cut their grass and not look at our house, but looking at our house very closely when a car pulled up. They were very reassured when friends from the department came over, we knew white people, so we were probably OK. And they were reassured by the middle class appearance of our black friends. So, they saw that clearly these were not people who were going to be having shoot-ups in the front yard!

Such accounts suggest the price black families pay for white stereotyping and paranoia. But there are also costs to this behavior for the fearful whites. Working with a graduate student, the first author has done some research on an upper-middle-class, predominantly white suburb in a southeastern city into which two formerly poor black families moved after winning millions in a state lottery. The suburban subdivision of expensive houses experienced some turmoil and rumor mongering, and several white homeowners on the street with the lottery winners put their houses up for sale. Rumors circulated inside and outside the subdivision about alleged drug dealing in the houses of the black families. Many white real estate agents steered white clients away from the subdivision, and in an interview with the first author the white developer estimated that because of this steering he had lost a million dollars in home sales. In this case, as in the respondent's account above, there was no substance to the rumors of criminality on the part of the black families, but again the negative association of "blacks and drugs" had seized the minds of many of the white homeowners.

White suspicions of black men as dangerous result in more drastic defensive actions than glaring. A television anchorperson in an eastern city recounted an incident that occurred on the day of his interview:

I've been in my townhome in this particular city; I bought it as probably one of the first owners in the complex I'm in . . . and I just recently returned to this city, moved back into my home here . . . And these people know who I am. Little [white] girl riding her bicycle in front of my house on the sidewalk. Well, her home is just a little ways off, can't be anymore than like thirty yards away. And I was coming

257

out of my house to get into my car to come back to the
station, and as the little girl was riding past me, I noticed
that her mother ran out of the house in what appeared to
be a fluster to keep an eye on her little girl who was in
close proximity to me. Now here I am a black professional
man. I'm a homeowner who's been in this complex longer
than these people have, probably make ten times the
amount of money that their household does. But at the
same time the stereotyping of a little white girl in proximity
of a black man, regardless of whether he's professional or
not, whether he's wearing a suit or not, that's ignorance.
Now if I had let something like that get me angry, I'd be
miserable. I like to turn it around and think, if they want to
be miserable worrying about the imaginary, then let them
be miserable. I mean, the little girl knows who I am. I said,
"Hi Sally, how you doing'?" And she says, "Hi Sam, see
you on T.V. tonight!"

It appears that the conception of the menacing black man
haunts the mind, not of a stranger, but of a neighbor. White
imaginings about blacks not only prevent real neighborhood
integration but also have a significant psychological impact on
victim and perpetrator. While this newscaster tries not to let
such episodes anger him, the intensity of his comments here and
elsewhere in his interview signals the impossibility of that.

Many whites, including one's neighbors and local police officers, often assume that blacks in traditionally white neighborhoods are not residents. An optician in a southwestern city
noted how a wealthy friend was treated by neighbors: "She was
at the door. And she was approached—because of the type of
house that she was in, it was about a $350,000 house—they
said, 'Well, are Mr. and Mrs. so-and-so, are they here?' And she
said, 'I'm that person.' And they said, 'Oh, well, we were just
coming to meet our neighbor.' They had no idea that their

[black] neighbor could afford, in this day and time, that price range." Similarly, a college counselor in a western city described her experience with occasional salespeople in an exclusive white suburb: "I live in a middle- to upper-class neighborhood. It's my home. Oftentimes, though, when I go to the door, for those salesmen who come around, they are shocked. They ask if 'the lady of the house' is at home."

Not all slights suffered by middle-class pioneers in white neighborhoods are so obvious. Many white slights seem to be linked to prejudices that are half-conscious or even unconscious. Recounting the mixed signals given off by his white neighbors, an engineer provided this account:

> Well, when I first moved in and to buy a house, our white neighbors came down and made us feel welcome. Brought cakes and cookies and brought sandwiches down when we were moving in. It was great! . . . [My wife's] white neighbor friend came down after everything was moved in and said . . . she was speaking to her husband—and I'll never forget this. . . . "Honey, do you see that? They have a brand new house, brand new furniture, and his wife doesn't even work!" And she was amazed. [How did you feel about that response?] I laughed. I said to myself, "Hmm, we're not supposed to have nice things. Or I'm not supposed to be able to put on a tie or a shirt and go to work, too? I'm not supposed to be able to manage and save like the other people." I just laughed at it because I knew that most of them think like that; we're not supposed to be able to live like them.

Perhaps the white neighbor did not recognize the implications of her comment; this type of ostensibly sociable reaction indicates the subliminal character of some white images of black men and women. Usually one thinks of home and neighborhood as places where one can relax and enjoy the fruits of his or her

259

labors. For blacks coming to a home and neighborhood can mean not peace and enjoyment, but frustration, anger, and emotionally generated illnesses. Even within the confines of family space, frequently purchased at great cost, middle-class blacks may find themselves threatened with psychological, if not physical, harm.

In these historically white residential areas black children can bear a heavy burden. In our interviews we observed a range of white reactions to black children, from harassment to friendly acceptance. A college administrator recalled the behavior of one of his white neighbors: "Well, when they were smaller and they were out on the sidewalk riding their bicycles and throwing the ball and things like that, if they happened to kick the ball into his yard or something, he would get into a heated [rage]. He had an encounter with one of the fathers out there in the neighborhood about one of the kids, and this was a Hispanic family. And it only happens with the Hispanic and black kids."

Commonplace neighborhood tensions can be aggravated by an overlay of racial tensions. An attorney in an eastern city who had just moved in described her and her child's experience with their new white neighbors:

They were like, "Maybe you should lock [the door] when the [black] neighbors are outside the door," like, "Oh god, what is she doing here?" I think for kids it's hard. I have a five-year-old. And my neighborhood is, I guess, sixty-forty white. And I noticed, like the second week we moved there, there are like five or six kids on the block. And he went over and spoke with them and played with them for awhile. [A] mother invited the five white kids into the house for Kool-aid. . . . He was not invited, which to me was just outright discrimination. There was no other basis for it. It's just unexplainable what black people go through, be they middle class or low class.

260

Exclusion can begin at an early age, as this five-year-old learned. The exclusion was initiated by a white adult, but in other cases the discrimination comes both from adults and children, as in the case of a high school principal and his son in a southern city:

> I found out he's a KKK'er, but as I told him, I was here be-
> fore you came. . . . My son was on his bike out there. And
> [my neighbor] had three boys and a girl. And he [my son]
> was riding up and down the sidewalk. And the wife would
> be standing inside the screen porch watching them push
> him off the bike. I said: "I don't want to talk to you; I'll
> wait until your husband comes." They had a KKK meeting
> over there one day. They were barbecuing out there because
> the air conditioner broke down, so they had to go outside
> so they could have some kind of air and everything. So they
> didn't have on the sheets or anything; they just had their
> arm bands and things like that. So, I told them, I said:
> "The next time your kids put their hands on my child, I'm
> going to sue you."

He later added that the neighbor eventually "moved to the city where the Grand Wizard lives." This black man took strong action against adults who were organized racists, but again the price in terms of personal energy was high, for this principal knew that he was risking serious reprisals. Implicit too is the perspective on black rights we have seen in numerous accounts of black responses to maltreatment.

White children can also cause pain for black adults, as a flight attendant in a western city illustrated:

> Well, the neighborhood that my sister and my mother live
> in is, I guess you would say, 95 percent white. When my
> nephew and my sister first moved onto the block, the little
> children, the little white kids wouldn't play with him. . . .
> In fact, though, I was walking up the street one day, not

long after they had moved there. And a little boy, he couldn't have been more than four years old, he was walking with his mother, and he turned around and looked at me, and he said, "What are you doing in this neighborhood?" And his mother turned around and she was appalled and she apologized to me. And I thought, well, where could a little boy of four years old even think of something like that if he hadn't heard it in his house.

There is more than white prejudice evident here. The mother did apologize for her son's behavior. The mixed, often unpredictable messages given off by whites in neighborhood interactions can confuse black residents and may signal the difficulties many white families have in casting off the legacy of racism. A dentist in the South described his son's experience at a local country club in an established white area: "Well, my son, as I told you, when he was a youngster about eight, he experienced probably his first direct confrontation with racism. I say that because *he* realized it was a racist situation. He was denied the opportunity to eat lunch during a tournament break in the country club that had invited him to play tennis, and that was something that he had never, ever experienced before. . . . He had never faced the overt name-calling." Discrimination is doubly damaging when there is no warning and when a youngster has never encountered flagrant discrimination before. The boy's experience was probably especially painful because he was expecting a pleasurable experience.

White neighbors' acceptance of black families varies from one neighborhood to the next. In many cases some type of *modus vivendi* is worked out. A minister in a southwestern suburb characterized his white neighbors as "kind, in their own way," going on to explain,

I think they're as kind as their perceptions of blacks will allow them to be. I think many of them have an institutionalized racism; whether they want it or not, it's there, it seems. And when they see us coming, the stereotypes come with us. They try, they try, but they keep their distance. We've not been invited over for dinner. There was not a welcome committee or anything like that. But the same can be said of us. We didn't invite any white folk over, either. But my wife goes walking with this one woman who happens to be white sometimes in the evening, and they claim to have a pretty good relationship. But it's always in the back—and maybe I'm projecting, but it's always in the back of our minds. My wife is going walking, not just with a *woman*, but with a *white woman*. And I think that my wife knows she's just been walking with a white woman. It's there, at all times.

The consciousness of race hovers as a constant presence between blacks and whites, even in a friendly relationship. Another black minister, this time in an eastern city, described the effects of residential integration more hopefully:

I have white neighbors on each side of me where I live now, and I guess the initial reaction when we first moved in, was hostility, and "Uh, oh, more minorities in the neighborhood." But the one thing that I think is important, is when any neighbors, no matter what color they are, that we learn to live together, and work together. And there's a kind of bonding now with the neighbors, if they see anybody at our door, they want to find out if that's a strange person or whatever. Once you live together with people, they sort of learn to live together.

This man's view, perhaps because he is a minister, may be unduly optimistic, but time and familiarity can engender the possibility of bonding. The willingness to "learn to live together" marks a dramatic change from the recent American past. Some black

263

and white residents in certain historically white neighborhoods like this one and the community of Shaker Heights mentioned earlier are beginning to renegotiate traditional black-white relations. However, it is possible the racial atmosphere described in this comment marks the positive limit of relations among black and white neighbors for the foreseeable future.

Black Residential Areas

Numerous popular and social science commentators on the state of black America have argued that middle-class families have been moving out of traditionally black residential areas and that huge numbers are now living in isolation from other black families.[28] This view of urban reality is exaggerated, for while housing segregation decreases for most American ethnic groups as education and income increases, it does not do so for black Americans. The national report on U.S. racial relations, *A Common Destiny*, cites data showing that blacks at every income level are to a substantial degree segregated from whites of similar income. In metropolitan areas affluent black families are about as residentially segregated from whites as those with lower incomes.[29]

The majority of middle-class black Americans live in substantially black or resegregating residential areas. Some choose black communities because of fear of whites; others, out of pride; and yet others, out of a concern for preserving black institutions. Expressing this sense of pride, a supervisor of vocational education programs described her neighborhood: "I've lived in a black neighborhood that's at least a hundred years old. And there's no discrimination in my neighborhood." A school board member in a northeastern city echoed this comment in her reply to a question asking if she had faced discrimination in housing: "No, only because the area where we live is predominantly African American." Living in a predominantly black neighborhood provides protection from the hostility and harassment faced by the middle-class families who venture into historically white residential areas. With a strong sense of territoriality, a dentist in an eastern city commented on his neighborhood: "Well, I don't have white neighbors. Well, this is funny. I got whites a block away. I live in the inner city, the Sugar Hill area, but I haven't been discriminated against. I'm there, and they know I'm there, I'm not going anywhere. We outnumber them, so I don't have to worry about any crosses being burned or anything like that!"

Those middle-class families who live in mostly black communities provide living contradictions to the argument that middle-class black Americans are abandoning traditional communities for white neighborhoods. Yet, the lives of middle-class black families, wherever they live, remain constrained by patterns of institutionalized discrimination. The anguish stemming from the choice between a traditional black community and a white residential area was poignantly described by a judge in the Southwest:

I guess that one of the problems of being black [is that] I stay in a black neighborhood. And you know, staying in a black neighborhood, that's discrimination. Well, what I'm saying is, I think it's important being a black judge, being a black person, that I identify with the black community and that I reside in the black community. But with regard to services, not so much city and government services, but [with] regard to private services, in terms of grocery stores, department stores and that type of thing, that is not available in the black neighborhoods. So I feel shortchanged, and my family feels shortchanged because we're not able to do some things here, we have to ride across town to get these services. If I stayed in a white, middle-class neighborhood, all the services would be right there.

265

While this respondent affirms his support for the black community and its value to him as a psychological and political anchor, he acknowledges that his choice means some inferior services. There are other tradeoffs to living in black areas as well, as a university administrator stressed in describing her choice to live in a central area of a northern city:

> My friends that have done that and have moved into some areas of the suburbs are very uncomfortable, particularly if they have young black sons, you know, and the dating situation. And they're driving back and forth all the time. But I opted to live near the center of the city because I want to be near the things that I enjoy doing. The concerts, the films, I love to go to plays; the things that I like to do are in the city. Plus, I try to do business with blacks as much as possible and to be near. I like living among my own people, so I live in a mixed neighborhood. And I like that, and I'm respected because I'm a Ph.D.

Comparing her situation to that of friends, this administrator highlights a troubling feature of the landscape for black families moving into traditionally white districts. Even in relatively liberal white residential areas, interracial dating and marriage are probably anathema to most white parents.

Relatively poor services may be part of the price a middle-class family pays for staying in black communities. The dean of students at a black college in the South described the mistreatment and neglect of his neighborhood by white officials:

> You get discriminated not necessarily in that you are denied use of this house, but if you live in a black neighborhood, you'll also see that they will allow a salvage yard, as an example, right down the street to be organized in your neighborhood. Even though the neighbors protested, they didn't want this. And they [city officials] said, "Well we'll require

266

them to put up a fence, a side-barring fence." And of course someone ran into the fence and knocked a hole in it, and it's been like that for five or six years now, where you can see through it. Plus the junk got piled up so high it came up over the top of the fence. So these are discriminatory acts that happen in your neighborhood. Also there is a code that requires vacant lots to be cleaned up and grass cut and underbrush cut, but somehow in the black neighborhoods these things don't get done. So you get discrimination in public services, public utilities and so forth, which also affects your housing. It affects the value of your property and things of that sort.

This respondent's difficulties with weak zoning enforcement are not unusual. Zoning processes often discriminate against African Americans. Research by sociologist Robert Bullard on what he calls "environmental racism" has shown that in many U.S. cities the location of dump sites, including toxic waste facilities, tends to be in or near minority residential areas.[30] We can see in this dean's comments how poor public services not only bring immediate costs but also reduce the value of property, making it difficult for black Americans to accumulate family wealth in real estate, a result with serious consequences for the mobility of future generations.

Conclusion

From a distance the racial ecology of U.S. cities is not unlike the geography of legal segregation, with most African Americans living in mostly black areas and most white Americans living in almost all-white areas. But up close, the patterns have changed in substantial ways. The racism of the late twentieth century is somewhat different from the racism of earlier decades, for at least a few black families live in some historically white areas in most cities in the United States. Equal housing opportunity has been a major goal of the civil rights movement, and state and federal laws now make housing discrimination illegal.

Contrasting the real experiences of African Americans with the ideal embodied in civil rights laws, one of our respondents, a professor at a western university, noted that "There is legislation. And there are policies that say it's one way, but in actuality it's totally different. Take any of the services—housing. They say there's no discrimination in housing. Yet, many blacks will show up to buy housing, or to rent an apartment, and they will be told it's filled." As we previously noted, middle-class black Americans rarely turn to government enforcement agencies to deal with discrimination. Although the 1968 Civil Rights Act banned most housing discrimination, it included weak enforcement provisions. The Department of Housing and Urban Development could negotiate settlements only in response to complaints; the Department of Justice could go to court only if the case showed a pattern of discrimination or was of "general importance." The 1988 amendments to the 1968 act added stiffer penalties and new enforcement mechanisms, and between 1989 and the early 1990s there was an increase in the number of housing discrimination complaints filed. In 1990 there were 7,664 discrimination complaints filed with the federal housing agency; about half have involved racial discrimination.[31] There have also been a few successful lawsuits brought under the 1988 act, especially in regard to rental housing.

Nonetheless, most whites who discriminate need have no fear of being punished. The enforcement of fair housing laws remains weak, and state and federal enforcement agencies are often handicapped by a lack of political will on the part of officials and legislators to provide adequate funding and to pursue substantial remedies for discrimination. As housing expert John Goering has commented, "So while the federal government now has a unique and powerful set of tools to attack housing discrimination it is less and less clear that there is any comparable responsibility or willingness to affirmatively expand this mandate."[32] The magnitude of the problem can be seen in the testimony of the HUD general counsel before a federal hearing, in which he estimated there are *more than two million cases* of housing discrimination each year in the United States. Federal agencies bring only a handful of "pattern and practice" suits each year, and the number of enforcement officers is very modest compared with the magnitude of the housing discrimination problem in the United States.[33]

Weak government enforcement puts the burden on black individuals. If African Americans wish to expend the energy and resources required, they can consider going to court as individuals. Since the 1968 housing act only a few hundred fair housing cases have been decided. Massey and Denton have assessed the current situation succinctly: "Whereas the processes that perpetuate segregation are pervasive and institutionalized, fair housing enforcement has been individual, sporadic, and confined to a small number of isolated cases."[34]

As a result, racial polarization is still fundamental to the residential layout of U.S. towns and cities. The consequences of this polarization are many, and we have observed in the comments of black men and women what happens when they try to break out of the traditional confines of housing segregation and seek homes in historically white areas. Some whites vehemently object to their presence, even fleeing as they move in, while white realtors and lenders have too much power over middle-class blacks' housing alternatives. Many black Americans seeking housing in traditionally white areas must struggle assertively to get better housing. They must often repeatedly call back, change realtors and banks, confront racist whites, or secure legal assistance. John Goering has noted that blacks' residential "choices reflect a complex overlay of fears of white rejection and hostility, desires for better residential services for themselves and their children, preferences for those like themselves, and dislike of deteriorating conditions in older, segregated neighborhoods."[35]

Washington Post journalist Joel Garreau has written of the suburban black middle class as "remarkable only for the very ordinariness with which its members go about their classically American suburban affairs."[36] Yet our respondents report that their lives as pioneers in white suburbia are often anything but ordinary and easy. For many the housing struggle brings anger mixed with resignation. The costs of this struggle were described by a counselor at a western university:

> First of all, just the attitude of taking you out to look at property. They take you to what they think you can afford based on the color of your skin. We did this three times; we had to *ask* to be taken, or to be shown, what they were calling middle-class homes. . . . Once you realize what's happening, you become so resentful. But then you figure, well, I can't spend my life [being upset]—I was born this way. I'm going to be black for the rest of my life, and I'm going to encounter discrimination. So for it not to have a negative [effect] on my life in terms of health, I think that you have to adjust. I wonder who else in this world has two, you might say even two lives, or two ways that they have to live, in order to function.

Housing problems will likely provoke much frustration, anger, and conflict for African Americans at all class levels for many years to come. The major 1992 riot in Los Angeles, the four major black riots in Miami since 1980, and the serious riots in other cities in the years between 1980 and 1993 were precipitated in part by anger over housing problems in racially polarized cities. Some time ago, the 1968 National Advisory Commission reporting on riots in the 1960s warned that the

270

United States was resegregating itself into two "separate and unequal" societies.

Racial segregation poses serious problems not only for black Americans but also for white Americans. Take the city of Chicago, a city with one of the most aggressive fair housing groups, the Leadership Council for Metropolitan Open Communities. In spite of much fair housing activity and a number of major court victories for fair housing, Chicago remains one of the most segregated of the nation's metropolitan areas.[37] In a 1992 *New York Times* series profiling two adjacent, highly segregated working-class suburbs of Chicago, one white and one black, journalist Isabel Wilkerson reported that the whites live in an insulated world where they "live out entire lives without ever getting to know a black person." Wilkerson found that there was racial fear and suspicion of the other racial group in both suburban communities. Yet the blacks were "fearful because much of their contact with white people was negative," while "whites were fearful because they had little or no contact."[38]

Housing segregation has costs for whites. A leading white scholar of school desegregation, Gary Orfield, has argued that future white leaders who grow up in suburban enclaves will have "no skills in relating to or communicating with minorities."[39] This social isolation will become even more of a serious handicap for whites as the United States moves into the twenty-first century, during which whites will eventually become a minority in the U.S. population. Even today, living in all-white enclaves does not prepare white Americans for dealing with a world that is composed mostly of people of color.

Chapter Seven

Contending with Everyday Discrimination: Effects and Strategies

A FEW months before he died of AIDS in 1993, the black tennis star Arthur Ashe was asked if that deadly disease had been the most difficult challenge he had faced in his life. Reflecting on his battle with AIDS, which he had contracted through a blood transfusion, Ashe replied that another challenge was greater: "Being black is. No question about it. Even now it continues to feel like an extra weight tied around me."[1] In previous chapters we have seen the extra weight that discrimination imposes on black lives. We have discussed the character and impact of specific instances of discrimination in public places, businesses, schools, and neighborhoods, and touched briefly on countering strategies middle-class African Americans have used in particular cases. In this chapter we focus in detail on the important lifesaving skills and coping strategies that African Americans rely on to survive the ordeals of modern racism.

To our knowledge the recent social science literature contains no systematic analysis of the survival skills African Americans have developed in confronting bigotry. A few psychological studies have recognized the stress caused by discrimination and identified some of the psychological strategies devised in response. Humphrey noted that "an ethnic group's perception of another ethnic group's effect on the distortion of the rules of distributive justice will predict a sense of anomie among its members and consequently disturb their emotional homeostasis."[2] He suggested that facilitating a sense of powerfulness in a group reduces psychological anomie. Similarly, Thomas and Sillen have noted that racial stress can stimulate important coping mechanisms. Individual reactions to this stress may range from constructive adaptation to a breakdown of normal functioning. Significantly, many victims of discrimination have marshalled resources that were not previously obvious or strengths of which they were not aware.[3] Much more social science research, in our view, needs to be done on black approaches to bias and discrimination.

Among middle-class African Americans there is much discussion of survival strategies. The oral tradition is a major source of the wisdom that has helped our respondents in struggling against everyday racism. Some programs within black organizations teach defensive survival tactics. A sophisticated repertoire of methods and tactics that have helped overcome racism becomes critical in a black person's life approach and life perspective.

With great persistence and patience, middle-class blacks pursue personal dreams of achievement and prosperity in the face of discriminatory encounters. Dreams must not, a hospital administrator argues, be given up in the face of discrimination. He explained forcefully what is it like to persevere despite meeting racism:

Being aware that the opportunities are there for black
Americans to achieve, and also realizing that though the

273

opportunities are there for achievement, the types of block-
age or the types of pitfalls that are there—and also recognizing that the opportunities may be there to excel, but you
may not have all the working tools and all the necessary
mentors to open the doors for you. . . . There's going to be
discrimination and racism out there, and as long as you can
accomplish what you have set forth to accomplish, recognize it for what it is, understand it for what it is, and don't
let it deter you from your dreams, don't let it deter you
from your goals. When that *does* happen, though, then you
have to formulate a plan of action to still accomplish your
goal and let that be your number one priority. Don't let attacking racism and attacking discrimination cause you to
lose sight of your goal. You keep that aside, and understanding that this is something that you had to deal with as
you continue to pursue your goal. Because what happens
when you start putting all your energy in trying to deal
with a racist act that is preventing you from trying to accomplish something, you won't accomplish it. You have to
understand that this is an obstacle that you're going to have
to deal with, but while I'm dealing with this, I'm going to
keep moving straight ahead.

He continued emphatically: "And I'm saying that we can't afford to get caught up in just attacking racism without pursuing
on a continued basis our goal to accomplish our goals and to
accomplish our dreams. My thoughts and my feelings are, yes,
recognize racism, recognize discrimination, try to deal with it as
you are continuing to pursue your dreams and your goals."

The Array of Situational Strategies

Prior to the 1960s the legalized mistreatment of black Americans, especially in the South, often demanded that they subordi-

nate themselves to whites and routinely respond to them with obsequiousness. Today, even when whites expect obsequiousness, most middle-class blacks do not oblige. Indeed, as many of our respondents have described, there has been a significant increase in the number of African Americans with the professional and financial resources to fight discrimination, often directly. In examining specific examples of discrimination, we have seen that responses to everyday prejudice or mistreatment range from careful assessment to withdrawal, resigned acceptance, verbal confrontation, physical confrontation, or legal action. We will now turn to the more general discussions in our interviews of the impact, character, and meaning of these anti-discrimination strategies.

One way to deal with discrimination is to try to avoid situations where it might occur, even at some personal cost. A physician in a southwestern city responded to a question about dealing with discrimination this way: "It just depends on what the situation is, whether or not it's personal, business; it just kind of depends on what, you know, exactly what it is. I usually don't go places where I'm not wanted, so I'm not the kind of person that trailblazes—where people tell you that they don't want you in a certain situation and you persist. It's kind of a hard question to answer." Seen here is the tragic legacy for black Americans of having to "know one's place." One senses fear of physical harm and psychological pain in his words.

Yet avoidance helps only in certain situations, since being middle class almost by definition means venturing daily into a white-dominated world. As we have seen in accounts of discrimination in previous chapters, in that white world a common initial response to discrimination is to carefully evaluate or read the situation. A teacher commented on this evaluation procedure:

First of all, within myself I try to analyze it. I try to look at all the pros and cons, all the ways in which the situation

275

could've happened. Did I do my part, not necessarily as a black person but just as a person? Did I do everything that I was supposed to do in the particular situation, whether or not it was a conversation, whether or not it was being hired for a job, or whatever. . . . Then what I do is, again, I just say what I think, in a very professional way. I try not to get into stereotyping myself by becoming very loud, and loud and aggressive, because I think that's the way white people feel as though we are going to handle ourselves. But if I'm faced with it, I try to be professional and assertive. Because I believe with whites you have to deal with them the way that they are accustomed to being dealt with. And that is, putting something on paper, and being professional, assertive but not aggressive. And that's the way I deal with it. I identify the problem. I say, "This is what I feel has happened here." And I give the steps or the reasons that I feel like it has happened, what has drawn me to this conclusion.

This woman captures well the preference of many black Americans to see, if possible, negative action against them as rooted in some factor besides color. Discrimination creates a psychological dilemma. A standard psychological recommendation for dealing with life problems is to face them head on.[4] From this perspective it may be healthier for blacks to say internally about mistreatment, "Yes, this is racism," for once a problem is named, it is often easier to solve. As we have suggested previously, many whites feel that black people are paranoid about discrimination and rush quickly to charges of racism. But the reality is often the opposite, as most middle-class blacks seem to evaluate a situation carefully before judging it discriminatory. We judge from our interviews that much discrimination is overlooked if possible. There is white hostility that blacks must ignore just to reduce the pain and to survive. If one can name racial discrimination something else, it may not hurt as much. For example, if blacks can attribute discriminatory acts to economic causes, then they can envisage how conditions might be changed to eliminate the negative behavior. They cannot change the color of their skins, and it is most disheartening to be damned for something over which one has no control.

Accuracy in assessing whites is usually necessary, as an administrative clerk in a publishing firm stressed:

> I'd say don't open your mouth and say anything that you're not 100 percent sure of. Don't have doubt. If you know this is where you want to go, and you know that these things are accurate, you shouldn't have doubt about it, no matter who comes through. . . . I don't care what the next person tells you. I've had people on my job to tell me, "well, it's your imagination." [Even] black people now, that say, "Maybe it's just your imagination that this is going on." No, it's not my imagination. . . . Take Susan, one of the supervisors. [They say] "This is just her nature to treat people this way." No. That didn't make me doubt for a moment. It didn't make me have a second thought and say, "Well, is this really the way she is and that she's really not discriminating?" No. She's discriminating.

Beneath the surface we sense the psychological toll taken on a person who must fight to have her view of what is going on in her workplace acknowledged. Having to assess potentially discriminatory situations carefully before responding can create a strain on the energy and psyche of African Americans. What is at stake is often more than whether one is right in a particular assessment. A less obvious aspect of modern racism is the great difficulty black victims often have in establishing their perceptions as legitimate. Full racial integration of historically white institutions requires a change in white views and practices, as well as an increase in power for blacks. Such a major change will result in the power of African Americans to establish their own situational readings and constructions as legitimate in interactions with the whites. In addition, some black Americans say, "The right I want most as an American of African descent is the right to be wrong." Blacks in white institutions feel constantly scrutinized and that they can never "let down" or make a mistake. True racial integration would include the right to make a mistake without abnormal or racial repercussions.

Several respondents discussed how they reassess maltreatment after it has occurred. A manager in an electronics firm described how he applies a self-evaluation technique he learned in a management program:

> When something happens, I'll take it and toss around in my head, replay it like a recorder, and see if there's maybe something that I did that could have caused it, or something I could have done differently that would have made the outcome different. Then once I feel comfortable with what I've analyzed, the one thing I'll do is I'll present, if need be, my argument to whoever it is that I'm dealing with, be it my manager or someone else.

Not every situation requires the same reaction. Punctuating his comments with some laughter, the owner of a chemical company described how he sometimes chooses to ignore minor incidents:

> It depends on the importance of the situation that I'm dealing with. If it's in the grocery store, hey, I don't get upset about somebody [who] gets in front of me, tries to pretend I'm not there. It depends on how I'm feeling that day, but, you know, life is too short to get upset about something like that. If it meant that they wanted to short-change me in the line, you know just because I'm black, then we've

278

got some problems. And we will deal with it head on. So we have to put it in the proper perspective because, like I said, there's always going to be discrimination and you just have to learn to deal with it; you just don't jump up and down in every instance.

A theme throughout many discussions of coping in our interviews is the struggle to keep some kind of balance and to contain one's frustrations in searching for the best response. In one situation, resigned acceptance is preferred; in another, active confrontation.

After the initial assessment of a situation one possible response is to retreat. Some street incidents, such as those discussed in Chapter 2, allow only for a quick exit. Some type of acquiescence is another response forced on black Americans. A computer specialist for an East Coast bank described one such response, a "blocking out" method:

> My first way of dealing with discrimination is usu-
> ally . . . acting like it doesn't exist. Back in the sixties, in
> my parents' days, Martin Luther King's days, it was out-
> ward, it was blatant. Now, you can't holler discrimination,
> because they're going to think that you're trying to get a
> lawsuit, or trying to [get] a free meal or something, so you
> really can't come out and say, "I'm being discriminated
> against." You've got to handle it in a more mature, more
> adult way, a more, I guess you could say, a more timid
> way. You've got to just know it's there, do all you can to
> avoid it.

Such acquiescence may sometimes be necessary, yet, as we suggested earlier, it may not be a psychologically healthy technique. It is possible too that by "a more timid way" he refers to an indirect or subtle means of deflecting discrimination.

The heavy price paid psychologically for this adaptation strategy can be seen in the comments of a banking executive in an eastern city:

> You become a chameleon. You take on the characteristics of what's going on there. It goes everything from patterns of speech, your philosophies, your thinking. Because I don't think all the time you're openly, I mean, you're not totally honest. You know what [white] people want to hear more than anything else and you give them back your feedback; you regurgitate back to them what you think they need to hear. There are times when you go against it, bucking the system, and then you just tell them your gut feelings or how you really feel about something, but most people that I know will hold that back until it's at the point when it needs to be said. But they don't normally, as a routine basis, do it.[5]

Some agree that the struggle with whites requires acquiescence, but only up to a point; that is, they take the "run to fight another day" approach. In an earlier chapter we discussed a black lawyer's measured response to a white attorney who used the word "nigger" in his presence. Although he appeared at first to ignore the remark, when the white attorney later came by to ask how he was, he with some humor pressured him by suggesting that many white people need "help" in dealing with their sickness called racism. In his interview the black lawyer added these words:

> I think many blacks have lost out because we have become frustrated. We see what we're dealing with. And then it appears so hopeless, and we just say, "Oh, I can't help it." And we just throw in the towel. . . . It's a world in which they may have the advantage, but there's nothing that says it has to continue to be that way. And so our job then be-

280

CONTENDING WITH EVERYDAY DISCRIMINATION

comes: How do we turn whatever disadvantages may be ours into advantages. And I think there're certain ways to do it. But the strategy must sometimes vary, and we must control our tempers and our emotions. And then there are some times when we must just hide to live another day, which means, "I see what you're doing, I don't particularly care for what you're doing, but nothing will be gained by me pointing it out to you today." So I'll take it, and there'll be another day.

Confronting White Racists

Withdrawal and acquiescence are by no means the only strategies our respondents described. Confrontation is a common strategy for dealing with the racist attitudes and actions of white Americans. Indeed, there has been a long history of active resistance to racism on the part of African Americans, from the time the first Africans were enslaved on ships bound for the new American colonies. Historian Herbert Aptheker found evidence of 250 American slave revolts or conspiracies to revolt, a count that did not include the numerous mutinies aboard slave ships.[6] Later, during legal segregation, some blacks took great risks by confronting whites openly. In Blauner's interviews with blacks and whites in California, several black respondents reported acquaintances reacting aggressively to racial discrimination prior to the 1970s.[7] After saying that "you have to choose your battles," a professor at a New England university commented on how she deals with racist remarks: "I would say, 'I don't think that's very funny,' you know. 'Look at what it is that you're [saying].' And they would say, 'Oh, it's *only* a joke.' But it isn't *only* a joke, you know. And I think it's really not uncommon even if it's not jokes given about blacks, but given about Arabs, for example. And I think that black people need to say, 'I don't think that's funny.'" Some whites have told the authors that the "black jokes are harmless" and that blacks should "lighten up" and laugh at them, the suggestion being that said jokes are a sign of integration into the core culture. While some middle-class blacks find themselves in situations where they feel pressured to laugh at antiblack and other ethnic jokes told by whites, this professor does not agree with such assent to joking.

By regularly confronting whites verbally, black Americans run the risk of being ostracized or labeled. Emphasizing an aggressive approach, a professional who directs a social welfare program in the Midwest spoke of confronting discrimination:

> There was a job that I just went through and filed a grievance like a big dog. And I called up all of the people that I know that would help raise hell—hell raisers—and that's what, really, what I did. I have never taken the back seat intentionally if I knew that I was taking the back seat. And I tell them. You know, when I came out of high school we had—in the seventies—we had a lot of pride, and one of the things we were taught is that you fought for what you believed in, regardless of how people felt about you, you did that. So as far as discrimination, you know, in my city people know me as a hell-raiser.

Called a "troublemaker," a social worker in an eastern city described her approach to white denial:

> Generally, I get myself into difficulties because I deal with it head on. And generally, I'm considered a troublemaker, or someone who's constantly looking at race, and someone who's looking to argue. . . . And what disturbed me and continues to disturb me is that whites will try to tell you that they're not being racist, when they can't tell you what you perceive, or how you've experienced something. And what they try to do is to deny your experience, and then invalidate it. And then in other words, you walk around like,

well, I know this is happening to me, but you're telling me this is not happening to me, so it's not? No, it means you don't want to acknowledge that it's happening, so what I tend to do is say, "you are doing this to me," and whether you acknowledge it or not, that's the way I experience it. So, I try to deal with it head on.

Again and again in the interviews we see that living with modern racism is a matter of accumulating experience. And it is the extensive experience that most African Americans have that makes them outraged at the common white denials of the reality of everyday racism.

A bank manager characterized her direct, but careful approach: "Being very direct, I tend to put them on the defensive. I don't, I'm not argumentative, but I always try to ask questions. I'm very direct with my accusations. I just don't fly off the handle. I usually have facts. I go right to the people involved, and I let them explain to me why things are happening. And it seems to shake them up a little bit, that someone can be as direct about the black-white issue."

A lawyer quoted previously sometimes deliberately uses a matter-of-fact but casual retort to racist comments: "Instead of just throwing temper tantrums, say, 'Oh, that's just because you're a racist.' They don't like to be called racist. . . . That's the exciting part. It's not always bad being the underdog. It's not. It's good to see people go through the mental gymnastics, you know." This lawyer characterizes his white antagonists as racists with a smile, using humor as an equalizer, but from the white point of view such a direct yet unheated accusation is disarming and it can provoke vigorous denials.

It is remarkable how many middle-class African Americans see it as their task to educate white Americans about racism and to remind them of the implications of the "liberty and justice"

283

creed whites supposedly honor. One theme in some interviews is calling whites on the carpet, as a southern newspaper publisher explained:

I think most people don't know what racism is. They consider it just part of the way of doing things. I think the most horrifying thing to me has been that when people have been racist and I have turned around and said, "That was very racist," it's almost been shocking to them. "Racist! I'm not a racist!" And then you explain to them how that's racist, and it's like, "Oh, I never thought of it like that." That's always been mind-boggling. Their perception is that it's not racist—that's the way they think, that's the way they function. So, if I had a choice, more black people would educate white people about what is racist.

The experience of being a victim often seems to generate considerably more thought and reflection about the character of U.S. racial relations than the experience of being white victimizers.

In Chapter 2 we discussed a television anchorperson's account of being discriminated against while attempting to buy a luxury car. In his interview he also described the educational approach he sometimes uses:

I have found that probably the most effective way—at least it makes me feel better—you realize that basically discrimination is based on ignorance, so you try to educate people. And the best way to educate people I have found is to point out in a very subtle way, and a very intellectual way, the stupidness—I don't know how better to put it—the ignorance basically of why they are prejudiced. For example, the incident that I cited to you about my buying the car, and the people, based on the [casual] way I was dressed, based on the fact that I was black, assuming that I was

284

not in a position, or was not interested in purchasing that car. That's based on ignorance, and that's based on stereotyping.

As we have seen in every previous chapter, racially insensitive or hostile remarks are the scourge of middle-class African Americans moving into formerly all-white situations. With an air of disapprobation, a management assistant in an eastern county government office recounted her reaction to a colleague's remark:

> Another incident in that same department—somebody had said that an ambulance company had picked up a person that was so dirty and had lice, and they were appalled. And the next comment was, "And the person wasn't even black." Well, again . . . and they looked at me, because they knew that that would be offensive to me and they also knew that I would have a retort for this person. And I said to him, "Do you think black people have a monopoly on dirt?" And the comment was made by the others in the group, which was said in jest, but probably very true, that the person who made the comment had no idea what the word monopoly meant. But they knew that he had offended me, and it was interesting. The refreshing thing about that was that the other people in the group were white and had very little exposure to blacks but because of my presence had become more sensitive.

Her presence and her quick response to racially barbed remarks apparently sensitized other whites in her work circle who had no experience with blacks.

For some middle-class black Americans, this desire to educate whites about a range of issues informs their everyday professional activities, as in the case of this professor who has taught at universities in the North and the Southwest:

285

Most of my class isn't black, two-thirds of any class I teach is white. And so when I'm politicizing black students, I'm also politicizing white students. And I do that because I think that as folks who are going to be participants in the big middle class, they probably won't be as well-off as their parents were, they might be at some point people who are interested in breaking the stranglehold that ideology has on the way we see the world. I think for example that a white male, who is just going to be the equivalent of a middle manager in an insurance company, can see the fact that what is happening to him is not tied to black people, but tied to the way the economy works, that individual will then be someone who in his own life interrupts the process of scapegoating another group. It's the only way I can think of to intervene, short of becoming part of a revolutionary group. Do you know what I mean? I mean, if I wasn't teaching, I'd be standing on a street corner with a machine gun, because I can't imagine what else I would be doing.

Mixing her commentary with occasional laughter, a black professional in a northern state discussed how her approach to educating whites depends on the situation and who the white person is:

I have very little tolerance for white people who expect me to change my behavior to make them comfortable. They don't change their behavior to make me comfortable. I am who I am. Either they sit with me and work with me respecting that, or you can't sit and work together. But I don't—and I see them uncomfortable, and I think to myself, "Well, that's unfortunate." But, no, I don't go to any great lengths to make them any more comfortable in dealing with me. I sometimes see them choking on words, trying to find ways to say things. And I let them choke! But

286

I'm serious! Why should I help them phrase it. Sometimes I think they're trying to say something about, "Well, do you think the other black members . . ." "Excuse me?" And I wait for them to come forward with it, and often times they end up not saying it because they're afraid of what my response will be. So they work around it, and I say, "Well, I think that's inappropriate." Then there are other people, who are personal friends, who may make a racist statement, and it's really based on their ignorance and their lack of understanding, and I'll take the time to deal with it. There's a young white woman that I work with now, and she's really not worked with a lot of different people of color, and she uses the term, "you people," and I bring it to her attention, and she's like, "oh, oh," and so it's an education, we're working together.

Differentiating between whites whose statements reflect ignorance and those whose comments show hostility, this professional takes the time to educate the former. Such a response seems to us to be psychologically healthy, for it offers a real solution to a chronic problem and gives the individual black person a sense of accomplishment.

In their everyday rounds some middle-class African Americans have the moxie and opportunity to create situations in which whites must come face to face with their racist views and assumptions. A manager for a southwestern computer firm described a "victory march":

One thing that used to always happen to me—[white] customers don't see me a lot, and their assumption is that I'm white when I talk to them over the phone. . . . I would go to a customer site, with one of my engineers. And they would come, and they would always talk to the engineer as though I was working for him. And what I would always do is have a game: I would make sure that I would walk to

the other side of the room. And then the conversation
would soon come to a point where the engineer would say,
"I'm not the one that's going to get your problems resolved,
that's my boss over there." I would make them come to me,
sort of like a victory march!

Although calculated, the manager's response is more one of
teaching a lesson than of seeking revenge—and again is
wrapped in the commonplace black humor rather than in overt
hostility.

Judging from our interviews it is very rare for black Americans to set out to annoy whites just out of vindictiveness. However, we did find a somewhat humorous example of a "payback
time" reaction. A student at a predominantly white university
recounted, with some laughter, how she and her black friends
set up situations and took chances in taunting whites:

> It's, I don't know, it's a sense of control in a way, I guess.
> And it's an acceptable way for me to lash out at white peo-
> ple, you know "acceptable." Because my friends and I,
> we'll do that a lot. We'll go to a restaurant and we'll talk
> so loud about racial issues, and we will just trip people out!
> We did that last Sunday at a restaurant as a matter of fact,
> no joke. And they would just turn around, and look and
> drop food and stuff! We would make sure that we sat
> around the most white people that we possibly could; and
> we would just talk about them, and just talk about them.
> And have the best time! I mean, I know it's mean, I know
> it's evil, but hell. Ok, I have no justification for it, I don't. I
> admit it, but I can't help it. I can't help myself. It's pay-
> back!

Specific incidents of racial discrimination often provoke a personal and collective sense of powerlessness. This pay-back action gives this young woman and her friends some sense of

power and the confidence that they often do not feel in the white university environment. The retaliation strategy works, it should be noted, only because some whites overreact to loud black comments on racial issues. Significantly, the young respondent shows concern over the meanness of her actions. Judging from our interviews—surprisingly, perhaps, given the scale of the racial hostility they face—even more aggressive revenge against whites is not an openly expressed goal of middle-class African Americans.

Many if not most whites grow up with few significant or intimate contacts with African Americans. Some may have had contact with a black domestic or yard worker; and some may have had fleeting contacts with black clerks in stores or one or two black employees in the workplace. Some have no contact at all. For that reason white preconceptions about black Americans stem mostly from parents, friends, teachers, and the mass media. Still, white prejudices can change with greater contact with black Americans, but the character of that contact is very important. Contact between those of unequal status, such as between servants and employers, will seldom have major positive effects. The racial "contact hypothesis" discussed in social science research proposes that contacts between blacks and whites must be between those of roughly equal social status for the contact to lessen white prejudices and stereotypes.[8] A research administrator at a southern university talked about how he helped a white associate deal with his prejudices:

> I'll tell you something that happened to me when I was in banking, I worked in the commercial finance division and I was supposed to go out and interview with somebody. I was the trainee, and this guy who was going out was an old-timer and stuff like that. But he told me, he said, "Listen, I never worked for black people." And in fact, he

didn't like black people because he told me that his grandfather told him black people were no good and to watch
out for them, that they were cheats and liars. I said, "You
know, my mother told me the same thing. Watch out for
white people. They're cheats, liars and thieves, and I've got
to be very careful around them!" And he realized over the
course of our relationship that all the things that he had
been taught was just rhetoric, but he says, "I can't change.
I've been taught this all my life." And by the time my little
tour of duty in that area was over, we became very good
friends. And that happens over and over and over again.
I've worked with people, I was almost the only friend of
this particular white guy that worked in this company. But
all he had seen, because he grew up in areas—people may
not believe this—but there are areas where white people
haven't actually seen a real black person.

Some of the whites described in this section belong to that
segment of white America for whom equal status contact with
middle-class blacks seems to have changed certain antiblack
attitudes. Yet a striking characteristic of the black middle-class
experience is that so many middle-class whites seem to be little
affected, especially in deep and lasting ways, by an increase in
contacts with these middle-class black Americans. The attainment by the black middle class of a status more equal to that of
the white middle class has not brought the fully integrated society that equal-status theory, and equality of opportunity laws,
would seem to have foretold.

Using Official Channels and Court Suits

A more formal or official response to discrimination can
range from writing a letter of protest to complaining to the
relevant government agencies or filing a lawsuit. An administra-

tor at a western university told the story of his wife driving past a white police officer who had given her an unclear signal. The officer hit her car hard with his fist, held her up in the middle of traffic, and then told her to get "that junk out of here." Reviewing the story, the administrator commented on how he prefers to handle mistreatment by working through channels:

> When I was younger, I dealt with it confrontation-style. But when I got older and smarter I dealt with it nonconfrontational-style. I deal with it through calling the proper people, writing the proper authorities, going through the proper channels and so forth. . . . Oh, for example, that same situation with that police officer who beat on the car and told her it was a piece of junk and told her to pull over. What she should have done was written down his badge number and then phoned it in. And enough people do things like that, a pattern clearly develops against policemen who do things like that.

This emphasis on using proper channels of institutional authority is remarkable given the problems that Africans Americans, including some in our sample (see Chapter 2), have with white police officers. In the recent past this type of protest would probably have been futile, if not dangerous. Yet this man's style signals how many middle-class African Americans have come to feel that the police system should be there to serve them. His resources have given him the grounds to demand respect as a citizen and taxpayer.

As we have documented in previous chapters, a number of our respondents have had to resort to threatening lawsuits or actually going to court to rectify maltreatment. A strong sense of justice and legal rights is evident in many of their specific accounts of discrimination. One account was given by an unemployed corporate executive in a northern state, who explored the implications and consequences of the litigation approach:

I got to a certain level, which is to say a middle-management level of the corporation. I was in line for a *major* increase in position, and that position was given to a white male who was brought from outside the area, outside the area of expertise of the project. . . . He had lesser education, he had lesser experience, so it would seem fit to use the old boy network to bring him into it and to see evidence that that probably happens to many people. And I believe the reaction on the part of a lot of the other blacks is to either resign themselves to putting up with it, and a large number of others end up simply quitting and going elsewhere, and all the effort that they've put into getting where they've gotten at that point in time goes down the drain. . . . Now in my particular case, I am currently unemployed; you know, I'm pursuing a lawsuit. And I'm unable to gain other employment since it's well known in the area where I live at that I am suing my previous employer. And since there is a protective order in place whereby I cannot discuss the specifics of the case, specifically what information we got from the various interrogatories and discovery material laying out what was done to me. But I cannot properly defend myself in front of potential employers, and, as a consequence, I'm affected so far as not being able to get employment. . . . It just kind of pulls you in and further essentially isolates you. . . . It's affected the way former associates, in the town I live in, particularly white associates, perceive and deal with me. It's a very overt avoidance at this point in time. It's even made black friends somewhat hesitant—black friends prior to the time I had to sue my previous employer, black friends who were very friendly toward me—after I had to sue and go into the situation I'm in right now, has made them hesitant so far as their relationships with me.

Seeking redress from discriminators in court, even if one wins, can be devastating professionally and personally. Given the isolation and possibility of retaliation, it is surprising that some middle-class black employees muster the courage to seek legal redress and jeopardize their current situations. Yet the black tradition of civil rights drives many to seek fair play. Despite the few legal recourses available to them, middle-class African Americans have in recent decades provided great and reinforcing support for the old U.S. tradition of protesting injustice.

Personal Coping Styles and Defenses

In addition to strategies for countering specific instances of white discrimination, middle-class black Americans have developed broader personal philosophies, coping styles, and protective defenses for dealing with the accumulating impact of racism on their psyches and lives. Broader life philosophies and perspectives are required because of the harshness, intensity, and prevalence of modern racism. Some costs of white racism are material; others are psychological. Psychiatrists William Grier and Price Cobbs have written that "people bear all they can and, if required, bear even more. But if they are black in present-day America they have been asked to shoulder too much. They have had all they can stand. They will be harried no more. Turning from their tormentors, they are filled with rage."[9]

Most white Americans do not have any inkling of the rage over racism that is repressed by African Americans. Asked how often she got angry about actions by white people, a professor at a western university replied:

Any time there's any injustice either done to me, or I see it or read about it, it makes me angry. I don't think any human being has the right to feel superior, or act superior, or

293

do things that say they're better than someone else, just because of the color of their skin. And every time I hear [about] incidents I get angry, it upsets me greatly. [So, would you say that's once a day, once a week, once a month?] In my profession you can hear it fifteen times on some days, it just depends on who you're seeing on that day, and what's going on in their lives.

The level of intensity this anger can reach is revealed in this vigorous comment of a retired professor in reply to the question, "On a scale of one to ten, where do you think your level of anger is?"

Ten! I think that there are many blacks whose anger is at that level. Mine has had time to grow over the years more and more and more until now I feel that my grasp on handling myself is tenuous. I think that now I would strike out to the point of killing, and not think anything about it. I really wouldn't care. Like many blacks you get tired, and you don't know which straw would break the camel's back. . . . And I'm angry at what's happening to our young people. I call it impotent rage, because it's more than anger, it's a rage reaction, but something that you can't do something about and that makes it even more dangerous when you do strike out.

Repressed rage over maltreatment is common, this professor argues later in the interview, to *all* African Americans. The psychological costs to African Americans of widespread prejudice and discrimination include this rage, as well as humiliation, frustration, resignation, and depression. Such high costs require major defensive strategies.

One strategy African Americans in all income classes use to cope is to put on their defensive "shields," the term used in a

294

conversation the first author had with a retired music teacher. Now in her seventies, this black informant contrasted her life with that of a white woman, who, like her, bathes, dresses, and puts on her cosmetics before leaving the house each morning. Unlike the white woman, this black woman suggested, she must put on her "shield" just before she leaves the house. When quizzed about this term, she said that for decades, before leaving home she has had to be prepared psychologically and to steel herself in advance for racist insults and acts, to be prepared even if nothing adverse happens on a particular day. One of our respondents, a physical education teacher, spoke to us of her "guarded position" in life: "I feel as though most of the time I find myself being in a guarded position or somewhat on the defense. I somewhat stay prepared to be discriminated against because I never know when it's going to happen to me." A teacher in the Midwest put it this way: Middle-class blacks "can't sit back and relax at all; you have to be vigilant at all times; if you don't you'll be back in chains." Psychologists Thomas and Sillen have argued that such a defensive approach is realistic; in order to survive, they suggest, a black person should assume that "every white man is a potential enemy unless he personally finds out differently."[10]

The high energy costs of this vigilance and of actually dealing with white racism over a lifetime were described by the retired professor quoted earlier:

If you can think of the mind as having 100 ergs of energy, and the average man uses 50 percent of his energy dealing with the everyday problems of the world—just general kinds of things—then he has 50 percent more to do creative kinds of things that he wants to do. Now that's a white person. Now a black person also has 100 ergs; he uses 50 percent the same way a white man does, dealing with what the white man has [to deal with], so he has 50 percent left. But he uses 25 percent fighting being black, [with] all the problems being black and what it means.

One way that African Americans consume personal energy is in determined efforts to succeed in the face of racism, including overachieving to prove their worth in the face of whites' questioning black ability and competence. A college graduate in a western city described how he felt about having to prove himself:

It's being constantly reminded that you're different, that you're not good enough, that you have to prove yourself, that you have to be better than average, just to be considered normal. . . . I am to the point now where when someone has a problem with my race, or my color, or my ability to be a human, and they only see me as an object, a black guy, a "blackie," I deal with it. When they have a problem, I leave it as their problem. I make sure that they understand that this problem that they're having is only theirs. If they have a problem with how I look, who I am, then maybe they should stop looking at me, stop associating with me.

The distress that comes from having to prove oneself in most situations has led this young black man to develop a defensive repertoire that includes making whites aware of who is at fault.

The professor quoted above explained a general approach many employ in dealing with whites:

I think sometimes I use the same strategy I've seen others use. I'll say that doesn't bother me, knowing it does. It's a matter of not letting it destroy you. So it's a matter of psychological strength. And I think most blacks have a tremendous amount of psychological strength. We're able to say this is unfair, but I won't let it destroy me. And that bulldog determination that you will not be destroyed, you will not be torn up, helps you to get over what I call many of the humps.

He tells blacks to recognize that discrimination is unfair, but to work to prevent it from destroying them.

Several respondents felt that it was common for black employees trying to prove themselves in white settings to overachieve, doing more than white employees with similar resources and credentials would have to do. Sprinkling his comments with some laughter, a professor at an eastern law school expounded on this strategy:

There's a lot of pressure, but one thing that there is, there is a byproduct of that that's good, because once you succeed, you *know* that you have the ability. There's no question about it, because you've had to do a little bit more than the next guy to even get through. Whereas we used to say when we were growing up, "If you're white you don't have any excuse for not succeeding in America." And if you're black and get into a position to pursue a certain goal, yes, you might have to work much harder, but that makes it a little bit better in the end, and a little bit more assured of your own ability. The way that things are done now is that everything that a black person does—not everything, but most of the things that some black people do—they try to discount it, say it's not as good, which is not true. And if you fall for that you really have a problem, but it's all a little game.

There is clearly a psychic cost to such an approach, yet there is also the benefit of knowing one has substantial ability when forced to demonstrate it.

Our interviews repeatedly demonstrated the importance of the inner strength required when African Americans enter indif-

297

ferent or hostile white worlds. A professor at a historically white university underscored the need for a healthy self-concept:

> You must develop some skills, but you also must develop a love of yourself, a liking of yourself. It's very important for you to do that. Now, the skills, that's difficult, because that's a very broad subject. You've got to put yourself in a position where you can learn, and sometimes you may be in a painful position, but once you have that confidence and the skills, you can make it. The liking of yourself is broader than just skills. . . . When you go to a predominantly white situation where people don't care about you, or a lot of them, and it's maybe even hostile at times, you need to love yourself. You truly need it. You need to get up in the morning and feel very self-contained.

This respondent links avoiding self-blame to liking oneself. Several of those with whom we talked discussed working to overcome excessive self-blaming inclinations, including this executive officer at a predominantly white chamber of commerce:

> Well, I think the thing that works for me is I know it's not me. And you're right, a lot of times when these crazy things happen, I'll sit down and call a friend. And then not even discuss that issue, but talk about something else. But the first part of my coping is to realize that I'm not the problem. I don't internalize it. And realize that I'm the victim, and so I don't blame the victim. I'm gentle on myself.

Psychologists Thomas and Sillen have suggested that, among blacks, anger at whites may be replacing self-derogation as a response to oppression. They suggest that this shift is a healthy sign, for it is saying, "I am condemning you for doing wrong to me."[11] From this perspective a positive means of coping results from a realistically targeted anger.

Young or old, the need to buttress one's self-image is a constant problem for our respondents. One college student, who has had epithets hurled at her by white students, explained that Stokely Carmichael's book *Black Power* had helped her strengthen her sense of self worth:

> This is crazy because I'm twenty-four, and all along I was
> thinking, "OK, he called me 'nigger,' he was just one,
> there's not a whole lot of them here." . . . But reading
> *Black Power*, I mean, we've always heard about the civil
> rights movement, and we've always heard about this, that,
> and the other, but *Black Power* to me was a little bit more
> in-depth than that. This man had a plan of what we needed
> to do in order to, I guess, consolidate or to establish some
> kind of solidarity. And he explained in a very, just rational,
> manner why it was needed. Because before, yes, we need to
> get together, you'd hear that all the time, "Unity, unity."
> But it seems like we've been doing OK without it—that
> was a lot of the older attitude. I can see that attitude. But
> reading that book I understand a little bit more about just
> how hard it [unity] is.

Exposure to the black power literature provided the student with a stronger sense of linkage to other black Americans and thus more confidence in dealing with the white campus culture.

Our respondents reported an array of creative approaches they find effective in keeping their sanity in the face of white racism. For some a candid dialogue with God is one approach, as in this statement of a state legislator:

> It's quite frustrating. I chew God out sometimes. I don't
> mean it in a blasphemous way, or cursing, but I mean like
> some of the minor prophets did, you know, "God what's
> your problem? You're not moving; you're not acting.
> What's the deal here? Why aren't you doing something

299

about this?" You see what I'm saying? You know, that kind of thing, and it's very frustrating. It's very hurting, because you go through the [black] community and when people say, "Oh, there's legislator Jones," and you tell people about being a good American, and doing this, and doing that, and you know really, you can't promise them much, not very much at all really.

Taking a Jeremiah-like stance, this legislator has addressed God to express her anger over how little she can do to help her constituents. Reflecting the deeply-felt religious heritage of African Americans, a probation officer in the South emphasized the importance of prayer and positive thinking:

Oh, I get angry. Frustrated. And then again, I pray. I remember back, I don't know, someone said, "What the mind can conceive and believe it can achieve." I've been a student of positive thinking, and I know if anybody can, I can. And that's the type of attitude I have to reach deep within myself to deal with that. . . . If not, it will eat you away and you'll wind up doing what we're seeing more and more of. I can remember when I grew up and I was growing up as a little kid, we didn't hear of suicides among blacks. But the older I get, the more prevalent suicides among blacks has taken place. A little godchild of mine, three months ago, took his life. Prime of his life. All because of these outside pressures, and he wasn't able to deal with them, a twenty-one-year-old kid. That's what I'm saying. You have to have an innermost strength to reach down and draw [on].

Using religious insights and resources to face racism has been at the core of black survival since slavery. The slave spirituals and much other prized religious music often refer to such conditions as a "home in Heaven" or to "rest, peace, and no more pain." Religion remains very important for many because the present

300

life is so difficult that African Americans hope that somewhere there is a better life. African American religion, including spirituals and other religious music, has long spoken of comfort and hope, as well as of resistance to oppression. From the beginning African American religion has been a foundation from which to critique white oppression and to work to try to transform a racist society.[12]

One other resource is often critical for black survival—the ability to laugh at one's fate and one's tormentors. In *An American Dilemma* Myrdal discussed the ways in which black southerners in the 1930s and 1940s used humor to deal with the gaping discrepancy between the American creed and discriminatory white behavior.[13] Throughout this book we have seen middle-class black respondents using humor and laughter to deal with poor treatment by whites. With great amusement a political consultant described how she and her husband were a fighting team: "Matter of fact, our hobby is to fight discrimination and challenge discrimination; that's a hobby for us. We've been doing it all our lives. We like it!" In conversations reviewing their encounters with whites, blacks sometimes say things like "I cut him, and he didn't even know he had been cut", or "I cut him so sharp, he didn't even bleed." In a particular situation such humor can be a means of covert retaliation, sometimes not even recognized by the white party but totally understood by other blacks. Such humor can help defang the white enemy, thereby protecting against retaliation. In difficult conditions humor can function to take some of the sting out of a situation or to side-step an action so that it goes by relatively harmlessly.

Numerous respondents chuckled or laughed as they gave accounts of encounters with whites. A college counselor at a western university explained this coping strategy:

Well, you know, one of the things that we've been able to use as a survival method is laughter. And there have been

301

times and situations where friends, feeling like I do now, we've been able to talk about something that was quite serious, but we've been able to make light of it. Well, not to make light of it, but to laugh at it, at how bad something really is, just turn it over. That's a survival method. . . . It's very important, in order not to be a statistic in terms of stroke or heart attack.

Chuckling at painful events helps lessen the stress and perhaps decreases the probability of greater anguish. Here laughing at tragedy is part of social interaction; this circle of friends is trying to manage psychologically the effects of mistreatment.

The ability to laugh at pain rather than being overwhelmed is at the heart of heroic advice a lawyer in a southern city had for younger blacks:

Having said all that, enjoy life. That'll get worked out over all these problems. There's a time to be serious, and there's a time to build, and there's a time to enjoy your life. And when all is said and done, don't be overcome by what you see, and by all means, don't let anybody else steal your joy. . . . And my attitude is real basic and simple, and that is, I may not live to see the struggle, the battle won, but my joy is just being right at this day in the struggle. We know how to get to the Promised Land. I just want to live to be in the fight.

Sources of Social Support

As we discussed briefly in Chapter 6, social and psychological support from family and friends is crucial in surviving daily struggles with whites. This may appear surprising to some white readers who have seen much discussion of black families as pathological, dysfunctional, and unable to provide their members sufficient sustenance.[14] However, the everyday reality is usually different, for most black families in all income classes have been strong enough to provide havens of refuge for generations. A law professor described this heroic heritage:

> Well, the love and the support and the understanding, they're important. It just happens that this past weekend, I went to a family reunion. And we traced our families' roots and we had a chance to all sit around and talk about the kinds of values that are important. My family comes from the South, and they were slaves. And we talk about the people who were slaves, but [with] a great sense of family, and a real understanding of the meaning of the concept of fear. Again, as I said, my people were slaves, they lived through Jim Crow, through the Depression, and found their way to the sustaining concepts, the sustaining philosophies, the sustaining wisdom, love, family, and support. Understanding the concept of emotional and psychological healing, then you are always making a move to make the wound heal. You also understand how to avoid wounds. You know there are situations where you may not go head on against racism, you may step aside, you may deflect it. And I think that my family has put a lot in me that has helped me to be able to at least lessen some of the effects.

Family support as a means of coping with oppression has a long history among African Americans. Harriette McAdoo has researched the family in many areas of Africa and compared it with the African American family. Among the salient dimensions of African family life are (1) an emphasis on kinship groups and tribal survival and (2) a guiding principle of humanitarianism and interdependence of members. Historically, there was a xenophilic rather than a xenophobic dimension to many African societies. Strangers were not automatically considered enemies.[15] Long before the intrusion of European slave traders and the enslavement in the Americas, the family system in west

Africa generally encompassed every person. This system proved its importance during slavery in North America. Despite the many and varied tribes, customs, and languages, and the inhuman destruction of many family bonds by white slaveholders, enslaved African Americans forged strong bonds in order to survive and escape. The importance of strong family bonds under slavery and segregation has been demonstrated by Herbert Gutman and other historians over the last two decades.[16]

A woman who worked as a clerical employee in the Midwest, then moved to the South where she holds a personal service job, discussed the role of family and friends:

> Oh, we discuss, you know, naturally blacks always get together and talk about it and what we're going to do. It's discussed, but most of my friends and even my family, my mother has always been afraid for me. Especially when, me moving here, because she knows that I'm not going to take anything, you know. So, she would always say, "Now, Jane, you know they're not like they are up here. You have to watch your mouth. You have to watch the way you say things to people because you know, you can be real cutting verbally." And I know I can. And she's just afraid that I might be one that they hang on a tree. Like my sons. I've always taught them to be proud and strong and they've had a couple incidents down here we had to discuss it, you know.

The half-joking reference to lynching is striking as a reminder of the psychological currentness of brutal practices that persisted into the 1980s.

Emotional support in the face of everyday racism is critical, as a corporate executive quoted earlier made clear: "[My family has given] me the, I guess, warm emotional support one needs that says, 'Keep pushing. Don't give up. Hang in there, and don't let things make you do things you'll regret later. Just do

304

the positive thing and recognize that it's going to take a long time.'" In managing encounters with racism middle-class black Americans are beginning to go to psychologists and psychiatrists. Until recently the great majority of mental health professionals have been white. These professionals, tending to make judgments in the form of white-normed diagnoses, have sometimes been considered the "enemy" in black communities. For example, for many years the anger and suspicion seen in black patients was too often diagnosed as paranoid schizophrenia. In recent years, however, mental health workers have examined these diagnoses more carefully and have found that for many black patients the feelings of anger and suspicion are reality-based and do not signal a psychosis. Very often the emotions have been generated by experiences with whites.[17]

The social support of black friends is grounded in shared experiences, a point accentuated by a social worker:

Well, I think I have some friends who validate my experience which keeps me sane. I think it's real important that you have blacks that you can go to, that you can say, this has happened to me, it is disturbing me. The [white] person will not acknowledge what they have done. Can you help me validate whether this is off or not? Having somebody that you trust, that's objective, that will tell you, "Hey, you were off there, you shouldn't have said that. They probably were being racist, but you should have dealt with it a different kind of way." But I think that my friends help me balance, because when you're in the midst of it, you get so hurt and so angry. It's like these two emotions running at the same time. It's like how dare they do this to me, that's the anger. Don't they realize that I'm a human being too? So, you have all these emotions happening at the same time inside of you, and you just need somebody to say, yea, this probably is happening to you, and this is how you can deal

305

with it. And my family, I was raised in a Christian home, and raised that you treat people the way you want to be treated.

Discussions with friends help by validating a black person's experience, as well as confirming one's sense of what is right and just.

Black organizations can also be places of refuge and sources of support. For example, one important survival tactic for black students encountering poor treatment at predominantly white colleges is to link up with local black organizations. A hospital supervisor and civil rights activist who lectures to black college students offered the following advice to those newly arrived at white campuses: "They should look up the black student organization on campus. . . . It is very important that they do this. A lot of what happens to black students that come to this university—I'm sure it happens in all of the big universities—is that their parents have mislead them. That's the reason the majority of them can't survive on that campus." She felt strongly that black students must join together on a white campus:

It is important that they hook up and become a very strong black organization member, to be there for each other. You can't walk that alone. You cannot be a lone black in a group of whites, because eventually that's going to wear so thin. . . . you need to first and foremost develop a real close relationship with the black organization. Go into the community, that's important, whether it's to the church, church activity, or a black organization in the community, but be a part of the community as well as part of the school community. Those are things that parents should tell their children.

From this point of view survival as an individual alone is impossible; only collective efforts ensure success. Thinking in a similar vein, one engineering student we interviewed on a white campus said: "I would have sought out more support groups."

The Role of Helpful Whites

In discussions with middle-class black Americans one senses a recognition that the problems of color discrimination in the United States will not be solved by either white or black Americans acting separately. Cooperation is deemed essential by most. On occasion, white reporters and colleagues of the authors have asked how helpful whites have been to middle-class African Americans as they have sought their personal goals in this society. Our respondents' answers to this question vary but most seemed to fall into two general categories: either they said they had not been helped by whites, or they cited one or two whites who had been important to them, often at a specific point in their lives. Into the first category fall respondents like this salesperson for an electronics firm, who was asked if any whites had been helpful in achieving his goals: "I wish I could think of someone, but realistically I really can't. And God forgive [me] if there was, and I don't remember. Maybe the system's had that much effect on me that . . . I can't bring it up to a conscious level."

Other respondents had a mixed reaction to the question. A human services manager in a northern city initially replied, "I can't think of any," but then qualified her answer with this comment:

> I've had white colleagues who have been very helpful in
> skills development. I tend not to be a numbers person, and
> hate dealing with the financial part of my job. I'm getting
> better at it, but there's a white woman at work who's been
> very good at helping me to do that. And at my old job,
> there was a white woman who—it's very funny, from a

very, very, wealthy family in the United States, worth millions, but acted very much in the manner in which it was comfortable for me, did not flaunt that station or position in life, and we got to be very close personal friends. In fact, she worked with me, and no longer lives in this city, but at that particular job, she was very helpful in helping me, in fact, to gain the skills, computer skills, and connection skills, that I needed to do that job well, and for that I'll always be grateful.

The whites mentioned here were helpful in particular areas of skill development, yet this woman made it clear in her interview that no white person had been broadly and fundamentally helpful to her achievements.

The response of a clerk in a vehicle parts department to a question about whether whites had been especially "helpful to you in achieving your goals?" was positive:

Yes. I would think so. They encouraged me. In fact, when I was deciding that I would bring this lawsuit against the company that I work for, I talked to this young guy—he's about thirty—and I asked him, I said, "I've decided I'm going to sue the company, so who should I go to for support, since the company's so large and I can't possibly do this on my own. Should I go to the National Organization for Women or the NAACP?" He said, "Why not go to the National Organization for Women because they are very visible and vocal. The NAACP is an old organization and they haven't done anything in a long time." This is a young white guy, He's now supervisor down where I work, but he wasn't then. He's still my friend, though. . . . I have, oh, the French class that I have, I study, all of those ladies support me and what I do. . . . There's a lady who works with me, she's part-time on this job, and the regular women in there won't associate with her for some reason or another. She's a

Mediterranean lady, a white lady, and we've become very good friends.

This woman found a white male supporter in a workplace where a number of whites had racially and sexually harassed her. Similarly, a banking executive in an eastern city mentioned some white friends as helpful, but not as central to her goal pursuits: "I've had some white friends who were there if I needed help, but no one who's pushed me and said, you can do it if you do this and do that, and you can achieve what you want. I think it's my own inner self who really wanted to do it, and went for it."

White friends are usually not knowledgeable enough about, or sensitive enough to, the U.S. racial situation to relate in a truly intimate way to the problems that their black friends face. Thus black students have noted that it is difficult to make close white friends, since few whites are willing to listen to their detailed accounts of or frustrations about racism on campus. We suggested in Chapter 5 that many white males, including some who see themselves as liberals, are defensive in the presence of black men, a point emphasized in an interview with a security supervisor in a western city: "I don't feel that I have too many close white male friends. . . . Just associates at work, but I really can't consider them close friends, because there's nothing that we share together. Most white males have a tendency to be defensive and not honest as to their relationship with a black male." He added that he had an easier time relating to white women at work. An airline customer service representative in the South spoke of the limitations of white friendships:

As sympathetic as white friends are, they don't understand. They just don't. They think: well, because we're friends, then surely they're not racist, so what's the whole problem, why are you even bothered about it? So I can't discuss it with white friends, and I do have white friends. . . . in the industry, the neighborhood, the situations that I'm in, there just aren't that many black people. So my husband and my family become the stabilizing force for bouncing off situations. And I guess just knowing that I'm not the only one who's experiencing it, you know, that safety in numbers.

This woman spoke of the insensitivity of even sympathetic white coworkers and neighbors to racist speech and action. For black Americans the most trustworthy white people may be those who candidly see themselves as "recovering racists."

The effort on the part of middle-class black students and employees to find nonracist or antiracist whites who are helpful and supportive can be vital to survival because most historically white organizations, including colleges, corporations, and governmental agencies, do not have enough black Americans for there to be a critical mass and supportive social networks. A professor at a northeastern university recommended seeking out sympathetic whites, in spite of the difficulties.

And then I think the other thing that blacks have to learn to do is to find whites in the system who are supportive and helpful to them, and there are such whites. I think that you can. . . . Some, even if they may have some attitudes that aren't totally liberated, they can sometimes still be helpful to people. And I think blacks have to learn how to utilize those kinds of resources, because if we don't, we won't make it, because there just aren't enough blacks in the system to serve that purpose.

Some respondents suggested that their relationships with whites in the outside world were strategic, somewhat like a chess game. A professor at a southwestern university explained how in some cases she was able to outthink whites with whom she was dealing, then added:

I'm also very good at figuring out who has the power to make decisions—of someone I might be talking to. I'm pretty good at getting the occasional white person to be interested enough in what I do to intervene on my behalf. And I think that's a skill, [finding out] who makes the decision, who because of a particular idiosyncrasy might be sympathetic to your case. And then you learn how to go to those white people, and make your case before them, and get them to intervene.

Preparing Children to Face Discrimination

Black middle-class parents face the daunting task of preparing their children for racial slights and obstacles. Many know well what playwright August Wilson has written: "Blacks know more about whites in white culture and white life than whites know about blacks. We have to know because our survival depends on it. White people's survival does not depend on knowing blacks."[18] In an important research study James Jackson and his associates found that black parents took several different approaches to teaching children about racial issues. Some avoided the issue and gave no information; some imparted messages stressing the equality of blacks and whites; and some taught their children to distrust whites and stand up for their own rights.[19]

In our interviews we found a greater variety of messages. Thus a law school administrator discussed his parents' view of whites:

I think they have subtly prepared me for different things. My father was always very conscious and said, "There're just a lot of things that you have to do to make sure that things are going to be okay for you. You've got to be care-

311

ful of what people think and how people see you." And I think those are the basic things that they've passed on to me, not suggestions of how to deal with discrimination, but how to avoid it. It's just like preventive medicine. We waste a lot of money trying to cure people instead of spending more money trying to prevent illness.

The father's cautionary socialization was based upon the preventive medicine of avoiding difficult situations. His warning to be careful of what white people think suggests another dimension of the black double-consciousness. In their book on counselling black clients, Peter Bell and Jimmy Evans have argued that in normal social interaction whites need to think mainly of how they see themselves and how other whites see them.[20] For middle-class blacks, however, social interaction is usually much more complicated. Seeing themselves in relation to how other blacks see them is compounded by the requirement to orient themselves to whites' (mis)understandings. African Americans must work through a psychological maze as they develop the necessary relationships with white Americans. Not only must they determine how they see the variety of whites (from blatant racists, to covert racists, to the culturally ignorant, to the truly color blind), they must ascertain how they see themselves *in relation to* whites (as inferior, equal, superior, powerless, or powerful). Such determinations start at an early age, and parents are a major source of advice on how to handle white hostility and discrimination. This means devoting considerable time and energy to a task with which white parents are not burdened.

Lessons are taught by example as well as by mouth. And avoidance is not the only lesson taught by parents. A television anchorperson in a southwestern city described his mother's strong personal example:

The [white] lady in front did not have to have her I.D. checked, and my mother had hers checked. Now the wom-

312

an in front was not even from the town, but then they asked my mom. And my mom was like, "Wait a minute, I've been shopping here for X amount of years, been living here all my life." She didn't tell them who she was. And she said, "and you're going to ask for my I.D.? I don't even want the groceries." And she left. But then she thought about it and said, "No, I'm going back and get the manager." And [once there she] said, "hey, I supply some money to this store, and I've been shopping here for years. And my son's in town, and my people are from here." And the guy was like, "Mrs. James, I know that name." Because he knew me. She said, "don't give me the green light because of what my son does. He's younger than me. I was here before he was, so [don't] think because he's an athlete that that's going to be the green light for me to write a check in this store and not get my I.D. checked. So, I saw her do that kind of stuff. So, it's rubbed off on me.

Notable here is the discretionary character of white power in moments of interaction with black customers. Assertive adults can create outspoken children; this man reported responding aggressively to the discrimination he encountered in his own daily rounds as an adult.

The theme of a legacy of collective wisdom about racism was touched on or discussed by numerous respondents. Alluding to this inherited wisdom, a hospital administrator in a northern city discussed the conflict she felt:

My goals, in terms of for myself and for my family, are in trying to teach them those inherited ways that others have learned and the wisdom that was passed on as to how to overcome racism, how to overcome discrimination, how to make yourself as good as anyone else to achieve and to accomplish. And I guess I can get hung up on the racism and discrimination, which is going to be there, but I think that

313

I'd rather get hung up on *my* attributes, on *my* success, on *my* qualifications, on *my* skills, on *my* intellect, and being able to overcome with strengths within myself the racisms that might be, you know, some of the stumbling blocks.

In the socialization of children there is some tension between teaching an unclouded knowledge of racism's realities and communicating a sense of personal strength and capability. In this woman's view black children should be taught there are major barriers, but they also need to be taught that they can be overcome—a difficult balancing act for parents.

However, a newspaper publisher suggested a cautionary note about teaching children too much optimism about American promises of equal opportunity: "I think we owe an obligation to our children to teach them about racism and how to deal with it, instead of giving them the false impression that if you get a good education, if you go to the better schools, if you appease the white man, then you will not have to really deal with racism." In the United States there is much exhortation to work hard and strive to succeed as individuals. In this philosophy of life personal failure is to be accepted as one's own fault. But this philosophy only makes sense if the social game is fair. An executive officer at a white chamber of commerce spoke of teaching young blacks the hard lesson that the game is rigged against them:

I think that, again, our children have got to realize that things really aren't fair, that there are barriers out there, that there are additional barriers, there are barriers in this world, and that everything that we face isn't because we're black. But we're going to face a certain amount of things that are because we're black. And I think if we teach our children on the front end of that tunnel, that that doesn't have to stop anything. We may have to figure out a different strategy, we may have to decide that instead of running

IBM, we're going to run our own multinational corporation.

In her view, teaching black children about racial hostility is important, but so is teaching them how to circumvent the barriers they will face.

Not surprisingly, a number of respondents urged young black people to fall back on friends and family to bolster their sense of self. A university professor had the following recommendations for black youth:

> [I recommend] that they talk to other people about it constantly, because I think you need every sense of reinforcement that you can get—that you can get from your friends, people that are going through the same things, from your family, from your teachers, from any well-intentioned human being, who seems to have some inkling that when you say that things are happening to you, you are telling nothing but the truth, that you are not imagining that things are going wrong, that you are not imagining that you're being oppressed. What you need is to have constantly reinforced your sense that the world is not fine, and you are . . . fine, and doing the best that you can under circumstances that are fairly horrendous. That's what I tell my students all the time, because what they tend to do is blame themselves for what happens to them.

White denial that the discrimination individual black Americans face is serious adds the burden of reality testing and fighting self-doubt to the burden of the discrimination itself.

Emotional support is critical to the black struggle. One mother, a therapist at a hospital, was blunt about getting black children, and black males generally, to share their pain: "I encourage my boys to share feelings. Not none of that macho shit where you fall down, and your knee's hanging off and you say,

315

'Don't cry, be a man.' And that's where a lot of our black men have gotten totally messed up at. It hurts, you cry."

Sharing one's pain and frustrations about life's troubles, including white oppression, was also recommended for blacks of all ages. A drug program director in the Midwest made this point:

> There is a population of older blacks, though, that are—
> like, my grandmother died when she was ninety-one—that
> don't like to talk a lot about that emotional pain that's
> there. . . . But there's an older population of blacks, when
> you start asking some of those [discrimination] questions,
> and they will choose not to talk about it because it hurts
> too bad. So, I agree we need to talk. But we need to also be
> encouraged by, and encourage, those [black Americans] be-
> cause a lot of times they don't want to talk about it.

A social welfare program director, also in the Midwest, commented on the cost to all African Americans of repressing anger and rage over racism:

> [We need] to teach them, our people, how to talk about it
> and how to identify what it is. Because quite a lot of what
> we keep inside of us prevents us from being comfortable
> about who we are and where we want to go. I really be-
> lieve that. I feel that a lot of us hold back our frustration
> and emotional pain because either we have not been able to
> have that permission or learn how to talk about those
> things. . . . We can get out of that negative environment of
> feelings in the mind.

Conclusion

We cited in Chapter 1 the view of Brittan and Maynard that the terms of racial and gender oppression are "profoundly shaped at the site of the oppression, and by the way in which oppressors and oppressed continuously have to renegotiate, re-construct, and re-establish their relative positions in respect to benefits and power."[21] Today the interaction of blacks and whites in discriminatory situations has some similarities with that of the era of rigid segregation, but there are significant differences. The arrival on the scene of significant numbers of middle-class African Americans with substantial resources and power has created many situations where white Americans are forced into more explicit racial negotiation and where whites' assumptions of low black power are challenged. In the examples we have examined we frequently observe middle-class blacks establishing "power credibility," as whites realize that the blacks are not bluffing. Whether this perception will last beyond the particular incident is not clear, but it is a major change from the old racism.

Consequential too in this period of modern racism are the changing legal structure, the institutionalization of civil rights laws, and black Americans' belief in legal rights and civil justice. These statutes are momentous not only in themselves but also in the effect they have had of reinforcing the robust sense of justice that is a part of the black middle-class approach to everyday racism. In numerous accounts we have noted this black sense of justice due, of the right to fair play. The irony is that these African Americans are simply demanding to be treated like the average white person in this ostensibly democratic society.

Changes in interpersonal negotiation have not meant that the costs of discrimination have been eliminated. Throughout this book we have reported the individual and collective price paid in dealing with life crises created by the omnipresent white dis-criminators. The anger of many middle-class black Americans is intense, if often repressed, or channelled into overachieving and hypertension. We have also observed the remarkable and perva-sive ability of African Americans to laugh at adversity. And we have seen the vital support of family and friends. The tremendous energy drain caused by discrimination has taken a toll on black achievement and performance. The exceptional achievements of these Americans have come in spite of, and in the face of, energy sapping racism. A central dilemma in fighting the internal stress of racism is how to cultivate a strong self-image, not only in oneself but also in one's children. At the heart of this positive self-image must be an enduring appreciation of black achievement and group worth, an avoidance of self-blame, and a recognition of the persisting flaws in the U.S. social system.

Chapter Eight

Changing the Color Line: The Future of U.S. Racism

Today blatant, subtle, and covert discrimination against
African Americans persists in virtually all aspects of their
public lives. Racism is central to the lives of white Americans
too, even though many whites deny its presence or effects. Racial discrimination is pervasive, and cumulative and costly in its
impact. Is there any hope for significant change? Near the end
of most interviews with our middle-class respondents we asked
several questions about future U.S. racial relations: whether
they saw things getting better or worse for black Americans in
the next few years; what major changes they would most like to
see in white society; and what they feel black Americans should
be doing to fight discrimination. Their responses open up interesting windows into how they view this society's racial order
now and in the future.

But their responses offer more than just another view of the
racial order. Understanding their perspective is crucial to taking
major steps to combat white racism. Why should white Ameri-

cans listen to these black voices? When one considers the loss of prestige and honor for the United States when governments and the mass media overseas critique outbursts of U.S. racism; when one calculates the human costs and multibillion dollar property losses of racial riots in the last decade in cities from Miami to Los Angeles; when one reads numerous reports of escalating hate crimes against black and other minority Americans; when one becomes aware of the terrible loss of human energy, talent, and achievements that results from black struggles with every-day racism; and when one examines the disintegration of the social fabric of cities where many black youth have lost hope of attaining the American dream, a white person has excellent reasons to listen to the voices of those most affected by racism.

But these voices must not only be listened to, they must be *heard*. Sadly, black and white Americans mostly live in separate worlds and often do not speak the same language. Our respondents regularly show how they and other African Americans are often not "seen" or "heard" by white Americans in everyday settings. Too often whites see no reason why they should "know" blacks, except perhaps in a special situation where a token black person will be called on to speak for all black Americans. Unless we find better ways to communicate, for whites to listen to black Americans, the "two societies, one black, one white—separate and unequal" that the prophetic Kerner Commission envisioned will never change, and racial violence will become all but inevitable. The recent call of some Ku Klux Klan leaders and other white supremacists for a racial war against people of color comes doubtless because they feel the time is ripe to attack.

A first step toward change is for white Americans to admit the reality of current white racism, a point underscored by a university researcher:

I get sick and tired of seeing things on television, white people saying that "people aren't racist any more." That's a lie.
They are racist. They don't want to recognize it, they refuse
to recognize it. They say, "Let's not think about the past."
Well, how do you go forward in the future if you don't
think about the past? . . . You still have people in 1989
saying that same stuff. They do studies on the size of people's brains; they do studies on whether or not a black athlete is better than a white athlete, and this kind of stuff,
which in itself says that this place is still racist. So, I would
like for them to go ahead and, you know, it's almost like
being an alcoholic. Admit that you're an alcoholic and go
on to solve the problem.

Until whites recognize that they have been raised in a racist
society and harbor its hidden influence even when they deny it,
until whites recognize that they too must take action to deal
with personal and societal racism, no matter how subtle, and to
eradicate it, the racial situation in the United States will only
worsen. Once most whites recognize that they and the system
their ancestors created are deeply racist, then most black Americans will doubtless be willing to cooperate and be patient as real
programs to eradicate racism are created. This task of educating
white Americans will not be easy, but it is possible. Once the
problem is admitted, the solutions can at least be envisioned and
implemented.

The Present and Future

Few respondents were strongly optimistic about the future of
racial relations in this nation. The majority realistically and
candidly characterized the present and the immediate future as
bad or getting worse. Among those who expected the situation

321

to get worse, some pointed to internal community problems such as drugs and changing family structure, and some focused on racism in the external society. In a pessimistic comment a high school teacher in the North took the position that the larger society will continue to stagnate: "I don't see that there's going to be a horrendous amount of change. I think that if we had a president who was a little bit more dynamic, or a little bit more helpful to blacks, there might be some. But as it is, . . . I see no change in the way things have gone." Some made an even stronger argument that the progress in rolling back racial discrimination from the 1950s to the 1970s had been reversed between the early 1980s and the early 1990s. An academic counsellor commented: "It seems that things are getting worse. It seems like one minute things are going well, and we're progressing. But then within a short period of time, it looks like it's reverting and going back into a backwards kind of situation. One time we felt that prejudice and discrimination was in the past. But now, it seems like it's worse than ever." She continued with a mixture of hope and pessimism: "You would think that by now everybody would be loving each other and caring, but it's just not working out that way. There's always something bad to keep it from being what it should be. I think it's going to get worse before it gets better again. It's kind of bleak when you look at it."

Government action to eradicate prejudice and discrimination has oscillated in recent decades. From the early 1980s into the 1990s African Americans experienced a conservative backlash against an aggressive expansion of civil rights and economic opportunities for minority Americans. A survey of young Americans by Hart Research Associates found that the younger generation has a pessimistic view of the present and future. Among black youth a majority thought U.S. racial relations were "generally bad," and just under half of the white respondents agreed. On a related question, the black youth were more likely than the white youth (46 percent versus 30 percent) to feel that racial relations were getting worse.[1]

Our respondents mentioned specific reasons for being pessimistic about the future of racial relations. There was great concern about the conservatism on racial issues in the U.S. political and judicial systems, especially the decisions of the conservative U.S. Supreme Court since 1980. Several major decisions in the mid- to late-1980s made it much harder for blacks to sue for redress for racial discrimination. One of these cases was *Wards Cove Packing Co. v. Atonio* (1989), an employment decision decided in favor of the employer that made it more difficult for minority plaintiffs to establish a prima facie case of discrimination and reduced employers' responsibility to justify business practices that have discriminatory effects.[2]

Noting that things are "definitely getting worse," a bank manager in an eastern city explained the backward movement: "Supreme Court decisions are already reversing all the civil rights legislation. It's going to be harder for you to prove discrimination. Everything is being turned around." She observed that African Americans had become complacent rather than vigilant:

And I think that's becoming so because we have gotten so relaxed and laid back and thinking that everything is on the up and up, when it's not. I think that they have given us a false sense of security by letting some of us achieve our goals. We're being carefully manipulated by them, because I probably am a token. I know I'm a token. But you're going to have that in this society, because we don't have the economic strength to put ourselves in these positions. But I think we have a false sense of security, and they're just going to put a double whammy on us, because sooner or later they're going to start reducing whatever we had before.

323

A strong sense of the history of U.S. racial relations underlies most of our interviews, together with a sharp awareness of the possibility of retrogression in public policy. Numerous respondents explicitly or implicitly indicated that current gains, including their own, represented a tenuous advancement that was being, or could be, rescinded by whites in power. A law school administrator was explicit about the signal the Supreme Court was sending:

> I think I see it getting worse. I mean, the recent Supreme Court decisions will tell you that. Those decisions are eroding away or taking away all the gains that—when I was coming along, we used to march and protest to get the laws passed, Title VII and the laws against discrimination. Okay, that [court action] sends a signal to the rest of the, to the white community, that, "Hey, you don't have to treat them as well as you used to."

With some laughter he noted the gallows humor at his law school:

> And in fact that's one of the jokes around here at the law school, between whites and blacks, is that every time they come out with a new decision, they say, "You better start learning how to shuffle again." "Tap dance, or something, because it looks like they're trying to put you back into slavery, right?" And that's the attitude. And employers— once they see this, I mean, that's just a green light for them to not use affirmative hiring procedures and promotions.

Several respondents touched on the damage to the black cause done by the Republican administrations in the 1980s and early 1990s. The director of a midwestern drug treatment program denounced governmental cutbacks in safety net programs:

324

Worse, primarily because we just went through eight years, the last eight years presidentially have taken away everything that was done in the sixties and the seventies. I mean, like we were talking about how Bush's new drug plan, the money that he's allocating is not even putting us back up to where we were before Reagan came back. Educationally, they've taken away programs that we fought for in the sixties and the seventies. Head Start programs, programs like that, are consistently being cut out.

Since the 1960s the Republican party's stance on civil rights issues has been perceived by a majority of African Americans as retrogressive and inimical to black interests. The historical evidence, though not yet compiled in a systematic way, seems supportive of their view. In his research Chandler Davidson has shown that, during the lifetimes of our respondents, the Republican party has intentionally abandoned black voters for a strategy targeting the concerns of white voters. From Barry Goldwater in the 1960s to Ronald Reagan and George Bush in the 1980s and 1990s, the Republicans' political campaigns adopted a strategy of aggressively seeking the votes of white suburbanites and Southerners to reinvigorate the party. Racial codewords such as "quotas," "busing," and "crime in the streets" have often been used, and white-oriented media campaigns have been developed, even though they are often offensive to the nation's black citizens.[3] As a professor at a western university put it, one sees "in the Reagan and Bush administration a dismantling of the whole Civil Rights acts . . . [and] that says racism is alive and well and kicking, and we will allow it to flourish."

Questioning the Republican administrations' cuts in social programs, our middle-class respondents expressed their concern for poorer blacks. In recent years, authors on the right and on the left have been critical of middle-class blacks' alleged insen-

325

sitivity in forgetting the black poor or the larger black community.[4] In a 1980 *Newsweek* column Chicago journalist Leanita McClain, who saw herself as "uncomfortably middle class," replied to such critics of the black middle class: "The truth is we have not forgotten; we would not dare. We are simply fighting on different fronts."[5] Similarly, there is little evidence in our in-depth interviews of a lack of middle-class concern or sense of responsibility for blacks who are less affluent. Expressing a sense that things are getting worse, a psychologist in the Southwest was articulate on who suffers most:

> I worry. It really feels like a struggle. Yes, you know, the "good little colored folks," and those handful of folks that are bright enough, talented enough, and at the right place at the right time where they let the one in the door, they're going to do o.k. So, you and I will do fine. It's this other class of folks who are not quite as advantaged as we are, who didn't have quite the academic skill, who don't have quite the family money resources, or who come from a little more unhealthy families, that I really worry about.

In some of the later interviews we asked specifically whether the respondents felt that middle-class black people have a special responsibility for their poorer brothers and sisters. There was substantial agreement that the black middle class had such a responsibility, as role models, educators, supporters, and advocates. The range of "dues" owed was suggested by a college graduate working for a western telephone company:

> We owe them our respect. We owe them our identity. See, we owe them much more than what we can give them. We not only have to be role models for them, but we have to help them, we have to encourage them by any means possible. Not by financing their entire existence, not giving them

326

a hand out, but teaching them to beat the system, by study-
ing hard, getting good grades, and using this thing called
scholarships and grants and work study programs to get an
education. We need to educate them on how to build their
self-esteem and their self-respect, so that they can stand
firm and lift their chin and be proud of who they are and
what they are. . . . We have to break the arm of the oppressor on our necks. We have to lift each other up by
supporting each other, being a guide, a road map, a light in
the darkness.

In our observations many, if not most, African Americans in the
middle class have reflected regularly on their obligations and
duties to the larger black community. Many of our respondents
would agree with a central proposal in *Rethinking the American
Race Problem*, a recent book by Roy Brooks, a black law professor. Brooks proposes that middle-class black Americans
should take an even more active role in helping working-class
and poor black Americans, acting as role models, giving financial support, and teaching consumer savvy and racial survival
techniques.[6]

Evaluating the present and future, some of those we interviewed were concerned about the need for broad economic
changes. The drug program director commented on worsening
economic conditions: "I find it very difficult to be black in white
America. And I think that it didn't used to be that way, it's
changed. And the changes aren't positive. Anymore, you see
change and it's not as positive. There are fewer people working
in the workplace, there've been many replacements and remov-
als of blacks. It's just, you know, we need to make strides for us,
and we've seen some backwards movement." Reflecting on similar issues, the owner of a small business in the Southwest noted
the decline of U.S. industry and the excessive reliance on products from overseas:

327

I see things, unfortunately, I see things getting worse for blacks in the next few years. Not only for blacks. Things will get worse for America, for all Americans, over the next few years, as I stated earlier. . . . American industries are shutting down everyday. We're getting all our products from some other country, which means that those jobs that people had are no longer there. So, if America is going downhill in terms of job market and everything else, then certainly that includes blacks even more so, because unfortunately blacks are already behind in the job market and what their earnings are.

Economic restructuring, sometimes called deindustrialization, has been offered as one major explanation for the development of a black "underclass" in central cities by scholars as diverse as Sidney Willhelm and William J. Wilson.[7] The capitalist market has become increasingly global over the last two decades, and many U.S. corporations now operate and employ around the world. This global employment market has made cheaper labor available to U.S.-based firms, and as a result millions of industrial workers have lost jobs because of plant closings or employment cutbacks. Following restructuring layoffs, black and other minority workers have often had the most difficulty finding new employment.[8]

A staff assistant to a state legislator noted how deindustrialization has affected middle-class black Americans:

You know, manufacturing is no longer the thing, we're an information economy, whatever that means, and increasingly the economic opportunities that come open are going to be fewer and fewer for us on a lot of different levels for a lot of different reasons, so I think things are getting worse, so I think that's going to force us to get up off our butts and do something. I've often said that, I said back in 1980, I think Ronald Reagan getting elected is going to be the best thing in the world that could happen to black folks because it was going to jar us into believing that everything wasn't o.k. Well, eight years did a lot for us, I think. I think the Reagan presidency was the absolute most anti-African American presidency in recent decades. And I think that was good for us, because we had too many of our black middle class people saying that everything's o.k. now, I have mine, now you get yours, but they saw that they were only one paycheck away from those 'bobo niggers' that they always talked about on the east side. So, when they started to lose those paychecks they started to understand.

Mixing economic analysis with commentary on some middle-class blacks who, if only temporarily, turned their backs on the poor, this young activist emphasized a point most respondents seem to sense, that those who have moved into the middle class find themselves no more protected from racism than the less fortunate. As we have suggested earlier, there is a chilling political dimension to current U.S. economic restructuring, for since 1980 there has been a resurgence of white supremacy groups and perspectives, the latter only thinly disguised in the electoral campaigns of men like Louisiana's Republican senatorial candidate and presidential hopeful, David Duke, an ex-Nazi and an ex-Ku Klux Klan leader.

With some frustration a university professor commented on the broader implications of restructuring in the U.S. economy:

I see things getting worse, and that has to do with the way the dominant society is using and allowing blacks to be scapegoated. It's a market economy that's failing at certain sites, and that's at the life of most human beings, and succeeding wonderfully at the site of upper-class economic participation. Given that it's failing, and that one way to make sure that an economy that's failing that many people, is that you find a group or groups that you can blame for the failure. And black folks exist as a group that everybody can blame for what's going wrong. We can blame the economy on them, because we can say they're not a productive group and a lot of the economy is being spent taking care of them. Because, of course, Americans don't read that a lot of the economy is being spent taking care of wealthy people in the defense industry. But since most Americans don't see it that way, black folks are causing us to spend money because they're poor, and they don't contribute anything, because they're criminals and it costs a lot to maintain them, because they're drug addicts and drug pushers, and we have to spend a lot in order to stop the drug trade. With all that being played out, I don't see how things can get better, because Americans as a group are not taught to think about what's happening to them.

Thomas and Mary Edsall have explained the 1980s' white backlash against social welfare and civil rights programs in terms of what they view as the pro-black actions of liberals in the Democratic party since World War II. As these authors see it, the white middle class as a group has accepted equality of opportunity for black Americans and has accepted the civil rights laws of the 1960s, but has never approved of affirmative action and other aid programs for black Americans, programs that in the Edsalls' view were forced on white voters by liberal white elites. Adopting a white-voter strategy, the Republican party attacked these liberal-elite policies in order to establish a new conservative ideology radically opposed to "special preferences and quotas" for black Americans.[9] Widely accepted by other white commentators on racial matters in the United States, this argument views white liberals as abandoning the needs of other whites and cozying up to blacks, whose needs are somehow exaggerated. Few of our respondents show any inclination to buy into such an argument. They do not feel coddled by elite white actions and programs. They do not see the white majority as strongly committed to truly equal opportunity or the enforcement of civil rights laws. In the view of the professor above the central problem of U.S. society lies not in the modest social programs supported for a time by white elites, but in the fact that the capitalist market economy (capitalists' actions) has failed large numbers of workers and their families, in all racial and ethnic groups, while from 1980 to 1993 the rich often got richer under conservative economic and political policies. African Americans like this professor are aware that blaming the problems of a declining or stagnating capitalist economy on black Americans has a long history."

Changes Sought: The Dominant White Society

The solutions to racial conflict proposed by some prominent white scholars contrast sharply with the views of most of our respondents. For example, George Keller, a prominent white educator, has played down the centrality of racial discrimination and blamed black leaders for black problems in education: "Petulant and accusatory black spokespersons will need to climb off their soapboxes and walk through the unpleasant brambles of their young people's new preferences and look at their young honestly."[10] In recent years this blame-the-victim perspective has resurfaced with vigor, taking hold on much white thought about racial issues, yet it is fundamentally out of touch with the black experience of persisting racism.

The contrast with the social changes sought by middle-class black Americans is indeed striking. When we asked the respondents what they would most like to see changed in the larger white-dominated society, most of the changes fell into two broad categories: either political, economic, and educational reforms, or changes in attitude among whites. At the societal level they call, among other things, for new economic support

331

programs, for new educational programs that deal realistically with black Americans and white racism in U.S. history, for enforcement of civil rights laws, and for greater equality and the redistribution of power. At the personal level they call for major changes in whites' stereotypes about African Americans, in whites' understanding of the black struggle and the courage it requires, and in whites' commitment to fair play and equal opportunity. African Americans are clearly one of the important carriers of the radical American tradition of championing full social, economic, and political rights.

Only in times of national prosperity and expansion does it appear that the majority of white Americans are willing to consider serious government programs to address the needs of less privileged citizens, especially those who are not white. Even then, most whites do not view the stratified character of this society as especially problematical.[11] In contrast, the middle-class black Americans with whom we talked often think in terms of power and inequality and underscore the justice of redistributing resources from the privileged to those in need. A director of planning at a university called for restructuring the support system for those without adequate food and shelter:

> It's a easy answer, and an impossible one to achieve, probably. I'd like to see change [in] the process and structure of providing the wherewithal for people to live in the country. This society is . . . sufficiently wealthy to enable those who are less fortunate to live in decent housing, to be able to give birth to children who have a chance to survive, to be able to provide the kind of nourishment that will facilitate the growth and development of offspring and to be educated in a way that does not demean their children. This may sound revolutionary, and if that's what it is, then so be it. . . . You have children who . . . lack a lot of the basic

things that they need in order to survive. And you have a
system that says that they lack these things because they are
not as able as other children. What nonsense, what nonsense!

These words describe basic economic support programs as "revolutionary," only a quarter century after President Lyndon
Johnson's War on Poverty and a half century after President
Franklin Roosevelt's statement calling for implementation of a
broad economic bill of rights, which included the "right to earn
enough to provide adequate food and clothing" regardless of
"race or creed."[12] In a similar vein, a college professor commented on the economic education of affluent whites. In her
view these middle-class whites must experience the economic
misery of people of color in order to see who the real economic
oppressor is: "What I think, unfortunately, has to happen for
things to get better, is for large groups of white people to be even
more oppressed than, say, poor white people are oppressed now,
and for them to be oppressed to the extent that they can no
longer escape the fact that it's not the fault of blacks, or Chi-
canos, or Vietnamese boat people."

Real change requires many whites to make major sacrifices,
to give up power and privilege. A student at a historically white
university proposed that whites must sacrifice because of the
history of racial exploitation:

Oh, yes, they sit around and talk about, "Yes, we want
equality for everybody." They want it on their own damn
terms. They want it when they are ready. They want it
when they don't have to sacrifice shit. And that's why
they're mad about affirmative action because they have to
sacrifice. I mean to get any long-run gain, logically, you do
have to sacrifice. I'm sorry, black people have been doing
the sacrificing for the last couple of hundred years, I think
it is the white man's turn, thank you.

333

For many whites the image of Dr. Martin Luther King, Jr., is one of a moderate leader, yet in an interview not long before his death, King argued that whites must sacrifice for real change: "White America must recognize that justice for black people cannot be changed without radical changes in the structure of our society."[13]

In the last decade numerous media discussions have focused on the changing demographics of the United States; white Americans are projected to lose their voting majority in the twenty-first century, a diminishment of power that alarms many whites. Among those we interviewed, several saw the erosion of white power as underway; a manager in an East Coast firm was eloquent:

> I would like to see the [white] fear to be gone. Because it really is a matter of fear, in my view. And fear is really a false expectation about reality. But, you see, one needs to understand how this whole thing operates. The whole discrimination issue is really one of power. And it's one of money. And it's one of knowledge. And that white power base has been eroded over the years, because of some of those struggles of our parents, and their parents, and so forth. And now we are, we certainly have access to the knowledge, and to the education, in ways we never did before. And some of us are getting access to the money. But still, when you look at the statistics, we're not nearly where, we're not nearly comparable in terms of our earnings compared to our white counterparts.

In the United States the changing demographics, the growing number of Americans with non-European roots, do not necessarily entail a speedy shift of power to the underdog. This manager commented on the chilling prospect of a shift in the direction of a society such as South Africa: "When I look forward—you may be familiar with some of the information on Workplace

2000, when people of color in the population will exceed white people in this country. And unless that's really managed very carefully, at the worst end you could have a South Africa, where you have the whites still in power and the minorities just kind of out here trying to get it."

One institution targeted for change by our respondents is the U.S. educational system. A student at a mostly white university wanted education changed for the sake of black children:

> I think the educational system is very important because there are a lot of young blacks who go around in life not knowing a thing about themselves and their past, because all their days in school they've been taught about Christopher Columbus, the Greeks, Charles Darwin, and all the rest of these so-called great Europeans in history. And they're not taught anything about their own past dealing with ancient African history, the accomplishments of blacks in history in America, etcetera. And as a result, black people still have a deep inferiority complex when they go out in the world, which in effect in many ways affects their self-esteem, their self-worth, their self-pride.

Black children are not the only ones shortchanged by white-dominated school curricula. A southern newspaper publisher argued for more fundamental changes in how black and white children are taught:

> I think that if our children, and I say, our children, I'm not talking about just black children, I'm talking about white children, if they were educated with black history, not as black history, but as a part of American history, if black teachers were encouraged in the classroom, if parenting were taught in school as a class, then I think those factors would contribute more to changing America than anything. Because I have seen where you cannot legislate mental atti-

335

tudes, you cannot politicize mental attitudes, you cannot purchase mental attitudes, you have to educate. And education starts at a very, very early age, kindergarten. The point is that if we could ever get to that extent to where when you open the history book, you not only see the George Washington Carvers and the Booker T. Washingtons and the Martin Luther Kings, but you see the Charles Drews, and you see all the other people that we don't read about, and the fact that black people created mathematics—those things aren't taught.

Adding another angle to this perspective, a student at a private university felt strongly that whites must learn to respect black opinions and priorities:

The white world and the European world and the majority culture have to start taking the Third World and black people and minority cultures seriously and treat them as adults and respect them and respect their opinions. That's it. They're just going to have to stop telling us what's best for us and giving us what's best for us, and we're going to have to start making what's best for us and taking what's best for us.

Since the late 1970s some educators, black and white, have called for the integration of the school curriculum at all levels, and many discussions and debates have centered on the need for multicultural materials and teaching. Protesting the many multicultural courses and programs that have been implemented, white, especially conservative white, commentators in a series of influential books and articles have attacked multiculturalism as a bastardization of the curriculum.

In our view black demands for educational change are sensible and realistic—if this nation wishes to survive to the end of the next century. The so far modest changes in the direction of a multicultural curriculum in U.S. schools and colleges do not yet go nearly far enough. Much more multiculturalism in every aspect of U.S. schooling is necessary. Multicultural teaching must be tough and deep; it must examine the racist history and present of the United States. This type of broadened education is one way to begin to eradicate white racism. The attacks on multicultural education led by such white luminaries as Arthur Schlesinger, Jr., in recent years are shortsighted, even in terms of the self-interest of white Americans. We agree with some of our respondents that a better and broader education for whites is essential.

Changing White Attitudes

A better curriculum in the schools and colleges should ameliorate whites' misunderstanding of U.S. racial history, but white attitudes toward blacks derive from more than cultural and historical ignorance. Some opinion survey data on whites' racial views indicate a significant improvement in recent decades.[14] Yet there are problems with these data, as the lives of the African Americans we have examined document. The surface-level character of white responses often may not tap the deeper feelings of many whites in regard to black Americans. In addition, if one examines the blatantly racist responses to some recent survey questions, some 20 to 40 percent of whites show themselves to be very racist, if not segregationist. And other recent surveys show that a majority of whites hold some racist stereotypes of blacks as lazier than whites and as more violent than whites.

Middle-class African Americans, like other African Americans, express great concern about these racist attitudes; our respondents had several suggestions for bringing about changes in them. Whites must learn to understand the black experience with racism and to feel black pain and anger. A school administrator asserted the need for whites to walk in a black person's shoes:

> Whites need to become educated. White folks need to make
> an all out effort to learn what it is to be black. They need
> to see America from Africa to these shores; they need to
> live and process me. When I say me, I'm talking about
> what it is to be black. Learn me, try to process what I've
> been through. Try to understand what I've been through in
> order to think the way I think. Try to see things the way I
> see them, or I've seen them.

Answering a question about required changes in white society, a southern television broadcaster asked that, rather than "lumping us all together and still seeing us the way their mothers and their fathers saw us," whites abandon "ingrained attitudes about black people." She pled for a better understanding of the heroism blacks exhibit:

> I don't think they really understand how brave and coura-
> geous and strong and all those wonderful, positive things
> we are, but if they would just think for a minute how we
> were able to survive slavery, they would understand then.
> You know? If you asked them, if you sit down and let them
> look at "Uncle Tom's Cabin," which was on cable the other
> night, and say, "Do you think you could've survived that?
> Do you think you could've survived the beatings and the
> hangings and your daughter being taken away from you
> and taken to the massa's house to sleep in his bed?" And
> you know, I mean, we survived that, and we still came out
> reasonably sane.

A receptionist at a major corporation in the South expressed her wish that whites would understand the reality of racial inequality and oppression:

338

In the dominant white society I would like to just for one time in life, to see them be real, if they know what being real is. . . . Being real is to stop asking black people, "What do you want or what else do you want? We've given you this, What else?" Being real is that you have the jobs. Most jobs that you go on, the companies are white owned or foreign owned, or Japanese, etc., but even though you have the jobs, even though you are supervisors and all, to treat people not like underclassmen, noncitizens, but to treat them like they are real people, and to not feel like—and not only feel like—you know, like I'm in a class of my own. Because I think really white people do not really know that we all will live together or die together. . . . So I would say that same thing to white America. Whatever is good for him is good for me and in the same manner that he gets it. . . . I want to be wanted not by having to force the issue for affirmative action and all this sort of thing, but because the white man knows within his conscience that's just the right thing to do.

After commenting that she is tired of hearing that the United States is color blind, she concluded forcefully: "I don't think it's going to ever be color blind. You can always look at a person, and I look at a person, and I know that person's white and I know that person's black, but behind the blackness and the whiteness there is a mental mind that no one can put a color on. That's why I'd like to see white people come to grips with life." Our respondents also called for a renewed commitment to affirmative action and the enforcement of existing civil rights laws and lambasted the recent conservative notions of "reverse discrimination."

During the 1980s such conservative notions resulted in a restructuring of the U.S. Commission on Civil Rights and of the U.S.

339

Department of Justice, so that both formerly pro-affirmative-action agencies in effect became opponents of aggressive affirmative action. An aide to a state legislator commented:

> I got into a long discussion with a white guy here at the Capitol . . . he was bellyaching about affirmative action, which is the biggest farce. There's never really been any affirmative action in this country. It's never really been enforced, and it's only been on the books little more than fifteen years. And stack that up against four hundred years of slavery and another hundred years of Jim Crow, and you see how ludicrous the whole reverse discrimination argument is. There can't be reverse discrimination unless, miraculously, tomorrow for four hundred years white people were enslaved and then they had another hundred years of Jim Crow and then we were in charge of things, *then* you could talk to me about reverse discrimination. . . . And he was saying, "You know, well I didn't have any thing to do with what happened in the past, and I don't feel like I should suffer, and I should be penalized, and blah, blah, blah." And I told him, "What did your grandfather do?" [He said,] "My grandfather was a mechanic. He worked a good union scale job back in the 1900s." [I asked] "Then, what did your dad do?" [He said,] "Well, my dad went to college, and got out of college, and he's an engineer now." And I said, "Well, how do know—we won't even go back four hundred years like we should, but let's just go back three generations—how do you know that because of Jim Crow and because of segregation and because of overt racial oppression, the mechanic that your grandfather was and the job he had wouldn't have been held by my grandfather, had he been allowed to. How do you know that my dad would not have been able to attend Georgia Tech and become an engineer, had he been allowed to and had his

340

grandfather had a good union scale job and could afford to send him? How do you know?" So, yes, white people today, even young white people today, are still benefitting from past segregation.

It is discrimination, past and present, that requires the present remedy of affirmative action programs. We agree with our respondents that the U.S. government must enact and enforce them aggressively if traditionally white institutions are to respond adequately to the reality of racial discrimination in the lives of all black Americans.

In recent years there has been much discussion among white commentators and scholars about the alleged "immorality" and "destructive values" of black Americans, especially poor blacks in the so-called black underclass.[15] In contrast, some blacks with whom we spoke were critical of the values of whites, including those at the top of the social and economic pyramid. Reviewing events in the lives of Wall Street investors, a professor at a northeastern university commented on white values:

> I think that the dominant white society is driven by all the, what I consider the, wrong human values: competition, money is the top-valued thing. See, what we have in the dominant white society, you have the Ivan Boeskys, the white-collar crime, you have all of that being done. And it has a kinder, gentler face than people shooting people over crack in the neighborhoods, or a teenager saying, "Hey, if I can be a lookout for the drug guys, and just by standing on this corner and alerting them to the fact that the cops are coming I can earn a couple hundred bucks a day, you think I'm going to work at Burger King? No way." Well, that's the same set of values that drives an Ivan Boesky to say, "I can cut corners or I can do insider trading and all the rest.". . . We don't see how that relates to the behavior of

young people in this country, and particularly young blacks who may be involved in easy money from drugs and that sort of thing. And it just happens that the penalties are much higher for the young people who get involved in drugs and that kind of quick and easy money.

Important to a deeper moral analysis of the situation of young or poor black Americans is the character of the prevailing role models, and not just the black middle-class role models that analysts like Keller and Wilson examine. At least as important is the standard set by powerful whites in the society's dominant institutions.

Running through many interviews is a strong call for *all* whites to move in the direction of fair play and truly equal opportunity, as this bank manager emphasized: "I would like to see both black men and women just given a fair shot. I don't necessarily need anyone to give me anything. However, if I qualify and work for it, just let me move along. I feel that if possibly myself, I wasn't black, a black woman, I would be much further along than what I am now." Discussing white stereotypes, an East Coast public administrator said that one thing she would like to see is the "realization that blacks as a people are as capable as the majority, and that we deserve a fair share in this country, a fair share." She continued:

And that's all we've ever wanted, and somehow, that's gotten lost I think in all of this. An opportunity to have access to some kind of job, educational opportunity, some kind of housing. And there might be a lot of lip service to that, but then they change the rules of the game. What will happen is, "Yeah, you can move into my community." And then what will happen next is people will start selling their homes at twice the price, and move to another subdivision, up the price, and make it out of the reach of the average black American. I mean, there are all kinds of games that are played under the guise of equal opportunity, when in fact it is not.

The issue of opportunity and the theme of the rules of the game we have encountered in previous commentaries. Recall the sentiments of the black entrepreneur who was the first one interviewed for our project: "We learn the rules of the games, and by the time we have mastered them, to really try to get into the mainstream . . . then they change the rules of the game." From this perspective, whites in positions of authority must stop excluding blacks from the rewards that should accrue from having played the opportunity game according to the official rules.

How does one bring about significant changes in white attitudes? Only a few racial relations training programs have a record of success in the United States. And for the most part they are small or localized in one corporation or one community. Often they take the form of sensitivity training or group discussions between whites and people of color about prejudices and stereotyping. There are some inherent problems in much of this awareness training. Some training focuses on cultural differences and not on racist behavior. And one reason for the failure of racial relations education and training to reach large groups of white Americans is the lack of backing by most top corporate and U.S. government officials. One exception is the backing given to racial change in the U.S. military, especially the U.S. army. A computer engineer cited as a model for new programs to sensitize whites the relatively successful program of racial relations training conducted in the U.S. armed forces:

We need to let them [whites] know that racism and discrimination is still alive, even though we're not carrying the picket signs, walking up and down the street. We need to let them know that we want to be done equally. How do

343

we do that? Example, like in the military. In the military
you have a course called "Race Relations." This is what
you go through all the time in all branches of the military,
and I really believe that helps. They need to have more race
relations courses.

Many thousands of U.S. citizens who have served in the U.S.
military in the last two decades have received some training in
understanding racial and ethnic groups other than their own.
Although some African Americans have criticized this military
program as too brief or too modest, in this respondent's view it
does at least provide one model for broader application. It
seems ironic that the one large organization that currently is the
most racially integrated and has the most developed program to
improve racial understanding is the U.S. army. Clearly, however,
military organizations have the hierarchical structure to implement change that most civilian organizations do not have.

Noting that understanding should be a reciprocal process for
blacks as well as whites, a probation officer made this plea:

I see a sensitivity, I think, to all ethnic minorities, even by
ethnic minorities themselves. I'd like to see a much more
moral development take place in this entire country. . . . I
think by and large most often white America and black
America, too, I think is entirely focused on what we like
and what we need and not necessarily sensitive to what
other people's concerns are. I don't know that white males
are really in tune to the impact that unfairness can have
and how far-reaching it can be with black people generally.

Some respondents put their hopes for improvement in the
development of closer relationships between blacks and whites,
especially younger whites. Optimistic about current change, a
corporate sales manager in the Southwest commented that what

he would like to see changed in white society are some of the stereotypes about blacks:

> I think it's improved a lot and I think it's going to continue to improve because you have more and more exposure to each other. My kids have white friends that they are dear to, and it's pure friendship. And I was probably twenty-two years old before I had a real relationship, a one-on-one relationship with a white person that I considered my friend. And that person and I have had a friendship for twenty years; probably one of my best friends. My kids are experiencing that at four and five and six and seven years old. I think that's going to make a difference in white society, people having that exposure.

The "equal status" contact we have previously discussed may be increasing in some sectors of U.S. society. Studies have shown that white prejudices are most affected by such contacts if they are not highly competitive but informal and friendly.[16]

An airline representative, with some laughter, argued that the whites in control have to be replaced by younger whites before there can be real change:

> I think about Eddie Murphy's [spiel] on Saturday Night Live—"Kill the white people!" [laughs] I'm sorry. Let's see, what changes? I guess for the people in control to just fade away. Because I see some hope with younger people, I really do. And I think that the grandmothers still have the influence, and no matter how you feel in your heart and what you know is right and how you feel is right, the grandmothers still have the influence, and I think until the grandmothers die we're still going to have the problem. . . . And so I see some hope with young people, and I think that's the salvation, if they can stay on the right track.

Black Action to Bring Change

In our view the burden of changing this racist society should lie primarily on the shoulders of white Americans. White Americans and their ancestors created a racist society, and white Americans are most responsible for taking action to eradicate this racism. And changing the system of racial inequality will require much concerted white action. This fact is recognized by many African Americans, including our respondents. But it is also clear that our respondents ask of themselves what they can do to accelerate positive changes in the state of U.S. racial relations. In the preceding chapters we have discussed the tactics and strategies used by individual black Americans as they cope with everyday racism. From the beginning of slavery African Americans have gone beyond individual strategies to consider what they as a group should be doing to deal with external racism and its internal effects on black communities. Among middle-class black men and women today one still finds a recurring concern with community and collective action. According to a dentist in a southern city the battle against racism must be carried out at several levels: "I think it has to be something that must be approached at different levels with different people. Some people are able to handle it better in the board room, on the floor of the House of Representatives and what-have-you, but I think we as a race of people must begin to support and encourage people to deal with it on every level in black society."

The white and black neoconservatives who have dominated much recent writing about U.S. racial relations prefer to target black individuals and communities as the source of contemporary black problems. A few of our respondents articulated a similar theme, although they usually acknowledged the role of racism in the problems. An administrator at a western university accented the need for community action:

Stop this black on black crime. Start caring about being educated and start caring about their lives. Because a lot of
the problem stems from blacks themselves. See, black folks
are so busy killing each other and ripping each other, it's
the crab syndrome. It's like a barrel full of crabs, as soon as
one starts to crawl out, the rest of them pull him down,
and they all try to struggle to get to the top on each other's
back. We've got to learn cooperation, learn how to learn to
work together and help each other.

Recognizing the need to struggle against racism in the outside
world, the dentist quoted above emphasized the necessity of
blacks' dealing with such community problems as "hopelessness
and the despair that manifests itself in the black community
with all the illegitimate children.":

To many black young ladies, a baby is something to love
and to love back, and they have so little of it. And there's
no future in their eyes out there for them. I think we as
blacks have many, many, many roles and many, many,
many places to put our efforts and our time and our love
and our patience to help black people that "have not been
able to keep on keeping on."

This man's concern for the poor became clearer as he recounted
a story of counselling in his office a young black woman with
sexual and marital problems. In contrast to the neoconservative
perspective, the respondents' assessments of community problems generally show a greater awareness of the direct and indirect role of racism in black crime and illegitimacy. And they
envisage working on these internal problems while at the same
time confronting racial discrimination.

Building up community pride and increasing black assertive-
ness, especially among young people, are goals for many
middle-class black Americans. Community pride is an old con-

cern in the writings of black leaders from William E. B. Du Bois to Malcolm X, Martin Luther King, Jr., and Jesse Jackson. Assessing the need for black action, a bank manager emphasized the necessity of teaching young people: "I think our future lies in our young people. We're going to have to train them, teach them how to live in this world, how to deal economically, how to be proud of ourselves. And when I say proud, not necessarily meaning because you want to straighten your hair or what have you that you're 'being white,' but mentally being proud. Being aware of who you are."

In racial and ethnic struggles across the globe one sees the central role of collective memory in the maintenance and development of group pride and community solidarity. This collective memory includes a central recognition of the history of African Americans and of the scale of the continuing struggle against white racism. Discussing this historical perspective, a high school teacher cited the collective memory of Jewish Americans as a model:

> I think that we cannot let that [memory of racial oppression] hinder us, and I like to use the example of the Jewish people. You never, ever will be alive and be allowed to forget the Holocaust. But that group of people does not let the Holocaust keep them back. They just keep it in front of you because they don't want it to happen again and they want you to always be apprised of what that was and how terrible it was. And periodically it's on T.V., and they're this and they're that, and they're always doing something about the Holocaust to keep it on everybody's mind. But they keep moving along. They keep moving along. And that is the one thing that I think we don't do as well. I think that we should never forget slavery. We should never forget from whence we have come.

In one way or another all of our middle-class respondents reveal that they participate in the collective memory of African Americans. This man is aware of the way the collective memory of slavery and other oppression can be debilitating, but he advocates the Jewish model of using the memory of oppression as a spur to achievements and to fuel the fight in human rights struggles.

An emphasis on black pride, black solidarity, and the memory of historical oppression are major pillars of an Afrocentricity movement in the United States.[17] Since the beating of Rodney King by Los Angeles police officers in 1991 and the subsequent Los Angeles riots in 1992, we have seen a reinforcement of black middle-class interest in concrete solidarity-building actions and a renewed commitment to "buying black" among some middle-class blacks. For example, in a *New York Times* story based on seventy interviews with middle-class black people in Los Angeles after a 1993 trial led to the conviction of only two of the four officers who had brutalized Rodney King, reporter Isabel Wilkerson found that many of these middle-class Angelenos were bitter and spoke with resignation about the need for black community solidarity and separation.[18] Many were moving their patronage from white to black businesses. This buy-black, build-black response seems to have been triggered by the view that one major way to deal with white racism today may be for African Americans to create economically stronger communities less dependent on whites. A newspaper publisher in our sample put it this way:

> I feel very comfortable about putting black people on the spot about not asking for a black sales rep. Often times these people are paid on commission, often times they will be more supportive. But then you have a group of people, like my mother, who believes that a white doctor is better than a black doctor. But yet, her daughter is in business, and she pushes her in business. Now, to me, that's a double

standard. She's very critical of the black [emphasis], because I use all black doctors. And, anything I can get service-wise, I ask for a black person, because my thing is to keep that dollar within the black community. Now, for some people that may be interpreted as racist. I think often times our community says, "Oh, black people don't do a good job, or oh, black people are higher [in price]." And then after they try one black, they'll go to a white. The point is if they used a white, then if that white messed up they'd go to another white. So, my point is, why not go to another black? It's not a racist thing, it's a conscious effort to try to rebuild the economic structure of the black community.

The negative impact of western culture on African Americans reveals itself in the view among some black buyers that "white is better." The liberating strategy envisioned here is greater black solidarity.

One of our informants, a graduate student interviewed in 1992 after we finished the primary sample, called himself a "social revolutionary":

I am a social revolutionary. It is my belief that black people will never receive from this society the rights and privileges that others possess. Therefore, it becomes incumbent upon blacks, along the lines of Frantz Fanon's alternative-systems thesis, to develop mechanisms within their own communities which will redress the discrepancies between the realities of a racist society and communal needs and objectives. I am a future teacher in the sense that I am teaching my people the knowledge of Afrocentric values.

Interestingly, this young man sees a type of social revolution in pressing for community action and the inculcating of an Afrocentric perspective to enhance and expand black pride.

Throughout our research many respondents advocated explicitly or implicitly a personal strategy of confronting white discriminators: African Americans must act, must confront, must argue in dialogue with whites. A corporate secretary commented this way:

Speaking out, for one thing. Speaking out, but doing it at a minimum. Not doing it to get everybody angry. Do it with some sense. Stop covering it up. Stop talking about it only among your black friends. The black friends already know racism exists. The black friends are not the ones who created racism. Why talk to them about it? If you're going to talk to them about it, talk to them about which white friend you're going to go talk to about it.

An administrator at a northern university emphasized the need to continue a long-term dialogue with whites:

I think they have to continue the dialogue, because as people get older, like me, I'm no longer patient enough to stop and explain to ignorant older white folks the practical realities. I think I would rather spend the time that I have left working with younger people, who're going to bring along the next generation, who're going to be the next generation out there operating, keeping things pretty good, for my grandchildren. . . . Is it up to blacks? I don't think you have too much choice; you have to do *something*, but certainly it takes more energy than I really have at this stage of the game, more energy or more patience. But the dialogue has to continue; you have to have it. If you can't sit down and talk in a rational manner about some of the conflicts, and at least if people don't buy your ideas, they have been exposed to them. And they may go back and think about them and be more fair in their dealings with us.

Throughout our interviews there is a recurring concern for the education of children, black and white. An attorney for a

351

hotel chain, emphasizing that aggressive action against white barriers should be taught by example to children, argued forcefully that blacks should "be learning more about how to deal with the white racist world. Pushing ahead enough. Not making what these people think we are, or should be, come true:"

> A lot of people say, "Oh, I'm not going to get the job. Nobody's going to give it to me." So they don't even try. Or, "I don't care, I don't want to send my kid to that school." "To go to a school because it's all a white school," and "they'll take advantage of that kid and the kid's not going to learn." They should stop seeing that and look at it where I have as much right to be there as that white person. And teach the kid to overcome the obstacles that may stand in their way as they go about it.

His message, for black adults and young people, is not to be defeated by a sense of futility and to attack the barriers vigorously and assertively.

In addition to working for change within the African American community and for more aggressive individual protests, numerous respondents stand proudly within the distinguished black tradition of collective identification, organization, and protest in attempts to change white society. Over the last century organized black protest has ranged from legal strategies, to voter registration, to nonviolent civil disobedience, to violent attacks on the system. Some respondents called for more organization and more protest action. While they supported individual action, they assumed the importance of collective action in bringing social change. A human services manager in the Northeast commented about the benefits of activism among young people:

> All is not lost! There's hope! I'm encouraged by a new-found revolutionary spirit. I was very encouraged by the

352

Howard University students demanding the resignation of Lee Atwater [campaign manager for George Bush in 1988]. That was wonderful! That kind of revolutionary fervor was just exciting to me. I'm excited by seeing black students do the black college tour that some of the agencies in this city operate each year. And I'm encouraged when I see black young people looking to black colleges for higher education. I'm encouraged when I see local activists in our community fighting for eminent domain and control of the land in this city, and getting it. I'm encouraged by that. And people are organizing and people are fighting, so I'm encouraged by that. While I said that I think in the short-run things will get worse, it will only, I think, ignite our fire to struggle more, and struggle in the collective fashion.

Other respondents also noted revolutionary stirrings in black America. A self-employed political consultant felt major changes were coming in the 1990s:

The reality is, brothers and sisters have started moving toward Afros, towards the braids. We started moving toward the African attire. Okay, whenever you see that, revolution's on its way. But it's subtle, it's subtle. You see, I see it because I'm everywhere, you know; I'm not just locked up in this city, and I see it everywhere. . . . I'm telling you, girl; it's coming. And what's going to happen is, they're going to force us, America is forcing us . . . you're going to see a whole different America, because, honey, we're going to take names and kick ass. . . . So they're trying to hold on and control, but we saying, "Uh-uh, we not taking that anymore." And *we are*; I'm telling you, we're going to prove that in the '90s. And it's not going to be a whole lot of ranting and raving going on. Some cities, you might have to go through the '60s behavior.

Some respondents pressed for blacks to take political action

353

within the existing political framework, both as individuals and in groups. They were aware of the heritage of the 1960s' civil rights movement that forced Congress to pass the Voting Rights Act of 1965, which encouraged voting in the South. An administrative clerk at a publishing corporation spoke of determined political action:

> Stop letting white folks push them around. One thing, we need to get out and *vote*. That's our number one priority. We do not go to the polls. We can't get any changes if we don't take the numbers out there to change them. "Oh, I'm not going to vote because . . ." You know, I've heard people say that, and I had never thought about it until I really, in the last five years, started working with the voter registration. "Why should I vote? It's not going to help anyway." And I can't believe that they actually believe that their vote won't count.

Similarly, a telephone company employee spoke of the need for community activism and political organization at the city level:

> Well, I think that we need to get more involved with what's going on around us. We need to be involved with our school systems. We need to be involved with our city councils. We need to be registered to vote. We need to have some kind of power base. And when you're dealing with a society that is built on power, and the wielding of power, sometimes you have to respond with power. Responding hate for hate does not work. But the only thing that power understands is more power. We must become educated, we must feed ourselves, for if we are not fed we cannot look up, we have to look down. We have to help our fellow brothers and sisters.

When asked in a follow-up question if the need for civil disobedience is past, he answered: "No, I think that it is a very real thing today, for our world is in for many changes, very recently. And we will be forced to either make a statement or be crushed by our oppressor. The only way we can fight the system is to stand up and fight. We cannot sit down and wait for the other guy to step in. . . . No, power has to be taken by force." The low visibility of the civil rights movements in the early 1990s seems to have lulled many into the view that African Americans will take most any indignities that are handed out. Yet the level of anger in many of our interviews is high, and this man's response suggests that more of the aggressive black activism and civil rights organization of the past could return.

The search for effective leadership has been an issue for African Americans from the beginning of racial oppression. In the last decade numerous white commentaries on the state of black Americans have been very disparaging of, if not hostile to, current black leadership. None of the blacks with whom we talked was so disparaging of black leaders as a group, although the owner of a landscaping business did comment on the need for better leaders today: "Well, unless somebody comes along, unless the good Lord drops us another Martin Luther King down here in the next few weeks, I'll tell you what, it's still going downhill. . . . Ever since that happened, we haven't had a leader, you know. We've got some out there that's defending themselves as leaders, but it's for their own personal goals."

The memory of Martin Luther King, Jr., is strong among these middle-class black Americans, and the desire for new leaders of his caliber may be nearly universal among black Americans. Numerous respondents mentioned the importance of black leaders like King, Malcolm X, or William E. B. DuBois to their own perspectives on the continuing black struggle. A southern newspaper publisher noted how the leadership styles of Martin Luther King, Jr., and Malcolm X were complementary models for the black rights struggle: "Martin Luther King, his whole thing was, wage the racism battle. But the way he did

355

it; the finesse he did it with. Also the counterpart of the Malcolm X thing: take the racist monster and kill it. . . . I think the two balance each other off . . . if you had to choose between these two, which one would you choose?"

A professor at an eastern university called for inventive leaders, black or white, who could encourage intelligent thinking and action about racism in the United States:

Well, it's hard to isolate one particular thing that I would like to see the most. And this is asking the impossible, but it's to ask for, to try to see someone take the lead, like the president of the United States, take the lead in encouraging some sincere thinking about race relations. Martin Luther King did it. Timing was important, but he did it. I don't think that would ever occur, but that's what I would like to happen.

The International Oneness of the Black Struggle

Reviewing issues of color coding in ancient civilizations, the late St. Clair Drake argued that "Crucial in the Afro-Americans' coping process has been their identification, over a time span of more than two centuries, with ancient Egypt and Ethiopia as symbols of black initiative and success long before their enslavement on the plantations of the New World."[19] African Americans have long drawn on the history, spirituality, and symbolism of Africa as part of their individual and group strategies for coping with the white-dominated society. Since the early 1980s black writers and scholars have probed more deeply and extensively than ever before into the significance of African history and cultures for African Americans.[20]

Several of those we interviewed wanted all blacks to develop a stronger knowledge of and solidarity with Africa as a way of fostering group solidarity and strong self-concepts. After noting

356

the powerful ties of American Jews to Israel, a sales representative at a major corporation was persuasive on the urgency of developing similarly robust black ties to Africa:

> The way I see it is there is either conflict, or there is an understanding from black people that we are related to African brothers. We have to interact, the brothers have to see that also. For instance, my heart pains for what happens in South Africa. But I very easily have been able to accept the media's presentation of the issue now. And so, what I'm saying is, that should affect me, and I'm conscious of it, and most, a lot of other black brothers are conscious of it, it affects me. I know that shit is wrong, I know we ought to be doing more than we're doing. So, I guess what I'm saying is that the only way that gets better is we have to finally decide that we're one. We have to finally decide that black people around the world are one. I heard Stokely Carmichael say one time, that if you grow corn in Africa, it's corn. If you grow it in the U.S. it's corn. And what I believe he meant by that, is that the African Americans are dispersed all over the world, we're still Africans. You have some roots, you have some ties, . . . that are very important to you, in terms of you understanding the betterment of your life.

Speaking to the same theme, a nursing professor at a southwestern university said that things were worse now than a few years ago, but she found hopeful signs in the freedom movements in South Africa:

> Now, in order for it to get to be better in five years, something is going to happen. We see the crumbling of walls everywhere. The release of Nelson Mandela was a very big step forward, but not enough of a step forward. With the barriers falling in Africa, I *know* that something's going to

357

happen in this country, and it's just a matter of what and who will be the impetus for leading it. . . . African Americans have always viewed themselves as being the freed people and our brothers in Africa as being oppressed. Now, when you get to a situation where the oppressed have made the decision and are willing to fight and die to say, "I will no longer be oppressed, I will have more say." Okay. With the walls crumbling in South Africa, the oppressed are standing up and saying, "I don't want to be oppressed any more." Then we, as African Americans who have sup- posedly had all these freedoms, we have to start to open our eyes and take a look and see that we really, in actuality, don't have all these freedoms.

Significantly, the freedom struggle in South Africa has put many white Americans in a conceptual bind. One woman, an active community volunteer, noted that white criticism of South African apartheid is hypocritical: "And too often, I have found that white Americans are more comfortable dealing with the point of apartheid; and they cannot see the tip of their nose. That here they are living an all-white life themselves. And I think it's going to take saying that and having them realize that, you know, are you kidding?"

Conclusion

We hold these Truths to be self-evident, that all Men are cre- ated equal, that they are endowed by their Creator with cer- tain unalienable Rights, that among these are Life, Liberty, and the Pursuit of Happiness.

U.S. Declaration of Independence

We the people of the United States, in order to form a more perfect union, establish justice, insure domestic tranquility, provide for the common defense, promote the general welfare, and secure the blessings of liberty to ourselves and our posterity, do ordain and establish this constitution for the United States of America.

Preamble, U.S. Constitution

All too will bear in mind the sacred principle, that though the will of the majority is in all cases to prevail, that will to be rightful must be reasonable; that the minority possess their equal rights, which equal law must protect, and to violate would be oppression.

Thomas Jefferson, Inaugural Address

All persons born or naturalized in the United States, and subject to the jurisdiction thereof, are citizens of the United States and of the State wherein they reside. No State shall make or enforce any law which shall abridge the privileges or immunities of citizens of the United States; nor shall any State deprive any person of life, liberty, or property, without due process of the law; nor deny to any person within its jurisdiction the equal protection of the laws.

Fourteenth Amendment, U.S. Constitution

These pronouncements and constitutional guarantees form the foundation of our democratic government. They were initially written by whites, including some white slaveholders, but the intervening centuries have seen their meaning broadened to include justice and equality for Americans of all creeds and backgrounds. Writing in the 1940s in *An American Dilemma*, Gunnar Myrdal noted that most blacks, like most whites, were under the spell of the American creed, the "ideals of the essential dignity of the individual human being, of the fundamental equality of all men, and of certain inalienable rights to freedom, justice, and a fair opportunity."[21] The basics of the American dream include not only liberty and justice but also the pursuit of

359

happiness, which can be seen as including a decent-paying job, a good home, and a sense of personal dignity.

Can all Americans achieve this dream? The logic of equal rights and equal opportunity would dictate that a black person who has reached middle-income status should have no difficulty in realizing the promises of the American dream. Middle-class African Americans have paid their dues and are asking to be accepted for their contributions and their ability to contribute, rather than to be viewed in terms of skin color. Yet the experiences of these African Americans with discrimination in traditionally white institutions are often destructive of their hopes and ambitions, of their ability to achieve true equality of opportunity and the multifaceted dream of being middle class. Recall the television broadcaster who argued forcefully that there is "no black middle class, by the way. You know that's relevant. Every time I use 'middle class,' I know that. Because a black middle-class person is still not a middle-class person."

In this book we have reported on concrete black *experience* with everyday racism. As we suggest in Chapter 1, racial discrimination is not an abstraction for these Americans, nor is it mainly a problem of the recent past. For most of these Americans racial discrimination is not a matter of isolated incidents, but instead a succession of negative experiences with whites from the early years of childhood to the last years of adulthood. Our interviews also put whites into the spotlight. We observe in the accounts that a large proportion of the discriminators are indeed middle class whites with power and resources.

Mainstream discussions emphasizing the benefits to black Americans of expanded employment in white-collar jobs often neglect the fact that as a group middle-class blacks are subordinate to middle-class whites in wages, salaries, and workplace power.[22] Typically the white-collar workplace offers no shelter from white racism, for it is a site where white peers and supervisors may isolate black employees, sabotage their work, or

360

restrict their access to better jobs and good promotions. Nor does the university or college provide reliable security and support. Black students in mostly white colleges face many hurdles and pitfalls, from epithets to social isolation, professorial indifference, and, often, a Eurocentric curriculum. Even one's home and neighborhood may not be a place of refuge from white hostility; white realtors and homeowners may try to keep blacks out of white neighborhoods, and white neighbors may be insensitive or hostile. In public accommodations African Americans still experience a range of discrimination, from poor treatment in restaurants and department stores to hostility in pools and parks. In street sites white hostility can be especially dangerous and threatening, for a black person never knows when a racist epithet signals violence to come.

As of this writing, what is missing in the mass media and the mainstream intellectual literature is a single in-depth article or book on the role of white racism in creating the foundation for current racial conflict. What is missing not only in the mass media but in the nation is white Americans, especially middle-class whites and powerful white leaders, taking responsibility for the widespread prejudice and discrimination that generate rage and protest among black Americans. It was white Americans who created slavery and the segregation of African Americans, and it is white Americans who today are responsible for most continuing discrimination against African Americans.

Even some white liberals see the racial relations dilemma as a problem of everyone's prejudices. In 1992 the liberal organization People for the American Way published the results of a survey they commissioned on young Americans. They concluded from their research that "benign neglect" was no longer the answer for U.S. racial problems and that it was time to get young people in all racial and ethnic groups to reconsider their racial attitudes. They recommended that an "assignment of blame" should be avoided and that it was time to "find common ground." They continued by underscoring a vicious cycle of mutual resentment: "Minority citizens believe with more certainty that whites are responsible for the hostility between the races; whites believe the same thing about minorities with equal certitude. This is an exercise in bitterness that is bound to have no affirmative or beneficial end."[23] This important survey of young Americans provided valuable information and some useful suggestions for change, but its conclusions were much too weak. The U.S. racial problem, now and in its origin, is fundamentally a white problem, for whites have the greatest power to perpetuate or alter it. The conditions of antiblack discrimination have specific creators, and the creators are mostly white Americans.

As a nation we have been misled by an influential group of mainstream liberal and neoconservative analysts, most of whom are white, who have told us that the primary cause of persisting racial tensions and problems in this country is not white racism, but rather the black underclass, or black families, or black dependency on welfare. These apologists have blamed the underclass for its immorality and the black middle class for not taking responsibility for the underclass. To deny white racism and blame the black victims of racism have become intellectually fashionable in recent years. Our respondents call for a new racial education for most white Americans. White Americans must be exposed to the real history of the United States, including a starkly realistic revelation of the ravages of slavery, of the delay and failure of civil rights laws, and of the lack of courage of white presidents and legislators to demand equity in education, employment, housing, and other sectors of this society. What being white in the United States means can only be understood by delving deeply into the white-on-black history too often left out of the public discussions of American racial relations. Our respondents do not ignore the responsibility of black Americans to attend to problems of discrimination, but they

362

also stress that white Americans have to confront and fight against white racism.

In *Faces at the Bottom of the Well*, legal scholar Derrick Bell has argued very forcefully that "Black people will never gain full equality in this country. Even those herculean efforts we hail as successful will produce no more than temporary 'peaks of progress,' short-lived victories that slide into irrelevance as racial patterns adapt in ways that maintain white dominance."[24] For Bell, an African American and former professor at Harvard Law School, the goals of racial equality and justice have been laudable, but in the final analysis they are usually sacrificed by whites to their own interests in day-to-day political struggles. This veteran of legal battles for civil rights is very pessimistic, and as a result he provides little in the way of concrete proposals and plans, beyond writing a better history of black struggles and a contemporary "defiance" of whites, for continuing the black struggle. Our black middle-class respondents are also veteran grass-roots theorists of white oppression, and they too take a broad view of the past, present, and future of this society—its strengths and hopes, as well as its weaknesses and destructiveness. Although many seem to share, to some degree, Bell's despair over the permanence of white racism, for the most part they continue to believe in or work for practical solutions to some of the nation's major race-related problems: good jobs for all black Americans, decent housing for all black Americans, vigorously enforced antidiscrimination laws, the re-education of whites away from racist attitudes, and the strengthening of solidarity in black communities. Against all odds, and in spite of the terrible obstacles, most somehow retain some hope for change in the future.

In our interviews, as well as in other accounts, African Americans have often hinted at or expressed openly the hope for future empowerment, not a wish for black domination of whites, but rather a humanist vision of shared development, one that

363

stresses self-respect, self-determination, and self-actualization for all Americans. Indeed, expanding such an encompassing humanist and egalitarian vision *among whites* may be the only hope for a peaceful and prosperous future for the United States. Considering the discriminatory conditions black Americans face today, a majority of white Americans show little or no empathy; they seem to have lost the ability to "walk in another person's shoes."

Securing full human rights for African Americans will necessarily bring benefits for all Americans. Nearly a century ago Du Bois showed how the African slave trade not only dehumanized African Americans but also white Americans.[25] White racism has long been inseparable from white identity, white history, and white culture and has greatly demeaned and sabotaged the ideals of liberty and justice prized by all Americans. If a humanist and egalitarian vision is to be realized, whites must no longer deny the power inequality and the attitudinal imperialism at the heart of white racism. Giving up racism means not only giving up racist attitudes but also giving up substantial power and privilege. In a famous speech at an 1881 civil rights mass meeting in Washington, D.C., Frederick Douglass declared that "No man can put a chain about the ankle of his fellow man without at last finding the other end fastened about his own neck."[26]

Notes

1. The Continuing Significance of Racism

1. Lawrence D. Bobo, James H. Johnson, Melvin L. Oliver, James Sidanius, Camille Zubrinsky, *Public Opinion before and after a Spring of Discontent* (Los Angeles: UCLA Center for the Study of Urban Poverty, 1992), p. 6; Lynne Duke, "Blacks and Whites Define 'Racism' Differently," *Washington Post*, June 8, 1992, section A, p. 1.

2. Judith Lichtenberg, "Racism in the Head, Racism in the World," *Philosophy and Public Policy* 12 (Spring/Summer 1992), p. 3.

3. Nearly 4,600 hate crimes were recorded by the FBI for 1991. See "FBI Issues First Data on Hate Crimes," *The Race Relations Reporter*, March 15, 1993, p. 8.

4. Marian Wright Edelman, *The Measure of Our Success: A Letter to My Children and Yours* (Boston: Beacon Press, 1992), p. 23.

5. Quoted in Itabari Njeri, "Words to Live or Die by," *Los Angeles Times Magazine*, May 31, 1992, p. 23.

6. National Advisory Commission on Civil Disorders, *Report of the National Advisory Commission on Civil Disorders* (Washington, D.C.: U.S. Government Printing Office, 1968), p. 1.

7. Ibid., pp. 1, 5.

8. "Black and White in America," *Newsweek*, March 7, 1988, p. 19.

9. Thomas J. Bray, "Reading America the Riot Act," *Policy Review* 43 (Winter 1988), pp. 32–35.

10. Nathan Glazer, *Affirmative Discrimination* (New York: Basic Books, 1975), pp. 6–7, 71–72.

11. Ben Wattenberg and Richard Scammon, "Black Progress and Liberal Rhetoric," *Commentary* (April 1973), p. 35.

12. George Gilder, *Wealth and Poverty* (New York: Basic Books, 1981).

13. George Keller, "Black Students in Higher Education: Why So Few?" *Planning for Higher Education* 17 (1988–1989), pp. 50–56.

14. William J. Wilson, *The Declining Significance of Race* (Chicago: University of Chicago, 1978), p. 151.

15. William J. Wilson, *The Truly Disadvantaged: The Inner City, the Underclass, and Public Policy* (Chicago: University of Chicago Press, 1987), p. 146. Bayard Rustin, review of *The Myth of Black Progress*, in *The Atlantic*, vol. 254, October 1984, p. 121.

16. Shelby Steele, *The Content of Our Character* (New York: St. Martin's Press, 1990), pp. 151, 175.

17. Stephen L. Carter, *Reflections of An Affirmative Action Baby* (New York: Basic Books, 1991), pp. 249, 221.

18. Gerald D. Jaynes and Robin Williams, Jr., eds., *A Common Destiny: Blacks and American Society* (Washington, D.C.: National Academy Press, 1989), pp. 169–171.

19. J. P. Smith and F. R. Welch, *Closing the Gap: Forty Years of Economic Progress for Blacks* (Santa Monica: Rand Corporation, 1986); U.S. Commission on Civil Rights, *The Economic Progress of Black Men in America* (Washington, D.C.: U.S. Government Printing Office, 1986).

20. Andrew Rosenthal, "Reagan Hints Rights Leaders Exaggerate Racism," *New York Times*, January 14, 1989, section 1, p. 8.

21. *Wards Cove Packing Co. v. Atonio*, 109 S. Ct. 2115 (1989).

22. "Black and White in America," *Newsweek*, March 7, 1988, p. 19.

23. Thomas B. Edsall and Mary D. Edsall, "When the official subject is presidential politics, taxes, welfare, crime, rights, or values—the real subject is race," *The Atlantic*, vol. 267, May 1991, pp. 53–55; Thomas B. Edsall, with Mary D. Edsall, *Chain Reaction* (New York: Norton, 1992), p. 15.

24. Leon Wieseltier, "Scar Tissue," *New Republic*, June 5, 1989, pp. 19–20.

25. Jim Sleeper, *The Closest of Strangers* (New York: Norton, 1991), pp. 172–176.

26. Elizabeth Ehrlich, "Racism, 'Victim Power,' and White Guilt," *Business Week*, October 1, 1990, p. 12.

27. Joe R. Feagin, "A Preliminary Analysis of Media Treatment of White Racism," Unpublished research paper, University of Florida, January 1992. The analysis used Mead Data Central's Nexis database.

28. Max Rodenbeck, "Dashed Good Yarns," *Financial Times*, May 8, 1993, p. xix.

29. Bob Blauner, *Black Lives, White Lives* (Berkeley: University of California Press, 1989).

30. Jaynes and Williams, *A Common Destiny*, p. 84.

31. James R. Kluegel and Eliot R. Smith, *Beliefs about Inequality* (New York: Aldine de Gruyter, 1986), pp. 186–187.

32. Cited in Joel Kovel, *White Racism*, rev. ed. (New York: Columbia University Press, 1984), p. xviii.

33. Louis Harris Associates and NAACP Legal Defense and Educational Fund, *The Unfinished Agenda on Race in America* (NAACP Legal Defense and Educational Fund, 1989), pp. 6–10.

34. National Opinion Research Center, "General Social Survey" (Chicago: National Opinion Research Center, 1991). Tabulated by authors.

35. William Brink and Louis Harris, *The Negro Revolution in America* (New York: Simon and Schuster, 1963); William Brink and Louis Harris, *Black and White* (New York: Simon and Schuster, 1966).

36. Louis Harris did a survey for the NAACP Legal Defense Fund in 1988, but no personal questions were asked about discrimination respondents had faced; see Louis Harris Associates, *The Unfinished Agenda on Race in America*.

37. Cited in Lee Sigelman and Susan Welch, *Black Americans' Views of Racial Inequality* (Cambridge: Cambridge University Press, 1991), pp. 53–55.

38. Ibid., pp. 55–57. When the respondents in the 1986 survey were asked two similar questions rephrased in regard to "blacks generally," the proportions citing discrimination increased substantially.

39. Ibid., p. 59. Philomena Essed found in her Netherlands study that some blacks do not categorize certain negative experiences with whites as discriminatory, even though they are. Philomena Essed, *Understanding Everyday Racism* (Newbury Park: Sage, 1991), p. 78.

40. We are indebted to Hernan Vera for his insightful comments here.

41. On life crisis, see Lydia Rapoport, "The State of Crisis: Some Theoretical Considerations," in Howard J. Parad, ed., *Crisis Intervention: Selected Readings* (New York: Family Service Association, 1965), pp. 22–31.

42. "Why Race still Divides America and its People," *Time*, May 11, 1992, front cover.

43. Gunnar Myrdal, *An American Dilemma* (1944; New York: McGraw-Hill, 1964).

44. Hubert M. Blalock, *Toward A Theory of Minority-Group Relations* (New York: Wiley, 1967); Phyllis A. Katz and Dalmas A. Taylor, eds., *Eliminating Racism* (New York: Plenum, 1988), pp. 1–18.

45. Gordon Allport, *The Nature of Prejudice*, abridged ed. (Garden City, N.Y.: Anchor Books, 1958), p. 50.

46. Stokely Carmichael and Charles V. Hamilton, *Black Power* (New York: Vintage, 1967).

47. Thomas Pettigrew, ed., *Racial Discrimination in the United States*, (New York: Harper and Row, 1975), p. x.

48. Randall Collins, *Theoretical Sociology* (New York: Harcourt, Brace, Jovanovich, 1988), p. 406.

49. Arthur Brittan and Mary Maynard, *Sexism, Racism and Oppression* (Oxford: Basil Blackwell, 1984), p. 7.

50. See Samuel B. Bacharach and Edward J. Lawler, *Bargaining: Power, Tactics, and Outcomes* (San Francisco: Jossey-Bass, 1981), p. 74.

51. Allport, *The Nature of Prejudice*, pp. 14–15.

52. Jaynes and Williams, *A Common Destiny*, pp. 119–129; Howard Schuman, Charlotte Steeh, and Lawrence Bobo, *Racial Attitudes in America* (Cambridge: Harvard University Press, 1985), pp. 139–162.

53. Among whites, 39 percent favored a law permitting whites to *refuse* to sell a home to a black person; a fifth favored laws banning racial intermarriage between blacks and whites and favored the view that whites have a right to keep blacks out of their neighborhoods. National Opinion Research Center, "General Social Survey" (Chicago: National Opinion Research Center, 1991). Tabulated by authors.

54. National Opinion Research Center, "General Social Survey" (Chicago: National Opinion Research Center, 1990).

55. See, for example, the 1990 survey cited above.

56. Charles R. Lawrence, "The Id, the Ego, and Equal Protection," *Stanford Law Review* 39 (January 1987), pp. 317–323; T. Alexander Aleinikoff, "The Case for Race-Consciousness," *Columbia Law Review* 91 (June 1991), pp. 1060–1080.

57. Judith Rollins, *Between Women* (Philadelphia: Temple University Press, 1985).

58. Carol Brooks Gardner, "Passing By: Street Remarks, Address Rights, and the Urban Female," *Sociological Inquiry* 50 (1980), p. 345.

59. William E. B. Du Bois, "The Talented Tenth," in *The Negro Problem*, ed. Booker T. Washington et al. (1904; New York: Arno Press, 1969), pp. 31–75.

60. E. Franklin Frazier, *Black Bourgeoisie*, rev. ed. (New York: Collier Books, 1962), p. 195.

61. See Bart Landry, *The New Black Middle Class* (Berkeley: University of California Press, 1987), pp. 2–10; and John Macionis, *Sociology* (Englewood Cliffs, N.J.: Prentice-Hall, 1989), p. 263.

62. Bureau of the Census, *The Social and Economic Status of the Black Population, 1790–1978* (Washington, D.C.: U.S. Government Printing Office, 1979), p. 72. These figures include all employed persons ten years old and older.

63. Ibid., p. 74.

64. Landry, *The New Black Middle Class*, p. 3.

65. Bureau of Labor Statistics data, as cited in Bureau of the Census, *Statistical Abstract of the United States, 1991* (Washington, D.C.: U.S. Government Printing Office, 1991), p. 400.

66. See, for example, Roy L. Brooks, *Rethinking the American Race Problem* (Berkeley: University of California Press, 1990).

67. Bureau of the Census, *Statistical Abstract of the United States, 1991* (Washington, D.C.: U.S. Government Printing Office, 1991), p. 38.

68. Bureau of the Census, *The Social and Economic Status of the Black Population, 1790- 1978*, p. 32; Bureau of the Census, *Statistical Abstract of the United States: 1990* (Washington, D.C.: U.S. Government Printing Office, 1990), p. 450.

69. On journalistic views, see Edsall and Edsall, *Chain Reaction*, p. 16. The socioeconomic indices indicate a group about the same size as is suggested by answers to self-placement questions in surveys. In a 1989 survey two thirds of black respondents identified themselves as "working class," while 30 percent identified themselves as "middle class" and 3 percent as "upper class." Among whites, however, 51 percent saw themselves as middle class and 4 percent as upper class. National Opinion Research Center, "General Social Survey" (Chicago: National Opinion Research Center, 1989). Tabulated by authors.

70. Herbert Blumer, *Symbolic Interactionism* (Berkeley: University of California Press, 1969), p. 32.

370

71. Leanita McClain, "How Chicago Taught Me to Hate Whites," *Washington Post*, July 24, 1983, reprinted in *A Foot in Each World*, ed. Clarence Page (Evanston, Ill.: Northwestern University Press, 1986), p. 36.

72. Antonio Gramsci, *Letters from Prison*, trans. by Lynne Lawner (New York: Harper and Row, 1973), pp. 43–44, 183–185.

73. See, for example, Robert N. Bellah, Richard Madsen, William M. Sullivan, Ann Swidler, and Steven M. Tipton, *Habits of the Heart* (New York: Harper and Row, 1986), pp. viii–ix. This major analysis has been faulted for not involving any interviews with black Americans. See Vincent Harding, "Toward a Darkly Radiant Vision of America's Truth: A Letter of Concern, An Invitation to Re-creation," in *Community in America*, ed. Charles H. Reynolds and Ralph V. Norman (Berkeley: University of California Press, 1988), pp. 67–83.

74. There are no lists of the members of the black middle class, especially those in the upper middle class, and they live in areas scattered across major cities, sometimes mixed in small numbers among whites and sometimes segregated in middle-class black residential areas. In most cases the initial respondents were suggested by knowledgeable black observers of the middle class in the cities chosen; other respondents were suggested by our black interviewers and by those first interviewed. Few of those we contacted refused to be interviewed, although some were not interviewed because of scheduling problems. The number of respondents for the demographic distributions here and in the next paragraph varies a little (from 189 to 209) because of missing data. A substantial majority in the South/Southwest category resided in Texas cities at the time of the interview, although, like respondents elsewhere, their accounts often cover experiences in other cities and regions.

75. In most cases the income reported is household income, but apparently several did report only their personal incomes.

76. We are greatly indebted to these black professionals for their support and encouragement in this difficult project.

77. In most interviews we asked questions about racial barriers

encountered in housing, education, and the workplace (or business), as well as about the personal impact of discrimination and coping strategies and support networks.

78. To protect the anonymity of these respondents, some of whom are the only blacks in their fields in particular cities, we will not list the cities. We have also disguised place and company names, and occasionally occupation, in chapter quotes.

79. After testing questions for communicability, we secured black interviewers to conduct all but one of the interviews, using a set of mostly open-ended questions. We added a few additional questions as we proceeded with the interviewing; latitude was allowed for digressions, so not all questions were covered in each interview. The interviews, conducted in 1988–1990, averaged about one to two hours each. In a few cases several respondents, such as a husband and wife, were interviewed together. Five interviews were done by black respondents who answered protocol questions on tape without an interviewer. A few short quotes in the text are presented verbatim from a taped interview of the second author by a black interviewer doing an early pilot interview for the first author before the second author became involved with this book.

80. Leanita McClain, "The Middle-class Black's Burden," *Newsweek*, October 13, 1980, reprinted in Page, *A Foot in Each World*, pp. 12–13.

81. William E. B. Du Bois, *The Souls of Black Folk* (1903; New York: Bantam Books, 1989), p. 3.

2. Navigating Public Places

1. Lena Williams, "When Blacks Shop, Bias often Accompanies a Sale," *New York Times*, April 30, 1991, pp. A1, A9.

2. Names and places in interview quotes have been disguised or eliminated to protect anonymity. Some quotes have been lightly edited

for grammar and to delete excessive pause phrases like "you know" and "uh."

3. National Public Radio, "Weekend Edition," May 29, 1993.

4. Associated Press, "Denny's to Monitor Treatment of Blacks," *Gainesville Sun*, May 30, 1993, p. 7A.

5. Judy Pasternak, "Service Still Skin Deep for Blacks," *Los Angeles Times*, April 1, 1993, p. A1.

6. Martin Dyckman, "Lawyers can be Heroes too," *St. Petersburg Times*, April 11, 1993, p. 3D.

7. Bill McAuliffe, "Black Leaders Call for Boycott of Local Carsons Stores," *Star Tribune*, December 10, 1991, p. 1B.

8. Joel Kovel, *White Racism*, rev. ed. (New York: Columbia University Press, 1984).

9. Walt Harrington, "On the Road with the President of Black America," *The Washington Post Magazine*, January 25, 1987, p. W14.

10. "FBI Issues First Data on Hate Crimes," *The Race Relations Reporter*, March 15, 1993, p. 8.

11. Carol Brooks Gardner, "Passing By: Street Remarks, Address Rights, and the Urban Female," *Sociological Inquiry* 50 (1980), p. 345.

12. David C. Perry and Paula A. Sornoff, *Politics at the Street Level* (Beverly Hills: Sage, 1973).

13. John Howard Griffin, *Black Like Me* (Boston: Houghton Mifflin, 1961).

14. James E. Blackwell, *The Black Community* (New York: Harper-Collins, 1991), pp. 456–457.

15. See Kim Lersch, "Current Trends in Police Brutality: An Analysis of Recent Newspaper Accounts," Gainesville, University of Florida, unpublished master's thesis, 1993.

16. See E. Yvonne Moss, "African Americans and the Administration of Justice," in *Assessment of the Status of African-Americans*, ed. Wornie L. Reed (Boston: William Monroe Trotter Institute, University of Massachusetts, 1990), vol. I, pp. 79–86; and Dennis B. Roddy,

"Perceptions Still Segregate Police, Black Community," *The Pittsburgh Press*, August 26, 1990, p. B1.

17. Les Payne, "Up Against the Wall: Black Men and the Cops," *Essence*, November 1992, p. 74.

18. Michelle N-K [sic] Collison, "Black Students Complain of Abuse by Campus Police," *Chronicle of Higher Education*, April 14, 1993, pp. A35-A36.

19. Bonnie J. Morris, "The Pervasiveness of Campus Racism," letter to editors, *The Chronicle of Higher Education*, May 12, 1993, p. B5.

20. Isabel Wilkerson, personal interview with the author, 1992.

21. This quote includes a clarification from a brief follow-up interview.

22. Ralph Ellison, *Invisible Man* (New York: Vintage Books, 1989), p. 3.

23. George M. Fredrickson, *The Black Image in the White Mind* (Middletown, Conn.: Wesleyan University Press, 1971), pp. 251-275.

24. See Doris A. Graber, *Crime News and the Public* (New York: Praeger, 1980).

25. Bureau of Criminal Justice Statistics, *Criminal Victimization in the United States, 1991* (Washington, D.C.: U.S. Government Printing Office, 1992), p. 61, and *Sourcebook of Criminal Justice Statistics, 1991* (Washington, D.C.: U.S. Government Printing Office, 1992), p. 403.

26. James Kilpatrick, "Hate Crimes not Protected by the First Amendment," *Austin American Statesman*, May 19, 1993, p. A19.

27. For a discussion of major distortions in the Horton ad campaign, see Kathleen Hall Jamieson, *Dirty Politics: Deception, Distraction, and Democracy* (New York: Oxford University Press, 1992).

28. On the black image as threat, see Mark Warr, "Dangerous Situations: Social Context and Fear of Victimization," *Social Forces*, 68 (1990), pp. 905–906.

29. Judith Lichtenberg, "Racism in the Head, Racism in the World," *Philosophy and Public Policy*, 12 (Spring/Summer 1992), p. 4.

30. Gerald D. Jaynes and Robin Williams, Jr., eds., *A Common Destiny: Blacks and American Society* (Washington, D.C.: National Academy Press, 1989), p. 84.

31. Robert H. Lauer and Warren H. Handel, *Social Psychology: The Theory and Application of Symbolic Interactionism* (Boston: Houghton Mifflin, 1977), p. 330.

32. John Mirowsky and Catherine E. Ross, *Social Causes of Psychological Distress* (New York: Aldine de Gruyter, 1989), pp. 10–21.

33. Leanita McClain, "The Insidious New Racism," in *A Foot in Each World*, ed. Clarence Page (Evanston, Ill.: Northwestern University Press, 1986), pp. 20–21.

3. Seeking a Good Education

1. Eric L. Hirsch, "Columbia University: Individual and Institutional Racism," in *The Racial Crisis in American Higher Education*, ed. Philip G. Altbach and Kofi Lomotey (Albany: SUNY Press, 1991), pp. 199–211.

2. People for the American Way, *Democracy's Next Generation II* (Washington, D.C.: People for the American Way, 1992), p. 65.

3. Lee Sigelman and Susan Welch, *Black Americans' Views of Racial Inequality* (Cambridge: Cambridge University Press, 1991), pp. 55–58.

4. National Opinion Research Center, "General Social Survey" (Chicago: National Opinion Research Center, 1990). Tabulated by authors.

5. "Study Shows Social Mix Good for Blacks," *Newsweek*, September 18, 1985, p. 3.

6. Ansley A. Abraham, *Racial Issues on Campus: How Students View Them* (Atlanta: Southern Regional Education Board, 1990); and Leslie Inniss, "Historical Footprints: The Legacy of the School Desegregation Pioneers," in *The Bubbling Cauldron*, ed. Michael P. Smith

and Joe R. Feagin (Minneapolis: University of Minnesota Press, forthcoming).

7. Quoted in Itabari Njeri, "Beyond the Melting Pot; In America, Blending in was once the Ideal," *Los Angeles Times*, January 13, 1991, p. E1; see Arthur Schlesinger, Jr., *The Disuniting of America: Reflections on a Multicultural Society* (New York: Norton, 1991).

8 "Separate and Unequal," *Minority Trendsetter* 1 (Summer 1988), p. 4.

9. J. Eyler, V. Cook, and L. Ward, "Resegregation: Desegregation Within Desegregated Schools," Paper presented at Annual Meeting of American Education Research Association, as summarized in Russell W. Irvine and Jacqueline Jordan Irvine, "The Impact of the Desegregation Process on the Education of Black Students: Key Variables," *Journal of Negro Education* 53 (1983), p. 415.

10. Gunnar Myrdal, *An American Dilemma* (1944; New York: McGraw-Hill, 1964).

11. American Council on Education and the Education Commission of the States, *One-Third of a Nation* (Washington: The American Council on Education, 1988).

12. Gerald D. Jaynes and Robin Williams, Jr., eds., *A Common Destiny: Blacks and American Society* (Washington, D.C.: National Academy Press, 1989), pp. 338–339; for earlier studies see A. W. Astin, *Minorities in Higher Education* (San Francisco: Jossey-Bass, 1982); see also Reynolds Farley and Walter R. Allen, *The Color Line and the Quality of Life in America* (New York: Oxford University Press, 1989), p. 208.

13. George Keller, "Black Students in Higher Education: Why So Few?" *Planning for Higher Education* 17 (1988–1989), pp. 50–54.

14. William E. B. Du Bois, *The Souls of Black Folk* (1903; New York: Bantam Books, 1989), p. 3.

15. Chalsa M. Loo and Garry Rolison, " Alienation of Ethnic Minority Students at a Predominantly White University," *Journal of Higher Education* 57 (January/February 1986), pp. 64–67.

16. Hoi K. Suen, "Alienation and Attrition of Black College Students on a Predominantly White Campus," *Journal of College Student Personnel* 24 (March 1983), pp. 117–121.

17. See Philip G. Altbach and Kofi Lomotey, eds., *The Racial Crisis in American Higher Education* (Albany: SUNY Press, 1991).

18. Walter Allen, *Gender and Campus Race Differences in Black Student Academic Performance, Racial Attitudes and College Satisfaction* (Atlanta: Southern Education Foundation, 1986).

19. Howard J. Ehrlich, *Campus Ethnoviolence and the Policy Options* (Baltimore: National Institute against Prejudice and Violence, 1990), p. iii.

20. Denise K. Magner, "Blacks and Whites on the Campuses: Behind Ugly Racist Incidents, Student Isolation and Insensitivity," *Chronicle of Higher Education* (April 26, 1989), pp. A27-A29.

21. William Celis, "Hazing's Forbidden Rites are Moving Underground," *New York Times*, January 27, 1993, p. A19; William C. Rhoden, "College Football," *New York Times*, November 30, 1991, section 1, p. 29.

22. Myrdal, *An American Dilemma*, p. 101.

23. John O. Calmore, "To Make Wrong Right: The Necessary and Proper Aspirations of Fair Housing," in *The State of Black America 1989* (New York: Urban League, 1989), p. 89.

24. National Opinion Research Center, "General Social Survey" (Chicago: National Opinion Research Center, 1990). Tabulated by authors.

25. Reported in Ehrlich, *Campus Ethnoviolence and the Policy Options*, pp. 12–13.

26. Quoted in Magner, "Blacks and Whites on the Campuses," pp. A27-A29.

27. Philomena Essed, *Understanding Everyday Racism* (Newbury Park, Calif.: Sage, 1991), pp. 30–32.

28. In 1992 this liberal college of 700 students had about 55 black students. See Isabel Wilkerson, "Racial Tension Erupts, Tearing a College Apart," *New York Times*, April 13, 1992, p. A14.

377

29. Joe R. Fengin and Nikitah Imani, "Black in a White World," unpublished research report, 1993. University authorities requested that the university not be identified.

30. See Keller, "Black Students in Higher Education."

31. Ralph Ellison, *Invisible Man* (New York: Vintage Books, 1989), p. 3.

32. Feagin and Imani, "Black in a White World."

33. Catharine MacKinnon, *Feminism Unmodified* (Cambridge: Harvard University Press, 1987), p. 34.

34. Allan Nairn, *The Reign of ETS: The Corporation that Makes Up Minds* (Washington, D.C.: Allan Nairn and Associates, 1980).

35. Percy Bates, "Teaching Children to be Test Wise," *Breakthrough* 15 (Summer 1988), p. 23.

36. Joseph Katz, "White Faculty Struggling with the Effects of Racism," in Altbach and Lomotey, *The Racial Crisis in American Higher Education*, p. 193.

37. Feagin and Imani, "Black in a White World."

38. The second author and his black colleagues have had this happen to them.

39. Feagin and Imani, "Black in a White World."

40. James E. Blackwell, "Graduate and Professional Education for Blacks," in *The Education of Black Americans*, ed. Charles V. Willie, Antoine M. Garibaldi, and Wornie L. Reed (Boston: William Monroe Trotter Institute, University of Massachusetts, 1990), pp. 103–110.

41. Stephen L. Carter, "Color-Blind and Color-Active," *The Recorder*, January 3, 1992, p. 6.

42. Joe R. Feagin, Nikitah Imani, and Hernan Vera, "The Views of Black Parents," unpublished research report, 1993.

43. John S. Butler, *Entrepreneurship and Self-help among Black Americans* (New York: SUNY Press, 1991), p. 259.

44. Keller, "Black Students in Higher Education: Why So Few?" p. 55.

4. Navigating the Middle-Class Workplace

1. Bebe Moore Campbell, "To Be Black, Gifted, and Alone," *Savvy* 5 (December 1984), p. 69.

2. David H. Swinton, "The Economic Status of African Americans during the 1980s: 'Permanent' Poverty and Inequality," in *The State of Black America*, ed. Janet Dewart (New York: National Urban League, 1991), p. 63; see also Gerald D. Jaynes and Robin Williams, Jr., eds., *A Common Destiny: Blacks and American Society* (Washington, D.C.: National Academy Press, 1989), pp. 310–317.

3. See William B. Gould, "The Supreme Court and Employment Discrimination Law in 1989: Judicial Retreat and Congressional Response," *Tulane Law Review* 64 (June 1990), pp. 1485–1514.

4. James E. Ellis, "The Black Middle Class," *Business Week*, March 14, 1988, p. 65.

5. Lee Sigelman and Susan Welch, *Black Americans' Views of Racial Inequality* (Cambridge: Cambridge University Press, 1991), pp. 55–57.

6. The 1990 General Social Survey asked why blacks have worse jobs, income, and housing than whites. Choosing among alternative explanations, two thirds of blacks said it was "mainly due to discrimination," compared to 35 percent of whites. And 78 percent of college-educated blacks said it was mainly due to discrimination. National Opinion Research Center, "General Social Survey" (Chicago: National Opinion Research Center, 1990). Tabulated by authors.

7. Margery Austin Turner, Michael Fix, and Raymond J. Struyk, "Opportunities Denied: Discrimination in Hiring," Urban Institute Report 91–9, August 1991, Washington, D.C.

8. "The Black Middle Class," *Business Week*, March 14, 1988, p. 65.

9. Ed Jones, "Beneficiaries or Victims? Progress or Process," unpublished research report, South Orange, New Jersey, January 1985.

379

10. Ellis Cose, "To the Victors, Few Spoils," *Newsweek*, March 29, 1993, p. 54.

11. "The Black Middle Class," *Business Week*, March 14, 1988, p. 65; Sigelman and Welch, *Black Americans' Views of Racial Inequality*, p. 57.

12. Swinton, "The Economic Status of African Americans," in Dewart, *The State of Black America: 1991*, p. 67.

13. Elizabeth Higginbotham and Lynn Weber, "Workplace Discrimination for Black and White Professional and Managerial Women," in *Women and Work: Ethnicity and Class*, ed. Elizabeth Higginbotham and Lynn Weber (Newbury Park, Calif.: Sage, forthcoming).

14. Marcus Mabry, "An Endangered Dream," *Newsweek*, December 3, 1990, p. 40.

15. Kluegel and Smith report on a 1976 survey in which 71 percent of whites agreed that "blacks and other minorities no longer face unfair employment conditions. In fact they are favored in many training and job programs." Only 12 percent of whites agreed with the statement that "Discrimination affects all black people. The only way to handle it is for blacks to organize together and demand rights for all." James R. Kluegel and Eliot R. Smith, *Beliefs about Inequality* (New York: Aldine de Gruyter, 1986), pp. 186–187.

16. Rosabeth Moss Kanter, *Men and Women of the Corporation* (New York: Basic Books, 1977), pp. 50–61, 63.

17. Cited in Dawn M. Baskerville, "Are Career Seminars for Black Managers Worth It?" *Black Enterprise*, December 1992, p. 122.

18. Ibid.

19. Ed Jones, "What It's Like to Be a Black Manager," *Harvard Business Review* (May–June 1986), pp. 84–93.

20. See Kanter, *Men and Women of the Corporation*, p. 158.

21. John Mirowsky and Catherine E. Ross, *Social Causes of Psychological Distress* (New York: Aldine de Gruyter, 1989), p. 16.

22. See Baskerville, "Are Career Seminars for Black Managers Worth It?" *Black Enterprise*, December 1992, p. 122.

23. Joe R. Feagin and Clairece Booher Feagin, *Racial and Ethnic*

Relations, 4th ed. (Englewood Cliffs, N.J.: Prentice-Hall, 1993), pp. 237–239.

24. Kenneth B. Clark, "The Role of Race," *New York Times Magazine*, October 5, 1980, p. 30.

25. Kanter, *Men and Women of the Corporation*, p. 158.

26. Kenneth W. Jackson, "Black Faculty in Academia," in *The Racial Crisis in American Higher Education*, ed. Philip G. Altbach and Kofi Lomotey (Albany: SUNY Press, 1991), p. 143.

27. Sharon M. Collins, "The Making of the Black Middle Class," *Social Problems* 30 (April 1983), pp. 369–381.

28. John N. Odom, as quoted in Thomas B. Edsall and Mary D. Edsall, *Chain Reaction* (New York: Norton, 1992), p. 163.

29. Ella L. Bell, "The Bicultural Life Experience of Career-oriented Black Women," *Journal of Organizational Behavior* 11 (1990), p. 475.

30. William E. B. Du Bois, *The Souls of Black Folk* (1903; New York: Bantam Books, 1989), p. 3.

31. Everett Hughes, *Men and Their Work* (Glencoe, Ill.: Free Press, 1958), pp. 109–110.

32. Kanter, *Men and Women of the Corporation*, pp. 210–212.

33. Gunnar Myrdal, *An American Dilemma* (1944; New York: McGraw-Hill, 1964), vol. 1, p. 101.

34. Herbert Hill, "Critique of Chapter 6, 'Blacks in the Economy,'" in *Critique of the NRC Study, A Common Destiny: Blacks and American Society*, ed. Wornie L. Reed (Boston: William Monroe Trotter Institute, University of Massachusetts, 1990), p. 15.

35. Edward Irons, *Black Managers: The Case of the Banking Industry* (New York: Praeger, 1985).

36. Philomena Essed, *Understanding Everyday Racism* (Newbury Park, Calif.: Sage, 1991), pp. 30–32.

37. See Catharine A. MacKinnon, *Toward a Feminist Theory of the State* (Harvard University Press, 1989), pp. 2–10; and Joe R. Feagin and Clairece B. Feagin, *Social Problems*, 3d ed. (Englewood Cliffs, N.J.: Prentice-Hall, 1990), pp. 18–21.

38. Jaynes and Williams, *A Common Destiny*, pp. 169–171.

39. On skepticism about courts, see Julius L. Chambers, "Black Americans and the Courts: Has the Clock been turned back Permanently?" in *The State of Black America, 1990*, ed. Janet Dewart (New York: National Urban League, 1990), pp. 9–24.

40. Cited in John Hill, "Senate Race Showed State's Racial Woes," Gannett News Service, October 14, 1990, n.p., Lexis/Nexis database.

41. People for the American Way, *Democracy's Next Generation II* (Washington, D.C.: People for the American Way, 1992), p. 70.

5. Building a Business

1. Quoted in David. D. Porter, "What must blacks go through? An experiment will let you see," *Orlando Sentinel*, September 13, 1989, p. G1.

2. See Thomas Sowell, *Markets and Minorities* (New York: Basic Books, 1981).

3. Porter, "What must blacks go through?" *Orlando Sentinel*, September 13, 1989, p. G1.

4. John Sibley Butler, *Entrepreneurship and Self-help among Black Americans* (New York: SUNY Press, 1991), pp. 165–226, 282–330.

5. Lerone Bennett, *Black Power U.S.A* (New York: Pelican, 1969), p. 37.

6. *1987 Survey of Minority-Owned Business Enterprises -Black* (Washington, D.C.: U.S. Government Printing Office, 1990).

7. Walter L. Updegrave, "Race and Money," *Money*, December 1989, p. 162.

8. National Center for Education Statistics, "Expected Occupations of 8th Graders at Age 30 by Selected Student and School Characteristics: 1988," *Digest of Education Statistics* (Washington, D.C.: U.S. Dept. of Health, Education and Welfare, 1989), p. 130.

9. Shearson Lehman Brothers, "Life in America," telephone survey, as reported in Julia Belcher, *USAir Magazine*, October 1992, p. 13.

10. See James R. Kluegel and Eliot Smith, *Beliefs about Inequality* (New York: Aldine de Gruyter, 1986), pp. 186–196.

11. Emile Durkheim, *Suicide* (Glencoe, Ill.: Free Press, 1951), pp. 241–296.

12. We draw here on Hernan Vera and Joe R. Feagin, "Racism as Anomic Action: The American Case," unpublished research paper, University of Florida, 1992.

13. Richard W. Stevenson, "Blacks Push for Jobs Rebuilding after Riot," *New York Times*, June 10, 1992, p. A16.

14. John Mirowsky and Catherine E. Ross, *Social Causes of Psychological Distress* (New York: Aldine de Gruyter, 1989), p. 14.

15. The quotes are from Joe R. Feagin and Nikitah Imani, "Black Contractors and Subcontractors in the [Southeastern] County Construction Industry: A Portrait of Discrimination," unpublished research report prepared for the Board of County Commissioners, [Southeastern] County, July 1991.

16. Carmenza Gallo, "The Construction Industry in New York City: Immigrant and Black Entrepreneurs," Working Paper, Conservation of Human Resources Project, Columbia University, New York City, 1983, p. 25.

17. Ibid., pp. 22–33.

18. Herbert Blumer, "Race Prejudice as a Sense of Group Position," *The Pacific Sociological Review*, 1 (Spring 1959), pp. 3–7.

19. Butler, *Entrepreneurship and Self-Help among Black Americans*, pp. 125–142.

20. Cited in Udayan Gupta, "Cash Crunch," *Wall Street Journal*, February 19, 1993, p. R4.

21. The study is summarized in Updegrave, "Race and Money," *Money*, December 1989, p. 162.

22. Feagin and Imani, "Black Contractors and Subcontractors in the [Southeastern] County Construction Industry."

23. Updegrave, "Race and Money," *Money*, December 1989, p. 160.

24. Paul D. Reynolds and Brenda Miller, "Race, Gender, and Entrepreneurship," paper presented to American Sociological Association, Annual Meeting, 1990.

25. Gupta, "Cash Crunch," *Wall Street Journal*, February 19, 1993, p. R4.

26. Bureau of the Census, *Household Wealth and Asset Ownership: 1984* (Washington, D.C.: U.S. Government Printing Office, 1986), Table 4, n.p.; Billy J. Tidwell, "Black Wealth: Facts *and* Fiction," in *The State of Black America 1988*, ed. Jane Dewart (New York: National Urban League, 1988), pp. 193–210.

27. Gunnar Myrdal, *An American Dilemma* (1944; New York: McGraw-Hill, 1964), vol. 2, p. 816; Herbert M. Morais, *The History of the Negro in Medicine* (New York: Publishers Co., 1967), pp. 86–100.

28. Lois C. Gray, The Geographic and Functional Distribution of Black Physicians: Some Research and Policy Considerations," *American Journal of Public Health* 67 (1977), pp. 519–526.

29. James H. Jones, *Bad Blood* (New York: Free Press, 1981), pp. 1–23.

30. Tom Junod, "Deadly Medicine," *Gentleman's Quarterly*, June 1993, pp. 164–169.

31. Feagin and Imani, "Black Contractors and Subcontractors in the [Southeastern] County Construction Industry."

32. William H. Grier and Price M. Cobbs, *Black Rage* (New York: Basic Books, 1968), p. 178.

33. Alexander Thomas and Samuel Sillen, *Racism and Psychiatry* (New Jersey: The Citadel Press, 1972), p. 54.

34. Thomas Pettigrew, *Racially Separate or Together?* (New York: McGraw-Hill, 1971).

35. See Gerald D. Jaynes and Robin Williams, Jr., eds., *A Common Destiny: Blacks and American Society* (Washington, D.C.: National Academy Press, 1989), p. 422, note 3.

384

36. See E. Yvonne Moss, "African Americans and the Administration of Justice," in *Assessment of the Status of African-Americans*, ed. Wornie L. Reed (Boston: William Monroe Trotter Institute, University of Massachusetts, 1990), vol. I, pp. 79–86; and Melvin P. Sikes, *The Administration of Injustice* (New York: Harper & Row, 1975).

37. See John Hope Franklin and Alfred A. Moss, *From Slavery to Freedom*, 6th ed. (New York: Knopf, 1988), pp. 233–238.

38. Nathan Glazer, "Blacks and Ethnic Groups: The Difference, and the Political Difference It Makes," *Social Problems* 18 (Spring 1971), p. 459.

39. See George Gilder, *The Spirit of Enterprise* (New York: Simon and Schuster, 1984), pp. 110–112.

40. Alejandro Portes and Robert L. Bach, *Latin American Journey* (Berkeley: University of California Press, 1985), pp. 200–220.

41. Gallo, "The Construction Industry in New York City," p. 26.

42. Walter Rodney, *How Europe Underdeveloped Africa* (Washington: Howard University Press, 1984), p. 280.

6. Seeking a Good Home and Neighborhood

1. Census Bureau, *Statistical Abstract of the United States, 1991* (Washington, D.C.: U.S. Government Printing Office, 1991), p. 726. The black figure is "black and other."

2. Robert G. Schwemm, "Fair Housing Enforcement," *One Nation, Indivisible* (Washington, D.C.: Citizens' Commission on Civil Rights, 1989), p. 272.

3. Douglas S. Massey and Nancy A. Denton, *American Apartheid: Segregation and the Making of the Underclass* (Cambridge: Harvard University Press, 1993), pp. 221–223.

4. National Opinion Research Center, "General Social Survey" (Chicago: National Opinion Research Center, 1990). Tabulated by authors.

5. Cited in Gerald D. Jaynes and Robin Williams, Jr., eds., *A Common Destiny: Blacks and American Society* (Washington, D.C.: National Academy Press, 1989), pp. 142–146.

6. Margery Austin Turner, Raymond J. Struyk, and John Yinger, *Housing Discrimination Study: Synthesis* (Washington, D.C.: U.S. Government Printing Office, 1991), pp. ii-viii.

7. The polls are cited in Lee Sigelman and Susan Welch, *Black Americans' Views of Racial Inequality* (Cambridge: Cambridge University Press, 1991), pp. 57–59.

8. Another NORC question asked why blacks have worse jobs, income, and housing than whites. Choosing among alternative explanations, two thirds of blacks said "mainly due to discrimination," compared to 35 percent of whites. Seventy-seven percent of college educated blacks but only 41 percent of college-educated whites, said it was mainly due to discrimination. National Opinion Research Center, "General Social Survey" (Chicago: National Opinion Research Center, 1990). Tabulated by authors.

9. Gary Orfield, "Minorities and Suburbanization," in *Critical Perspectives on Housing*, ed. R. Bratt, C. Hartman, and A. Meyerson (Philadelphia: Temple University Press, 1986), pp. 223–225.

10. John Goering, Department of Housing and Urban Development, letter to senior author, May 1991.

11. See Joe R. Feagin and Robert Parker, *Building American Cities* (Englewood Cliffs, N.J.: Prentice-Hall, Inc., 1990), pp. 132–138.

12. Massey and Denton, *American Apartheid*, pp. 232–233.

13. Ibid., p. 232.

14. Margery Austin Turner, *Housing Discrimination Study: Analyzing Racial and Ethnic Steering* (Washington, D.C.: U.S. Government Printing Office, 1991), pp. ii–v.

15. See Joe R. Feagin and Clairece Booher Feagin, *Discrimination American Style* (Englewood Cliffs, N.J.: Prentice-Hall, 1978), pp. 87–105.

16. See Feagin and Parker, *Building American Cities*, pp. 129–147.

17. William J. Wilson, *The Declining Significance of Race* (Chicago: University of Chicago Press, 1978).

18. Massey and Denton, *American Apartheid*, p. 226.

19. See John M. Goering, *Housing Desegregation and Federal Policy* (Chapel Hill: University of North Carolina Press, 1986).

20. Goering, letter to senior author, May 1991.

21. Office of Thrift Supervision, *Report on Loan Discrimination* (Washington, D.C.: Office of the Treasury, 1989), p. 2; Statement of Jerauld C. Kluckman, Director, Compliance Programs, Office of Thrift Supervision, U.S. Department of the Treasury, Before the Subcommittee on Consumer and Regulatory Affairs of the Senate Committee on Banking, Housing and Urban Affairs, May 16, 1990.

22. Paulette Thomas, "Federal Data Detail Pervasive Racial Gap in Mortgage Lending," *Wall Street Journal*, March 31, 1992, p. 1.

23. ICF Incorporated, "The Secondary Market and Community Lending through Lenders' Eyes," prepared for the Federal Home Loan Mortgage Corporation, February 28, 1991.

24. Klanwatch Project, " 'Move-in' Violence: White Resistance to Neighborhood Integration in the 1980s," Montgomery, Alabama, Southern Poverty Law Center, undated (circa 1987).

25. See "2 Klan Leaders Indicted on Cross-burning Charges," *Atlanta Constitution*, June 27, 1992, section D, p. 7.

26. Major Garrett, "Democratic Hopefuls Unload on Bush," *Washington Times*, November 24, 1991, p. A4.

27. For a discussion see Theodore Cross, *The Black Power Imperative* (New York: Faulkner, 1984), pp. 114–116.

28. See Wilson, *The Declining Significance of Race*.

29. Jaynes and Williams, *A Common Destiny: Blacks and American Society*, pp. 144–146; see also Douglas S. Massey and Nancy A. Denton, "Trends in Segregation of Blacks, Hispanics and Asians, 1970–1980," *American Sociological Review*, 52 (1987), pp. 802–825. Housing discrimination has been neglected in national reports on the state of black America. In *A Common Destiny*, for example, fewer

than six pages out of 600 are devoted to housing issues, and half of that is on white public opinion.

30. See Robert D. Bullard, "Solid Waste Sites and the Black Houston Community," Unpublished paper presented at the Annual Meeting, Southwestern Sociological Association, March 17–20, 1982, pp. 6–20.

31. John Goering, letter to first author, May 1991; see also U.S. Department of Housing and Urban Development, *The State of Fair Housing* (Washington, D.C.: U.S. Government Printing Office, 1989).

32. John Goering, "Are Size of Place Differences Worth Talking About?" Commentary paper, Conference on New Perspectives on Racial Issues, 1991.

33. Testimony of John J. Knapp, General Counsel, U.S. Department of Housing and Urban Development, in *Issues of Housing Discrimination*, vol. 2 (Washington, D.C.: U.S. Commission on Civil Rights, November 13, 1987).

34. Massey and Denton, *American Apartheid*, p. 224. They cite a figure of four hundred resolved fair housing cases.

35. John Goering, "The Racial Housing Question in England and the United States," revised version of a paper presented at the Annual Meeting of the International Sociological Association, Madrid, Spain, July 11, 1990, p. 21.

36. Joel Garreau, *Edge City* (New York: Doubleday, 1991), p. 146.

37. Massey and Denton, *American Apartheid*, p. 225.

38. Isabel Wilkerson, "The Tallest Fence: Feelings on Race in a White Neighborhood," *New York Times*, June 21, 1992, section 1, p. 18.

39. Quoted in George J. Church, "The Boom Towns," *Time*, June 15, 1987, p. 17.

7. *Contending with Everyday Discrimination*

1. Rachel Shuster, "Arthur Ashe; 1943–1993; Ashe Legacy Goes beyond Sports, Race," *USA Today*, February 8, 1993, p. 1C.

2. James H. Humphrey, *Human Stress* (New York: AMS Press, 1986), p. 63.

3. Alexander Thomas and Samuel Sillen, *The Theory and Application of Symbolic Interactionism* (Boston: Houghton Mifflin Company, 1977); see also John Mirowsky and Catherine E. Ross, *Social Causes of Psychological Distress* (New York: Aldine and de Gruyter, 1989).

4. See, for example, Mirowsky and Ross, *Social Causes of Psychological Stress*.

5. This commentary on the requirements for survival reminds one of the black folk song: "Got one mind for white folks to see. Another for what I know is me. He don't know, he don't know my mind. When he sees me laughing, laughing just to keep from crying."

6. Herbert Aptheker, *American Negro Slave Revolts* (New York: International Publishers, 1943), pp. 12–18, 162.

7. Bob Blauner, *Black Lives, White Lives* (Berkeley: University of California Press, 1989).

8. Gordon Allport, *The Nature of Prejudice*, abridged ed. (Garden City, N.Y.: Anchor Books, 1958), pp. 251–253.

9. William H. Grier and Price M. Cobbs, *Black Rage* (New York: Basic Books, Inc., 1968), p. 4.

10. Thomas and Sillen, *The Theory and Application of Symbolic Interactionism*, p. 54.

11. Ibid., p. 54.

12. In his analysis of black slave revolts in the United States, historian Sterling Stuckey has shown that African culture and religion were one source of the revolutionaries' philosophy and inclination to rebel. Sterling Stuckey, *Slave Culture* (New York: Oxford University Press, 1987), pp. 27, 42–46.

13. Gunnar Myrdal, *An American Dilemma* (1944; New York: McGraw-Hill, 1964), vol. 1, p. 38.

14. See, for example, Daniel P. Moynihan, *The Negro Family: The Case for National Action* (Washington, D.C.: U.S. Government Printing Office, 1965); Ken Auletta, *The Underclass* (New York: Random House, 1982).

15. Harriette P. McAdoo, *Black Families*, 2d ed. (Beverly Hills, Calif.: Sage, 1988).

16. See Herbert Gutman, *The Black Family in Slavery and Freedom, 1750–1925* (New York: Random House, 1976).

17. See Peter Bell and Jimmy Evans, *Counseling with the Black Client: Alcohol Use and Abuse in Black America* (Center City, Minn.: Hazelden, 1981).

18. Quoted in Betty Sue Flowers, ed., *Bill Moyers: A World of Ideas* (New York: Doubleday, 1989), p. 173.

19. James S. Jackson, Wayne R. McCullough, Gerald Gurin, "Race Identity," in *Life in Black America*, ed. James S. Jackson (Newbury Park: Sage, 1991), pp. 246–253.

20. Bell and Evans, *Counseling with the Black Client*.

21. Arthur Brittan and Mary Maynard, *Sexism, Racism and Oppression* (Oxford: Basil Blackwell, 1984), p. 7.

8. *Changing the Color Line*

1. People for the American Way, *Democracy's Next Generation II* (Washington, D.C.: People for the American Way, 1992), p. 63.

2. *Wards Cove Packing Co. v. Atonio*, 109 S. Ct. 2115 (1989).

3. Chandler Davidson, *Race and Class in Texas Politics* (Princeton: Princeton University Press, 1990). Other research has demonstrated that at all three Republican conventions in the 1980s there were very few black delegates. Joe R. Feagin, "White Elephant: Race and Electoral Politics in Texas, *Texas Observer*, August 23, 1991, pp. 15–16.

4. See Shelby Steele, *The Content of Our Character* (New York: St. Martin's Press, 1990).

5. Leanita McClain, "The Middle-class Black's Burden," *Newsweek*, October 13, 1980, reprinted in *A Foot in Each World*, ed. Clarence Page (Evanston, Ill.: Northwestern University Press, 1986), p. 13.

6. Roy Brooks, *Rethinking the American Race Problem* (Berkeley: University of California Press, 1990), pp. 17–21.

7. Sidney Willhelm, *Black in a White America* (Cambridge: Schenkman, 1983); William Julius Wilson, *The Truly Disadvantaged: The Inner City, the Underclass, and Public Policy* (Chicago: University of Chicago Press, 1987).

8. See Joe R. Feagin and Clairece B. Feagin, *Social Problems*, 3d ed. (Englewood Cliffs, N.J.: Prentice-Hall, Inc., 1990), pp. 358–360.

9. Thomas Byrne Edsall and Mary D. Edsall, "When the Official Subject is Presidential Politics, Taxes, Welfare, Crime, Rights, or Values . . . The Real Subject is Race," *The Atlantic*, May 1991, pp. 53–55.

10. George Keller, "Black Students in Higher Education: Why So Few?" *Planning for Higher Education* 17 (1988–1989), p. 55.

11. James R. Kluegel and Eliot R. Smith, *Beliefs about Inequality* (New York: Aldine de Gruyter, 1986), pp. 287–302.

12. Franklin Roosevelt, "Economic Bill of Rights," in *The Human Rights Reader*, ed. Walter Laqueur and Bary Rubin, rev. ed. (New York: New American Library, 1989), p. 313.

13. As quoted by Mwatabu S. Okantah, "In Search of the Real King," *The Plain Dealer*, April 4, 1993, p. 1D.

14. See Howard Schuman, Charlotte Steeh, and Lawrence Bobo, *Racial Attitudes in America* (Cambridge: Harvard University Press, 1985), pp. 139–162.

15. See Paul E. Peterson, "The Urban Underclass and the Poverty Paradox," in *The Urban Underclass*, ed. Christopher Jencks and Paul E. Peterson (Washington, D.C.: The Brookings Institution, 1991), p. 9.

16. Gordon Allport, *The Nature of Prejudice*, abridged ed. (Garden City, N.Y.: Anchor Books, 1958), pp. 251–253.

17. See Chancellor Williams, *The Destruction of Black Civilization* (Chicago: Third World Press, 1987), pp. 320–331.

18. Isabel Wilkerson, "Middle-Class but Not Feeling Equal, Blacks Reflect on Los Angeles Strife," *New York Times*, May 4, 1993, p. A20.

391

19. St. Clair Drake, *Black Folk Here and There* (Los Angeles: UCLA Center for Afro-American Studies, 1987), p. xv.

20. For example, in *The Signifying Monkey* Henry Louis Gates explored the significant impact of African story-telling styles on African American thought and literature, while in *The Destruction of Black Civilization*, Chancellor Williams argued that the hope for African American unity lies in understanding the great African civilizations and their distinctive values. Henry Louis Gates, *The Signifying Monkey* (New York: Oxford University Press, 1988); Williams, *The Destruction of Black Civilization*.

21. Gunnar Myrdal, *An American Dilemma* (1944; New York: McGraw-Hill, 1964), vol. 1, p. 4.

22. See Anthony J. Lemelle, Review of *From Exclusion to Inclusion, Contemporary Sociology*, 22 (January 1993), p. 63.

23. People for the American Way, *Democracy's Next Generation II*, pp. 48–49.

24. Derrick Bell, *Faces at the Bottom of the Well* (New York: Basic Books, 1992), p. 12. Italics omitted.

25. William E. B. Du Bois, *The Suppression of the African Slave-Trade to the United States of America, 1638–1870* (1896; New York: Schocken Books, 1969), pp. 93–199.

26. Quoted in Emily Morison Beck, ed., *John Bartlett's Familiar Quotations*, 15th ed. (Boston: Little, Brown, 1980), p. 556.

Index